# HIGH-PA

Ric

Bob Teschke

Steve Thompson

Scott Primiano

# HIGH-PAYOFF SELLING

## Being Visible and Viable
## in the New Insurance Market

Richard Coskren

Bob Teschke

Steve Thompson

Scott Primiano

polestar
Performance Programs, Inc.

Polestar Publications
Cheyenne, Wyoming
2014

For information, contact Polestar Performance Programs at www.gopolestar.com.

This book includes information from many sources, gathered from many personal experiences. It is published for general reference and is not intended to be a substitute for independent verification by readers when necessary and appropriate. The book is sold with the understanding that neither the authors nor the publisher is engaged in rendering any legal, psychological, or accounting advice. The publisher and authors disclaim any personal liability, directly or indirectly, for advice or information presented within. Although the authors and publisher have prepared this manuscript with utmost care and diligence and have made every effort to ensure the accuracy and completeness of the information contained within it, we assume no responsibility for error, inaccuracies, omissions or inconsistencies.

ISBN: 978-0-9912141-0-5

ATTENTION: QUANTITY DISCOUNTS ARE AVAILABLE TO YOUR COMPANY OR EDUCATIONAL INSTITUTION for reselling, educational purposes, subscription incentives, gifts, or fund-raising campaigns.

Please contact the publisher at Polestar Performance Programs www.gopolestar.com.

# Table of Contents

# List of Figures

# Foreword

If this is your first experience with the team of Coskren, Teschke, Thompson, and founding author Scott Primiano... hang on for a terrific read. *High-Payoff Selling: Being Visible and Viable in the New Insurance Market* is not a compilation of sales and service theories. Rather, it is a collection of tools you can apply to systematically succeed in both your professional and personal life.

Over and over again, people tell us how our approach helps them to achieve significant increases in productivity, profitability, sales performance, efficiency, and client retention. Even more importantly, they say it helps them find new meaning, purpose, and dignity in their personal and professional endeavors.

*High-Payoff Selling* is based on the best-selling strategies found in *Hard Market Selling: Thriving in the New Insurance Era,* by Scott Primiano, whose insights and creativity have helped redefine insurance professionals' sales and service approach throughout both the insurance field and its peripheral industries.

Unlike other books you might have read about insurance sales and service, this one doesn't offer you a script to memorize; it doesn't rehash sales and service strategies you probably already know, and it doesn't focus on generating revenues for the sake of getting rich. It does, however, provide a method of defining specifically what you, as an individual, aim to achieve. It also: shows you how to cultivate needs-based expertise to offer clients; offers a relationship-oriented way to attract business; and builds integral value into your service proposition—ensuring your indispensable worth in the marketplace, no matter its current condition.

In other words, this book offers much more than sales tips. It is a holistic approach to integrating your life and work goals, customizing services, and securing your position in the insurance industry, based on quality rather than price.

Ask yourself these questions:

- Do you want to experience a greater sense of purpose in both your personal and professional life?

- Do you want to work and play more effectively?

- Do you want to increase your worth to clients and distinctively differentiate yourself from competitors?

- Do you want to stop chasing prospects and attract a steady clientele who seek out your expertise?

- Do you want to be able to measure your results and learn from your experiences?

If you answered yes to these questions, this book is for you.

In the pages that follow, you'll learn a simple, straightforward method to define both personal and performance objectives, develop an action plan to prioritize and accommodate these into a manageable schedule, and implement new activities and behaviors to achieve them. You will also come to understand how these actions ultimately synthesize to serve you and your clients. Rather than just selling products and services, you will learn how to monitor your progress and benefit from the learning curve (instead of expecting perfection). Finally, you will discover how much fun and rewarding the process can be.

One of the hallmarks of our approach to succeeding in this industry is the life-long, personal mentorships we establish, both with people in our workshops and others who seek us out for advice. While we aren't able to work alongside you as you read this book, we encourage you to share your process with us and with your colleagues. Supporting each other is as important and rewarding as the journey itself, and we never tire of hearing about your progress. Share your experiences with us, and who knows maybe your story will show up in our next edition! You will find all the forms you need to work this high-payoff selling program on our website: www.gopolestar.com. You may also contact us there at any time.

## New to this Edition

- Cross-selling/account-rounding chapter

- Pipeline-management chapter

- Carrier-connection chapter

- Additional content on personal lines

- At-a-glance key point boxes

- Social media marketing section

- Author snapshots

- Client testimonials

- Graphics

- Index

# Acknowledgments

Our grateful and sincere acknowledgment goes to Scott Primiano, the founder of this program, and to his self-proclaimed inspiration and support, MaryAnne DiCanto.

We wish to acknowledge the many participants and readers of *Hard Market Selling: Thriving in the New Insurance Era* for their contribution to *High-Payoff Selling: Being Visible and Viable in the New Insurance Market,* through their letters, e-mails, testimonials, and personal stories of triumph. And to all those people who have the courage to be introspective and the willingness to "change for good" their personal and professional actions—we thank you for your valuable input and ideas.

Particular and heartfelt thanks go to our executive team of Shari Norris and Steven Walker for their dedication, partnership, and friendship.

Special thanks and a big hug to all contributors: Bob Titus, Cathi Marx, Connie Merchant, Dan Hopwood, Deb Beddoe, Debra Parker, Harry Fine, Helen Kasper, Jeff Teschke, Jim O'Connor, Julie Donn, Kym Martell, Lynn Ross, Mike Murrah, Paul Michaels, Phaedra Buxman, and Terri Dittman. Their remarkable stamina and commitment continue to inspire and "give back" to our industry.

Finally, we want to thank our editor/author mentor, Celene Adams, for her patience and encouragement. Without her persistence and creative writing partnership, this book would not have happened.

# Introduction

*"When you're through changing, you're through"*

— Bruce Barton

L ike other monumental business trends, it was inevitable. The excesses created by what Alan Greenspan dubbed as an "irrationally exuberant" stock market and the soft insurance market that so typified the '90s had to give way to more sensible, secure, and economically favorable business practices. After the dot-com frenzy turned into a dot-bomb disaster for private and institutional investors, followed by the financial markets' collapse in 2008, portfolio income evaporated for many insurance companies and catalyzed an industry-wide examination of precariously high combined ratios. This, in turn, sparked a re-underwriting effort for many carriers seeking to bridge the gap between premium income and losses, first in the late '90s and again well into the second decade of the 21st century.

As the industry and the economy began to stabilize, as the "back-to-basics" cultural shift began to gather momentum, our world and our thinking were forever changed by the events of September 11, 2001. The insurance industry—tethered to the fortunes of our economy and culture—has changed with it. Americans have gone from coveting Internet stock options and window tables at Spago's to craving comfort, warmth, and security. Unprecedented losses from the attacks, combined with already poor combined ratios created by a short, hard market sandwiched between two very long, soft markets, have exacerbated what has always been a cyclical market—a market that continues to challenge clients, agencies, and companies alike.

As the new economy continues to emerge from the rubble, re-insurers, carriers, and agencies, along with millions of people working in the insurance industry, are scrambling to define their place in the market. Some see opportunity and are enthusiastically re-inventing themselves to harvest it. Others, still hanging on to dated perspectives and obsolete business practices, see only trouble and are fighting to survive.

If you are a member of our insurance industry, however you got here and however you feel about being here, this book will help you make the most out of where you are now, identify where to go next, and build a plan to get there.

Before we go any further in explaining what this book is, let us explain what it is not. *High-Payoff Selling: Being Visible and Viable in the New Insurance Market* is not another "how to" book about the process of selling and servicing insurance. There are already too many books available that offer technical descriptions of various selling methods and service gimmicks, and none of them effectively present any remedies for the real life, day-to-day struggles of the professionals for whom they are intended. There are an equal number of inspiring and insightful books that provide reasonable evidence of a universal order, promote spirituality, and delve shrewdly into the metaphysical forces that govern pre- and post-life existence—yet they neglect to address the importance of making a living during *this* life.

Compared to such books, *High-Payoff Selling* is a radical departure. How so? *High-Payoff Selling* is a "hands-on" book, designed to bring both topics (methods and motivation) together in the context of the down-to-earth reality the average producer, underwriter, field-marketing representative, account executive, agency principal, and customer-service representative experiences. It is an insiders' guide for survival and achievement within an industry that is rapidly and constantly redefining itself.

The advantages of this book transcend the ranks of producers, underwriters, and service providers. Although we wrote this book primarily for those directly involved with selling and servicing insurance programs, experience with our coaching and training program (upon which the book is based) proves that exposing the entire organization to these concepts sparks surprising results. Most non-service and non-sales people find the material quite easy to adapt to their situations, and almost all of them undergo a positive transformation.

By and large, insurance producers, production underwriters, field-marketing representatives, agency owners, and account executives stand to gain the most from this book. Why have we chosen to focus on these industry professionals? Frankly, we stand in awe of the really great ones, the *insurance fundamentalists* who go to work each day to make our world a safer place to live and work. Unfortunately, many don't recognize their contributions. It's the nature of the industry—do a great job of managing risk and. . . nothing happens: Buildings don't burn; employees don't slip and fall; trucks stay on the road, and so on. Our best work goes completely unnoticed.

This is particularly true of "producers," a term we use inter-changeably with "agents" throughout this book. People seem to forget that producers are people first. They are people with personal worth and integrity who are too often stereotyped as superficial and greedy. Not so. Producers are people with families, car payments, and mortgages, just like everybody else. Like career people everywhere, they are constantly torn between the needs of their families and the needs of their clients and em-ployers. They are people seeking acceptance, but who often meet rejection. They cannot be defined simply by their sales reports, yet they are driven by their sales success. These are the people we work with every day, and this book is about what we have learned from them and others in our industry.

The book is laid out in a handy, real-world manner that makes the information easy to understand and apply. Each section represents a specific topic or concept that every insurance pro-fessional wrestles with at some level—either personally or profes-sionally. Throughout, our authors share anecdotes—stories they have lived—with which you will identify and appreciate.

Unfortunately, too many of us feel powerless to resolve these problems on our own. Years of working furiously have left us out of balance and feeling disenfranchised from an industry that promised a career. The lingering effects of 9/11, natural disasters such as Hurricane Sandy, and the financial devastation of the 2008 stock market meltdown, for instance, haven't helped either. Each event has brought loss, including brothers and sisters in our industry, friends and colleagues whom we may never have met but know nonetheless.

We know we have a job to do, and we know it must be done in spite of political, social, financial, and military events. We know the "right way" to conduct business, provide value, and build proper insurance programs; however, prevailing insurance buying and selling practices do not encourage a principled approach or allow time to truly build integrity-based relationships. For too many people in our industry, the path that leads to personal and professional success has become either too difficult to find or too confusing to follow. Hence this book is intended to shake us up and get us moving toward a solution.

For the past three decades, we authors have been employed as agency principals, as well as carrier senior managers, performance coaches, and risk consultants. However, we have really been students of the people who sell and service—and the organizations for whom they work. Thousands of hours spent in private sessions with insurance professionals at all levels, combined with observing their selling and servicing experiences, confirm the need for a long-term strategy for personal and professional success. It is our intention that this book provide such.

Our premise is that our station in life, both professionally and personally, is of our own making. Once we can accept responsibility for where we are and where we have been, regardless of environmental conditions or outside influences, then we will begin to realize that we already have the solutions to most of our difficulties and problems. They reside within us and are available to us at any time, provided that we take the time to listen. We already know our strengths, our weaknesses, and the answers to most of life's questions. Call it instinct, Providence, or the voice of reason. We call it soul. The important thing is to learn how to call up this reserve of knowledge and strength when it is needed and to use it wisely.

Of all working people, insurance professionals are most in need of soul-searching guidance. We live lives of constant competition and disparaging evaluations. We are always on stage, always in motion, and always at the mercy of critics and supporters alike. All too often, while attempting to balance competing priorities and please everyone else, we lose sight of our own needs and fail to recognize their value. We take shortcuts we otherwise would not, make personal sacrifices we should not, and renounce our freedom of choice—not seeing that we still have options.

If you work in our industry, this book is written for you—to enlighten you, to empower you, to inspire you, to help you rediscover who you are and what is important in your life. Life's questions all have answers, and you should begin to find some of them here. History notwithstanding, the world is basically a neutral place; we and we alone are responsible for who we are and what we become. That is our message and the focus of this book. We have been lucky enough to make a career out of these ideas, and we have done so joyfully and successfully. We share them with you now to remind you, to refresh you, and to challenge you to simply listen and take notice of where you are, why you are there, and where you are going.

# Chapter One

# Industry Observations—The Dawn of the New Insurance Market

*"The essence of all growth is the willingness to make a change for the better, and then an unremitting willingness to shoulder whatever responsibility this entails."*

—Bill Wilson

For essentially the last two decades, the insurance industry has been facing significant change. Commoditization, technology, and variable market conditions have caused many clients to interact and work differently with the insurance industry, while pricing pressures have driven carriers and agencies to abandon sound underwriting practices and principled marketing strategies.

> "Upon reflection, after almost two years of working to implement its model and processes, [your program] continues to be a 'diving board' that is shaping my success."
>
> *Linda Starr Winans*
> *Agent/Producer*

In addition to changes in distribution channels and market consolidation of independent agencies, there are younger/newer clients, who are Internet confident, expect lightning fast interactions and take advantage of price opportunity at nearly every renewal.

In past soft markets, our behaviors forced the industry into an extremely price competitive position and caused some severe re-alignments of market share. For starters, carriers that were willing to live off of investment returns worked with agents to undercut reasonable pricing models and buy business in many markets—perhaps believing that rate increases could be applied at time of renewal to make up for the shortfall in pricing. Wrong. Producers in these agencies were taught to sell aggressively and to make price, rather than service, the top priority. Forced to compete against this strategy, other carriers and agencies followed suit, creating a gigantic decline in premiums and commissions across the industry.

Seeking to replace the lost capital, dramatic cutbacks in service and support personnel resulted in diminished, reactive, client-service strategies that fix problems and address complaints but fail to build quality, long-lasting relationships. The quantity of clients and their premium dollars became an industry priority, rather than the quality of the business. Impersonal marketing strategies and specialty programs focused on large audiences, pitching price and product, hoping to attract the critical mass that could justify the effort. Producers, underwriters and service personnel became stretched beyond acceptable limits, trying to pursue every hint of an opportunity while still attempting to manage an increasingly volatile book. An avalanche of paper, fruitless activity, and wasted proposals that are the unavoidable byproducts of this methodology resulted in slow suffocation.

As a market continues to harden, as it always will after an extended period of underwriting losses, premiums will continue to rise for all clients—regardless of claims experience. Like all market corrections, this market correction will stabilize at a lower level for client companies that have lower loss ratios and are considered healthy and therefore better risks, and at much higher levels for companies with higher loss ratios that are riskier. In addition to industry classification differences, carrier pricing for risk will be heavily influenced by the frequency and severity of claims, along with the functional presence of proactive client risk-management and loss-control programs.

In short, as markets harden, marketing people are often tossed out of the boardroom, and underwriting is put back in charge of pricing. And when markets soften and prices drop, those who have more to offer than price and product will prosper.

> *The "limbo" dance continues.*

## Who is to Blame?

Who is to blame? Clients? Carriers? Agents? The feds? The lawyers? The press? The economy? The answer is none of the above. There are two factors that heavily affect market changes: selling methods and buying habits.

These evil twins have created more chaos and misunderstanding in the market than all other disruptive behaviors. They have done so by patiently and shrewdly depersonalizing our connection with it and commoditizing not just our products and services, but the entire insurance buying experience. In the name of advancement and efficiency, they have cut people out of the profession and replaced them with processes, policies, and price. Needs-based selling, client consultation, and ongoing client education have steadily disappeared as business practices, while client, agent, and carrier apathy, ignorance, and mistrust have skyrocketed.

Who will navigate the choppy waters the industry is experiencing and survive to tell the tale? Client companies with active risk-control programs will justifiably fare better in the matter of premiums paid, while those without such programs will certainly pay more. Client service is critical too. Agencies and carriers that have proactively serviced their accounts will continue to do so and retain their book. Agencies and carriers that bring nothing more to the table than product and price will not be as fortunate.

The problem is that many in our industry have forgotten how to sell and service with value, integrity, and trust. Our approach—the one that you'll learn in this book—is designed to fix this problem.

## Client Reactions

- *Clients have come to expect slow or no service, renewal-based producer contact, and level or reduced pricing.*

- *Clients view their insurance program as a commodity without value.*

- *Clients rely on market pressure, rather than risk-management and loss controls, to contain insurance costs.*

As products, markets, and distribution channels swirl in chaos, clients often reel from the fallout of this transition. While clients certainly enjoy the financial rewards of a buyers' market, in a changing market, they consistently report feeling sold to and abandoned by producers and insurance professionals they trusted. That breach of trust compromises our most treasured asset—our personal integrity. As Peter Scotese, a retired Fortune 500 CEO once said, "Integrity is not a 90 percent thing, not a 95 percent thing; either you have it or you don't." Somewhere along the way, we seem to have lost it.

Consequently, buyers' remorse is high, service gaps are wide, and producers and our industry are collectively viewed as disingenuous. As a result, insurance buying practices shift away from consultative, relationship-centered, value-driven discussions and move toward commodity transactions that go to the lowest bidder. That, my friends, is a red flag of epic proportions for our industry.

In any market, we are obligated to explain the logic behind the pricing actions, but more importantly, we need to work with each client to develop effective risk-management and loss-control programs that will reduce loss ratios and contain insurance costs.

In short, selling value, integrity, and trust will work in *all* markets, and the pages that follow will provide the roadmap for success.

## What Next?

- *Carrier and agency consolidation will continue, as will cyclical pricing actions.*

- *Carriers will continue to re-underwrite books and consolidate service centers.*

- *Company combined ratios <u>will</u> continue to drive the process.*

- *Agencies and producers must step up proactive services to clearly differentiate themselves in soft and hard markets alike.*

In a soft market, many clients appear willing to sacrifice value-driven service to get a reduced rate. Often, they expect nothing more than the lowest price from their agent and their insurer. And that's what many producers offer. Dare to be different! Find ways to add value that matter to clients and prospects, yet with competitive pricing. In a hard market, the "lowest price" is at best an ambiguous term. All clients are going to expect agencies, producers, and carriers to justify their value and earn their keep. The question is . . . who is ready to deliver in all markets, hard and soft?

## Additional Challenges

- *Agencies will be squeezed toward a narrowing band of opportunity in the middle market.*

- *Personal lines (with the possible exception of the high net-worth account), auto, and Business Owner Policies (BOPs) will continue to migrate to the Internet.*

- *Lower middle-market and small accounts continue to consolidate in carrier service centers and with banks that have entered the market.*

- *Large accounts continue to seek alternative markets and self-insurance programs.*

- *Clients and carriers demand something more; producers must do more than shop a policy.*

- *Bad things will continue to happen. Agencies must <u>stop selling insurance</u> and start reducing risk.*

Complicating matters even further, the industry is currently experiencing dramatic changes in the distribution channels used to deliver products and service. Massive consolidations in small accounts and program business will continue to apply pressure at the low end of the middle market. Carrier service centers and Internet insurance providers will soak up what is left of the small market and push onward toward the middle market, leaving little room for an inefficient "legacy agency system," as defined below. As might be expected, large accounts will turn to captives and alternative markets, rather than stick with traditional insurance programs. We also see reinsurers dipping into the larger accounts at the top end of the middle market and actively courting some direct business.

Clearly, the middle market is shrinking. Inevitably, this means that the number of agencies and producers competing successfully in this market must shrink as well. Who will prosper and who will fail? Years of observation and experience in and around agencies of all sizes, specialties, and operating cultures give us a very clear picture of the type of agency that will be successful in the new insurance market. This type of agency we call "healthy and thriving." As producer behavior tends to mirror agency attitudes, it is important that *everyone* learn to recognize and demonstrate the habits and behaviors that make for a healthy and thriving agency. When this is done correctly, everybody wins.

We also have a good understanding of those agencies that will struggle, perhaps fail, and why they will do so. We have labeled this a legacy agency. Let's take a look at a legacy culture first.

## The Legacy Agency

- *Legacy agencies see the entire market as a potential opportunity.*

- *Legacy agencies use sporadic, traditional, volume-driven sales and marketing initiatives.*

- *Legacy agencies are loosely networked and randomly referred.*

- *Legacy agencies target new business during "harvesting season."*

- *Legacy agencies are policy, price, and product focused. Producers are "hit-and-run."*

- *Legacy agency service is reactive and often anonymous.*

- *Legacy agencies offer very limited client contact or involvement.*

- *Legacy agencies have limited or no community or industry involvement.*

- *Legacy agencies have an unprofitable or marginally profitable book of business.*

- *Legacy agencies have difficulty placing renewal business in a hard market.*

Legacy agencies often react adversely to varying market conditions and struggle to find some stability. They feel besieged by relentless competition, lack a strategic plan, and put most of their energy into chasing new business. They know that service is critical, yet they lack the time and the personnel to provide anything other than reactive service that repairs but never builds. They are rushed, exhausted, and worried. These agents sell rather than develop client relationships, and they do so during the traditional selling season, 90-120 days prior to renewal.

There are no proactive risk-management or loss-control programs for their clients, nor are they able to consistently deliver value-added services. Their book of business is inconsistent in regard to business mix or specialty, tends to run an above-average loss ratio, and is difficult to place at time of renewal. They focus on price and volume. Some of them are established agencies trying to replace the flow of departing clients; others are newer agencies trying to grow in an unforgiving market. They are desperately looking for some relief, and many honestly wish to conduct themselves like top performers but simply don't know how. Others can't or won't.

Now let's look at a healthy and thriving agency:

## The Healthy Agency

- *Healthy agencies are highly selective when choosing opportunities.*

- *Healthy agencies have little or no marketing.*

- *Healthy agencies rely heavily on networking and referrals.*

- *Healthy agencies conduct formal and comprehensive needs analysis.*

- *Healthy agencies do not "sell" insurance; they offer risk-management service.*

- *Healthy agencies are active on client committees and boards.*

- *Healthy agencies are active in community and industry.*

- *Healthy agencies develop proactive client-service plans for all clients.*

- *Healthy agencies have no timeline on the sales process.*

- *Healthy agencies are low volume and carefully coordinated.*

- *Healthy agencies manage a profitable, carefully selected book of business.*

- *Healthy agencies partner with carriers at renewal time and throughout the year.*

A healthy book of business is not discovered—it is developed. In a healthy agency, agents are able to avoid the feeding frenzy created by varying market conditions by investing their time and energy into the client organizations and activities that nurtured their success.

Such agents save their clients money through sound risk-management practices rather than shifting markets, and they have established a service reputation that is beyond reproach. New business opportunities flow to these agents through a referral network, and they are discriminating when selecting which opportunities to pursue. They tend to avoid the bidding process, as do their clients, choosing instead to build steadfast relationships that extend beyond insurance.

Through all markets, these agencies continue to thrive, as the integrity of their risk-management and loss-control programs greatly enhances risk evaluation, book profitability, and carrier relationships. They are proactive, efficient, creative, and energetic. These agencies are financially sound, expertly managed, and culturally nourishing for clients, carriers, and employees.

We developed our model to improve the way that insurance is bought and sold by injecting into the process an ever increasing level of value, integrity, and trust. Experience has shown that agencies and carriers that proactively seek, sell, and service clients by consistently demonstrating high levels of value, integrity, and trust, attract and retain desirable business. Unfortunately, this message has often been overshadowed by a widespread industry practice that myopically focuses on getting any and all business on the books as soon as possible, without regard for any long-term impact on agency or carrier prosperity.

If you then factor in the effects of inevitable market changes and channel-distribution disruptions that require ever increasing levels of account profitability and agent and client accountability, you begin to see an industry shakeout, in which uninformed and unengaged agencies and carriers will pay a serious price in lost profitability. The pendulum will always swing back to sound insurance principles that require all of us to manage the cost of insurance by managing the frequency and severity of claims. We can forecast stormy weather for agencies and carriers that are unwilling or unable to adopt a disciplined, proactive, consistent, value-added service strategy for their clients.

# Chapter Two

# A Winning Model—A Vision for You

*"Growth means change and change involves risks, stepping from the known to the unknown."*

—George Shinn

Top producers working in healthy and thriving agencies use a number of client discovery, development, and management strategies. We break the process into four distinct stages; however, it is important to note that the sales and service behaviors demonstrated during each stage of the model are on a continuum, overlapping and blending with each other throughout the process, as shown in Figure 1. This is the model that we suggest you follow when building your marketing, sales, and service programs.

"As I sit here in my office on this quiet Sunday morning I feel like the world has been lifted off my shoulders. I mean that because I feel like I have conquered what takes most agents years, and some agents never realize, the importance of value. … I have something different, something more to bring to the table and that is something to be proud of. I couldn't thank you …enough. You have energized me and the agency. I truly feel like this is a life changing experience."

*Mike Bulow*

*Agent/Producer*

**Figure 1: A Winning Model—A Continuum of Sales and Service Behaviors**

Success, as we define it, means consistent and efficient growth in new business, profit, and client retention over time. Therefore, the marketing, sales, and service activities that create and maintain the desired growth must also be consistent, efficient, and lasting.

Top producers know that a random and haphazard approach to marketing leads to random and haphazard results. They recognize that consistency is created when marketing, sales, and service plans are aligned, interwoven, and constructed to ensure that each client contact builds from the last and leads to the next. They see that traditional selling practices that identify a prospect, lead the prospect to a sale, and then drop the new client in the lap of an unknown service team while the producer moves on to the next prospect without maintaining "touch points" with the client, violate the integrity of the relationship and destroy producer credibility. Top producers understand that real opportunity is developed long after the initial sales event, because consistent, proactive, personalized, value-driven client contact beyond the first sale continues to build client trust and naturally develops into cross-selling, referral, and networking opportunities, while ensuring a stellar retention rate.

Top producers know that their success is only a byproduct of their clients' success and of the win/win relationship that they create and maintain. A top producer's service plan is almost identical to the sales plan. The activities used to create the relationship are the same ones used to maintain it, because that is what attracted the client and will retain the client. When clients hand over a broker-of-record letter, they are not buying insurance—they are buying into the relationship with the producer based upon a demonstrated level of value that met or exceeded expectations.

At a minimum, the client expects more of the same. Top producers know this and devote their time exclusively to activities that proactively build and maintain client relationships. The following provide a glimpse of what "business as usual" will mean for you, a top producer, at each stage of the process:

## Stage One—Marketing and Prospecting

Effectively communicating a distinctive message to potential clients is, by far, the greatest challenge that a producer is forced to contend with. Prospective clients are the constant targets of insurance salespeople and their intrusive and impersonal mass-marketing weapons, such as the cold call, spam, and the snail or e-mail blitz.

Recognizing that the problem with most sales and service plans is that they are the products of these inept, inefficient, and inconsistent marketing strategies, which are labor intensive and create a mostly wasted exposure and fruitless follow up, you will opt for a more refined approach.

Your creative, functional, and effective marketing plans begin with a narrow definition of who your clients are going to be. You research your target market in advance and limit your marketing resources to a discreet handful of pre-qualified prospects, specifically selecting your clients, rather than waiting to be selected by a prospect of unknown quality who is responding to a generalized marketing message. This enables you to build a highly personalized, disciplined, and manageable marketing strategy. You use a scalpel where others use a machete.

Your pre-scheduled, carefully coordinated marketing events build on each other and occur in consistent waves over time, rather than in random mass blasts. Each of your contacts will be directly linked with a follow-up plan that is equally precise and easily managed, due to the limited volume of prospective clients.

Rather than being aggressive, intrusive, and overwhelming, your approach is gentle and gradual, designed to attract prospective clients to you for the right reasons over time. Your marketing initiatives are not intended to sell but instead to inform and educate your selected pool of prospects so that they have enough information to make an educated decision about your capabilities.

No matter the prospect, your message is one of integrity, value, and trust. It is not about product, price, gimmicks, gloss, or glitter. You are establishing a rapport with dignity and professionalism—traits that will differentiate you from your competitors.

## Key Points: Stage One—Marketing and Prospecting

***Objective:*** *To inform and educate a selected group of prospects*

- ◦ Narrowly define who your clients will be

- ◦ Research your target market in advance

- ◦ Limit your marketing resources to a discrete handful of pre-qualified prospects

- ◦ Pre-schedule carefully coordinated marketing events that build on each other and occur in consistent waves

## Stage Two—Relationship Development

These are our moments of truth. What we do and what we say here will determine if we stay in the relationship or if we are asked to leave. If we have done a thorough job of pre-screening for desirable clients, we already have a good idea that our prospect is qualified and worthy of our time and attention. Now we must prove ourselves worthy of theirs.

Conventional wisdom would have you selling from the moment that you enter the prospect's home or facility. For example, others make nice with the receptionist, stand rather than sit in the waiting area, scan the office for hints of a personal life that you can make into small talk. You know this game, and they know this game. Because the game is as trite as it sounds, you don't play.

Instead, you are going to start developing your relationship by demonstrating the unexpected levels of value and integrity that you intend to use to maintain it. In other words, you continue to differentiate yourself from the pack at every turn. You know that there is a long way to go before you are ready to make any qualified insurance program recommendations, so you remove the sales event from your mind and focus on prospects' expectations.

Rather than wine, dine, and pitch to prospects, you are going to listen. Using an agenda that outlines your process, you request permission to conduct a thorough needs assessment. For personal lines, that may include a home visit and family interview to connect with the prospect's lifestyle. For commercial lines, that may include a tour of the facility, employee interviews, risk-management and loss-control program assessments, claims analysis, and policy reviews. You will review your service plan, your prospects' expectations, and your ability to measure up to them. You will provide references without being asked, invite prospects to tour your agency, and introduce them to your service team. You will talk about the markets when appropriate, and let them meet with the underwriting team, loss-control representatives, and claims personnel. You can, of course, entertain them as well. However, your definition of entertainment reaches beyond the golf course or the ballpark—it includes loss-control seminars, client roundtables, and attendance at their safety-committee meetings.

Having concluded your assessment, you know your prospect's corporate or family philosophy, structure and exposures. You have the information you need to look beyond issues of policies and rates, because you have gained a true understanding of your prospective client's organizational culture and specific needs. This insight will enable you to specifically tailor programs and strategies that meet or exceed your future client's expectations. Now it is okay to talk about insurance.

---

## Key Points: Stage Two—Relationship Development

***Objective:*** *Gain true understanding of your prospective client's organizational structure/home and family situation and specific needs*

- ○ Conduct a thorough but scaled needs analysis

- ○ Volunteer references

- ○ Invite prospects to tour your agency and meet your service team

- ○ Continue to educate prospects and clients

---

## Stage Three—Value-Added Service Delivery

It is at this stage that the breech of trust between the client and the producer usually occurs. The check is banked, the binder is in, and the policy and endorsements are on the way. The producer is feeling good, anticipating the commission and ready to move along to the next prospect looking for more of the same. The account is assigned to a customer-service representative—and off they go, whistling while they work, sorting through the next batch of targets.

But . . . what about the new client? How is the new client feeling now that the deal is sealed? Regardless of the job that was done to build the relationship and put together the program, despite the smiles, handshakes and pats on the back exchanged once sold, something mysterious is happening back at the client's office. Something that most producers don't learn about until it's too late.

Buyers' remorse—a sinking post-purchase feeling that casts doubt on the deal and raises suspicions about your character. It is a factor in every transaction, and it could significantly damage the relationship if it is left unabated.

You, of course, know this and have the time to do something about it. You know that it takes much more than a "thank you card" to clear this hurdle. You know that it takes an immediate and unsolicited demonstration of value that will evidence your commitment and help the client to remember why you have been selected as the broker of record. And this is just the beginning. From this moment on you will be proactively visible and viable. For personal-lines clients, you will offer timely family safety tips regarding holiday hazards or student risks, or write a disaster/home evacuation plan. For commercial clients, you will offer to sit on the safety committee, conduct claims reviews, develop a substance-abuse policy, conduct employment-practices audits, ensure that your client is OSHA compliant, install a driver-safety program, identify and act on cross-sell opportunities, and routinely and professionally seek referrals. You won't do all the work, of course, but you will see that it is done.

Your clients will finally feel in control of insurance costs and experience a tremendous sense of satisfaction from knowing that somebody else (you and your team) is thinking about their well-being, every hour of every day. And you will be rewarded with referrals and introductions to others who need the same level of integrity, value, and trust. Your work will uncover additional insurance needs, and you will effortlessly cross sell. Your status will be elevated from insurance salesperson to trusted advisor, and you will be immune to competition. You will also be quite unique. Only the best producers ever take the time to fully develop client relationships to this level. They know that their relationships are most vulnerable immediately after the initial sale, and they know that renewals are won and lost early on—not in the 60-90 days before the expiration date that most producers use as a guide. They know, and now you do, too.

## Key Points: Stage Three—Value-Added Service Delivery

*Objective: Make an immediate, unsolicited demonstration of commitment to avoid client doubts and prepare for renewal*

- **Be proactively visible and viable by:**

    **Personal-Lines Clients**

    - ➤ Forwarding timely family-safety tips
    - ➤ Writing disaster-/home-evacuation plans

    **Commercial-Lines Clients**

    - ➤ Sitting on safety committees
    - ➤ Conducting claims reviews
    - ➤ Developing substance-abuse policies
    - ➤ Conducting employment-practices audits
    - ➤ Ensuring clients are OSHA compliant
    - ➤ Installing driver-safety programs
    - ➤ Identifying/acting on cross-sell opportunities
    - ➤ Routinely and professionally seeking referrals

## Stage Four—Relationship Maintenance

Your relationship with your client is now on solid ground. As the harvesting season draws near and competitors start making their rounds, your team is busy comparing your performance to the benchmarks that you established early in the relationship. You are also developing new program guidelines and designing enhanced coverage for the coming year. Your renewal meeting with the client will not be the worrisome event that it is for many producers, because you have proven worthy and effective. For you, it is just another day.

Your value-added service programs are in full gear, and you are preparing for your renewal-strategy session. Taking nothing for granted, you revisit some of the steps encountered during the initial proposal process and design an enhanced, value-added service schedule for the coming year. You conduct a final claims review and analyze the reserves. You meet with the carrier and the client together to review the policies and establish new risk-management and loss-control objectives for the coming year. You do all of this because it is the right thing to do, and it is a natural extension of your value commitment to the client—not because you are afraid of losing the account.

As you review the year, you analyze your own performance and your personal objectives. A review of the overall plan clearly shows what worked, what didn't work, and how you can evolve your plans to find even greater productivity, efficiency, and success.

You see how the relationships with your clients blossomed under ever increasing levels of value, integrity, and trust. You see how careful client selection from the very start enabled you to devote the time required to manage your relationships proactively and consistently. You see how a comprehensive approach to developing your proposals enabled you to learn and understand your clients' family characteristics, operations, industry, culture, policies, procedures, and risk-management goals prior to developing your recommendations. Your awareness of your clients' needs and expectations allowed you to build a customized strategy to meet and exceed them. Clearly, you have broken from the crowd, differentiated yourself, and discovered not just a new way but the right way to create and maintain desirable client relationships.

---

### Key Points: Stage Four—Relationship Maintenance

***Objective:*** *Preparing for Renewal*

- Compare your performance to established benchmarks and personal objectives

- Develop new program guidelines

- Design enhanced coverage programs

- Design enhanced service schedule

- Conduct a final claims review and analyze reserves

- Meet with carrier and client to review policies and establish new objectives

---

# Chapter Three

# How to Use this Book

*"Start by doing what's necessary, then what's possible, and suddenly you are doing the impossible."*

—St Francis of Assisi

Because positions, responsibilities, and needs vary significantly between insurance agencies, carriers, and peripheral supporting industries, one book cannot address the specifics of each position for every line of business in our industry.

> "I have adopted the many facets of the program and it has made all the difference in the world. My book has doubled and high valued prospects for the next few years are already in place."
>
> *Tommy Farrell*
> *Producer*

Although we wrote *High-Payoff Selling: Being Visible and Viable in the New Insurance Market* from the perspective of a typical commercial-lines producer, we recognize that its key concepts also apply to personal, small business, health benefits, and life insurance lines at both agencies and carriers.

Now what about you? How do you apply the suggestions, strategies, and activities to your specific set of circumstances? Because we work with carriers, agencies, underwriters, and sales and service professionals from every segment of our industry, we are able to provide each participant in our in-person and online training and consulting programs with some techniques for personalizing the program. We're going to do the same for you here, to help you squeeze as much value out of the material as you possibly can. The following are your guidelines for personalizing your own program:

**Rule #1:**

You are unique. So is your perspective, environment, experience, personality, preference, lifestyle, and so on. Rather than adjust who you are to conform with our recommendations, we'd like you to adjust the recommendations to fit who you are and the circumstances that you face each day. It is not our intention to lock you into a prescribed process that might be inappropriate or inadequate for your needs. We have defined our objective—our ultimate destination. However, there are an infinite number of roads to take to get there. You are the navigator. We have presented you with a buffet of ideas and a range of strategies. Select those that you need and can apply; adapt them to fit your world, and move forward according to your plan.

**Rule #2:**

There is something here for everybody. Your work is only what you do; it is not who you are. The personal growth and development content is the heart of this book, and we believe it to be the most valuable. The personal objectives that you are encouraged to identify define you and the meaning of your life. Your satisfaction and happiness depend on your ability to accomplish these goals, and we want you to be successful. We have designed the goal-setting, planning, and priority-management tools to help *you the person* first and *you the professional* second.

## Guidelines for Underwriting Professionals

For underwriting professionals, a hard market leads to an avalanche of submissions, massive re-underwriting, strict appetite guidelines, and a disrupted agency plant. A soft market, on the other hand, creates its own submission issues, including a river of price shopping submissions, book "churning," and less client attention to quality risk management. At the time of publication, we are slowly returning to a slightly harder market, but over the past several years, we have been in a very soft market. No one really knows what the market will be like going forward. Even if we had a crystal ball, markets are always changing and depend on many factors, including geography, carrier, line of business, etc. Consequently, the bottom line is that, regardless of what market we are in, our behavior needs to be consistent.

Many of you are limited by the volume of processing that's required, and you are scrambling to provide baseline levels of service to your agents and clients. Endorsement processing is lagging; renewals are extraordinarily time-consuming and often late; new business opportunities are piling up; the phone and e-mail don't stop "ringing," and no matter how hard you work, there doesn't appear to be an end in sight. These are real issues that require real solutions.

An unnecessary but common response to this workflow crisis has been to focus on the processing. Field-underwriting and agency-management activities have taken a back seat to desk underwriting and processing files. Unfortunately, effective and strategic communication between agencies and carriers is abysmal, at a time when it should be a priority.

There is a solution, and it is found in the pages of this book. When reading the material, we suggest that you think of it in terms of carrier-to-agent relationships, rather than in the agent-to-client context that is presented. The parallels are quite apparent, and the strategies are easy to develop when viewed from this perspective.

For example, agents will be building a value-added service plan for their key accounts. You will be building an agency-management plan for your key agency relationships. We suggest in no uncertain terms that agents must protect their time (their most valuable resource) by allocating it only to those clients that are worthy of it. The same holds true for you.

You must make a determined effort to segment your agencies, evaluate which agency relationships truly qualify as partnerships, and then prioritize your investment of time and attention to these agencies. As we continue to deal with the legacy of the soft market or confront the operational challenges created by a hard market, recognize that legacy behaviors, assumptions, and procedures are no longer appropriate for this new insurance market. The first thing to go must be the erroneous assumption that you the carrier are able to provide and should try to provide the same level of services, proactive or otherwise, to every agency that hangs up your plaque. You simply don't have time, nor are you compensated enough for your effort. Agents pay for your time, and they pay for it with premium dollars from new and existing business. Spending time with those who attract and retain desirable business means less time spent with those who don't. Otherwise, you end up over servicing half of your agencies and under servicing the other half.

Here are some additional ideas to consider when implementing this material:

1) **Prioritize your new business submissions based upon the opportunity and the agent, rather than the old "first in first out" rule of thumb.** Your best agents bring you your real opportunities, and these should not be squandered while you work on submissions from other agents that don't fit your appetite, are incomplete, wishful thinking, or intended only to be sold off of, rather than sold. Triage your new business submissions, get rid of the junk quickly, and focus on taking care of those that will take care of you. The opportunity cost for not doing so is horrific, and the real goal is not to process paper, it is to write qualified, profitable new business.

2) **You don't have time to chase.** Too much time is wasted reminding agents over and over again that you have submission standards that mandate specific information to be included

in all submissions. Most of the required information is commonly requested by all carriers and should be obvious. Agents who consistently fail to comply and require chronic follow up to "remind" them of what you are missing are wasting your time—particularly if they don't sell the account, which is too often the case. The days of the "courtesy quote" and the "quote pending" need to end. You are better than that, and so are they. Let the incomplete stuff sit, while you work on the real opportunity. An agent who is serious about writing the account will get you what you need.

3) **Get back to the field.** Too many of you are caught behind your desk trying in vain to stay in contact with your agencies. It's not working. Most agencies need consistent coaching, training, and support if they are going to represent you effectively and with integrity. You must assume an active role in helping them manage their book of business. Carriers need to maximize their visibility and viability with their key agents by proactively supplying them with the loss-control and risk-management resources that they need to do the job the way that we suggest. Customer-service representatives (CSRs) need further training on submission standards, coverage changes, and appetite guidelines. Pre-renewal strategy sessions, joint calls for new business and renewal presentations, joint business plan reviews, and agency-performance evaluations are all essential elements of a true partnership, none of which can be done by exchanging voice or e-mail. Again, this means less or no time spent with those that are not productive, even if they are demanding more of it. Some of your lower tier, non-productive agents can rise to the occasion and become valued partners. Some will be worthy of your effort to rehabilitate them, but most won't. So pick your spots very carefully, and hold them accountable for improving their results.

Use the material presented in this book to formulate your agency-management plans. Develop a list of activities that will bring value to your key agency relationships by improving production, retention, profitability, and efficiency; then review these ideas with your agents.

1) Following the format outlined in the book, conduct your needs assessment, and develop these customized plans agency by agency.

2) Schedule the activities, execute and monitor the results. Carriers that have helped to develop this strategy are currently out-performing their expectations and their competitors, both financially and culturally.

3) Use the ideas contained in the channel-marketing section to create your agency marketing plans and to help your key agents create their value-added marketing strategy for their clients.

4) Build a needs assessment for them to use or, better yet, for your joint use on a co-developed opportunity.

5) Use the referral-harvesting strategy to develop a new agency-appointment plan that keeps a steady flow of quality, new agency prospects at your fingertips. These are new agencies that your best agents have recommended.

6) Use the priority-management system to organize yourself and your underwriting team, and use the goal-setting system to make sense of it all.

We assure you, adopt this method of conducting business and conducting yourself, and you will be well on your way to a more balanced, enjoyable, and successful personal and professional life.

## Guidelines for Personal-Lines Professionals

You can apply every strategy in this book to personal lines. While the large number of clients that make up a standard book of personal-lines business will not require elaborate service plans, they will still require dedicated attention. Putting individualized consideration back into personal lines is, in fact, one of the ways agents who deal primarily with them build their success. Knowing details, such as the family makeup and who is getting a driver's license, going to college, getting married/divorced, etc., allows for customized, relevant contacts that demonstrate your interest and concern for matters affecting them. Your information gathering (needs assessment) leads to building a value-added service plan. However, do not try to customize it for each client. Instead keep it simple, efficient, and effective, focusing on automated contact using e-mail, phone, and other methods. You can provide tremendous value by regularly mailing risk-management information, surveys, and industry updates, and you can conduct educational webinars and seminars for your clients and prospects at regularly scheduled intervals. The objective is to maintain consistent, personal contact over time with your clients. The contact does not have to be complicated or inefficient, but it should be unique and demonstrate a commitment to your primary purpose: saving lives, preventing injury and illness, and helping your clients avoid financial hardship.

## Guidelines for Employee-Benefits Professionals

As we go to publication, massive regulatory changes are advancing in the health care insurance market. Some call it regulatory evolution with opportunities; others consider it the end of benefits insurance as we know it. When multifaceted, employer-sponsored policies entered the market in the 1940s, employee-benefits professionals began to emerge as advisors to employers. There has always been financial and regulatory complexity in the employee-benefits market. Consequently, as we enter this age of change, what we said in 2003 remains true—almost every provider of employee benefits has a wide-open distribution network… so differentiating on price, product, or anything other than value-added service is out of the question. Because of these unique characteristics of your sale, it will be difficult to claim a "specialty" in any particular space in the market that isn't already well populated with competitors. However, with change comes opportunity. For example, some specialize in self-insurance programs for small and mid-size employers, while others are becoming advisors to large employers. Therefore, complete implementation of each strategy presented in the book is vital for your success—where your value-added service plans will be dominated by activities that educate and inform the entire client company. Whether it's obtaining a new certification or acting as consultant/advisor, it is essential for you to be consistently visible and viable to your clients and prospects. Client involvement includes participating in regularly scheduled online and in-person employer/employee meetings, brown-bag training webinars and on-site sessions, focus groups and other satisfaction surveys, help with enrollments, and so on. Your clients need a consultant much more than they need a salesperson—so . . . consult.

## Guidelines for Service Professionals

The traditional distinction between sales-related activities and service-related activities is removed in our model. We have clearly defined our reasons for doing so further on, so we will not elaborate here, other than to say that the old practice of a service person or service team coming into the client relationship to clean up after the producer when the deal is done is over. Your role in this model is as vital before the sale as it is after the sale, and your ability to differentiate yourself and your agency and to create and implement a value-added service plan is as important as any work that a producer will do. Whether cross selling, account rounding, or referral harvesting, all contribute to production of new business, retention of profitable clients, and the viability of your agency.

This material is appropriate for anybody, working anywhere, who is responsible for taking care of clients. We believe that you will find our approach to be especially refreshing and validating. It is not our intention for you to implement the systems and strategies exactly as we present them, nor should you attempt to embrace all of these ideas at once. To do so would only add to your burden, which would be self-defeating. Instead, ease your way into each new approach, one at a time, by adapting the material to fit who you are and the circumstances that you find yourself in.

Take your time, be patient with yourself, and let your plans and strategies evolve.

> *"A complex system that works is invariably found to have evolved from a simple system that works."*
>
> —John Gall

# Chapter Four

# Managing Your Objectives

*"Those who cannot tell what they desire or expect, still sigh and struggle with indefinite thoughts and vast wishes."*

—Ralph Waldo Emerson

Remember that old quote from Thomas Edison—the one where he explained the concept of genius as "1 percent inspiration and 99 percent perspiration"? We love that quote. What Edison is saying is that you have to work hard to achieve your goals—and so-called "geniuses" aren't exempt from applying a little elbow grease, too.

> "You have helped me to perfect the finer arts of Time Management, Referral Harvesting, and Goal Setting. I strongly believe these fine tuned skills will help me to achieve my objectives."
>
> *Nick Scamperino*
> *Broker*

We're reminded of Edison's quote because our objectives usually frighten people. Not because they are sinister—they're not. But their magnitude can shake people up. Aiming high and hitting the mark isn't easy and often doesn't seem worth the effort. That said, we have never been interested in settling for less. Nor are we content with mediocre results. We believe, and our experience has proven, that all well-conceived goals are attainable, regardless of size—but you've got to work hard to attain them. All goals, big, small, and other, represent nothing more than a series of well-defined, high-payoff activities linked together in a chain. The larger the goal, the longer the chain.

Although we define "high-payoff activity" in more detail in our chapter on Priority Management, we want to take a minute to do so here, too. Basically, a high-payoff activity is a specific action step that contributes to achieving our goals. Too often, we set lofty goals and even specific, measureable, achievable, relevant, and timely (S.M.A.R.T) objectives with ease—but that's as far as we get. Like so many things, the devil is in the details. Only when we identify the specific *actions* we need to take do we have much chance for success.

Look at Steve Jobs. He was all of 12 when he called Bill Hewlett, late founder of Hewlett-Packard, and asked if he could spare some new parts for a computer project Jobs was working on. That "project" was the personal computer. Even at a young age, Jobs knew that success is developed (not discovered) by starting early and working each link in the chain (or each high-payoff activity) consistently and thoroughly before moving onto the next step. A part here, some funding there, some advice over there—soon Jobs was on his way to building the first commercial personal computer—and making history in the process.

Here's another example. When Scott Primiano wanted to learn to fly, his quest for a license to pilot a plane began with finding a flight school. Finding the school encouraged him to find the money for tuition, which motivated him to allocate the time for study, which aided him in practicing the lessons, which developed his expertise, which in turn allowed him to pass the test that made him a licensed pilot—all according to plan. Well, almost according to plan. Actually, what began as a six-month plan turned into a three-year quest. As circumstances in his life changed (i.e. two relocations and a business start up), he had to change his plans to accommodate them.

*"In this life we get only those things for which we hunt, for which we strive, and for which we are willing to sacrifice. It is better to aim for something that you want—even though you miss it—than to get something that you didn't aim to get, and which you don't want! If we look long enough for what we want in life we are almost sure to find it, no matter what that objective may be."*

—George Mathew Adams

So it goes for most of our goals, particularly the large and long-term ones. Perfect execution according to plan is a nasty delusion—a monster myth that sets up lofty expectations that are bound to be disappointed. Disappointment leads to defeat—if you let it. There's an old story about the fabled 19th century British explorer Henry Morton Stanley, who, after fighting his way through a deep and dangerous jungle in search of Scottish missionary and explorer David Livingstone, was asked if he'd ever been frightened and felt like giving up. "I don't think about it that way," he replied. "I did not raise my head to see the whole. I saw only this poisonous snake in front of me that I had to kill to take the next step. Only after I had gotten through did I look back and see what I had been through. Had I taken a look at the whole thing beforehand, I would have been so scared that I never would have attempted it." It's difficult to imagine a higher payoff activity than "killing the snake," but it was certainly necessary if Stanley was to achieve his larger goal of finding Dr. Livingstone.

Okay, there aren't any snakes in the insurance profession—not that crawl on their bellies, anyway. But that doesn't mean you should forgo a plan that includes a list of high-payoff activities scheduled to be executed one at a time—just be prepared to create a flexible one you can change on the fly. "If you ever want to make God laugh, tell him your plans," as the saying goes. We would add that successful outcomes usually result from contingency planning and corrections to the original plan. Demanding strict adherence to your original idea and expecting perfect compliance with your initial assumptions is a guarantee of disappointment and frustration. Things change. Conditions change. You have to be ready to change too.

But change what—and when? After an idea bubbles to the surface, it's difficult to say which goals will be easy and which will have you reaching for an aspirin. Proper timing has as much to do with success as any other factor, and careful planning of each step in the process, although not always accurate, is still mandatory.

Patience is crucial. A need for instant gratification will derail projects that would have benefited from an even-tempered disposition. Even an occasional lapse of self-discipline will cause you to become distracted by other activities. Such diversions serve only to take your eyes off the prize long enough to damage a project's timeline and its success.

Regardless of the cause, the effect of living with an unrealized goal is unbearable. It is unbearable because a legitimate goal never goes away until it is achieved. Left undone, it lives on as regret. It invokes feelings of failure and resentment as we think about "what if?" and fantasize about "if only."

Over the years we've learned that one of the keys to success is not to become too rigid or too righteous about doing it "your way." Know at the beginning of any plan that unforeseen events and uncontrollable circumstances will occur and require you to change tactics and alter your plan. That's okay. Change is good. As George Bernard Shaw once said, "Progress is impossible without change and those that cannot change their minds cannot change anything." Change is difficult—as is achieving your goals. Almost every other major goal that we have set for ourselves has usually been difficult to achieve and, at times, seemed altogether impossible. Yet without goals we have no direction, no destination, no sense of purpose, and no hope of making the most out of life.

## Back to Business

Think about it. Think about the history of selling, and try to identify success stories that didn't involve goal setting. Actually, try to identify any success in life that didn't involve goal setting. Think about the late John Goddard. As a 15-year-old boy, the famous explorer established 127 "goals" he wanted to accomplish in life. They included navigating the Nile River, circumnavigating the globe, reading the Bible, and playing the piano, among others. During his lifetime, about the only thing he didn't accomplish was visiting the moon. Goddard understood the importance of matching vision with purpose and calculated action. So too, have many of you in the sales world. It's no secret that sales professionals are routinely exposed to various goal-setting systems, strategies, and techniques. Unfortunately, although logical in approach and principle, they all too often never grab hold long enough to become habit forming.

Why did the intrepid Goddard succeed where so many fail? The same reason our New Year's resolutions, made with such sincerity, dissolve by Super Bowl Sunday, and the same reason business plans, marketing programs, service contracts, and sales projections are sent to the recycle bin with such regularity.

Most goal-setting systems that break down, either partially or completely, do so very predictably. As salespeople, our tendency is to focus on activities that generate an instant return for our time and attention. Whether real or perceived, the anticipation of our return, usually in the form of commission dollars or recognition, motivates us to devote our energy to short-term selling events. We equate today's success with tomorrow's check and learn early that more prospecting activity means more checks. Calling on a new prospect might pay quicker returns than further developing a current client. This is not perceived as a problem, until the inevitable occurs—we begin to see clients slip away and our book of business beginning to erode.

As is the case with our personal relationships, our relationships with our clients thrive on our consideration or turn elsewhere for attention. Clients have demands for service, meetings, problem resolution, socializing, coaching, planning, training, and other contacts.

To provide this service, our focus must shift. If client retention is an objective, then we are forced to invest more time in relationship maintenance. The time we once used for pure sales production is now shared or even dominated by these service requirements. Adding to the burden, we have internal administrative requirements and external demands on our personal time. It seems that the more successful we become, the more difficult it is to remain a success.

How do sales professionals cope in such a chaotic environment? With uncertainty—and with mixed results. As new business production levels off or decreases, we struggle to find enough time to recommit to these business-building—and revenue-generating, high-payoff activities. Now our sense of work ethic comes into play, although often that's hardly the issue. Knowing that more activity means greater success, we extend our days and burn the proverbial midnight oil. We also add or request additional support and begin to take shortcuts or put off administrative work, hoping against hope that all bases are covered and all potential cracks are sealed. At this point, a mild sense of panic sets in. Panic is not good for anybody, especially a salesperson. As the unlucky-at-love 20-something career woman puts it in the movie "Singles," "Desperation—It's the world's worst cologne."

Our desperation sets in when we realize that the foundation isn't level, and the seals have cracks in them that are widening by the hour. We're in full reactive mode now, and we begin looking for a solution—any solution—that will turn us into the finely tuned, humming-like-a-Swiss watch production machine that we've been before. That quest for an alternative solution often ends at a goal-setting workshop, a time-management seminar, or with the purchase of a quick fix-type book. We read, listen, and absorb as best we can. Then we ring the bells and blow the whistles right on cue, and we wait for things to change. They don't. Our enthusiasm for the "new and improved" approach wanes with time, until we find ourselves unceremoniously dumped right back to where it all began—at our own desks.

Harsh? Maybe so. But not uncommon. Not long ago, Scott found a solution to this problem. This treadmill had played out once too often in his own life, with poor results. But what to do? Simple. Declare war on every know-it-all who ever sold a book or gave a speech. It was time to try something original.

He began with a look at his personal goals and found nothing peculiar, puzzling, or inappropriate. Maybe they were a tad optimistic, (i.e. XX dollars in savings by age 45). Still, they were balanced against others that were simple and less daunting, like learning to juggle. They were also equally divided between long-term objectives (run a complete marathon) and short-term ones (visit Gettysburg). Some were one-timers (finish *Hard Market Selling*), while others were repetitive (work out four times per week). Some were very specific and measurable (write a business plan), while others were less clearly defined (happy and healthy children). Finally, some were spiritual (meditate daily), while others were materialistic (a house at the beach).

A closer look revealed something interesting. In addition to being achievable and meaningful, each goal was in some way connected to the other (except for the juggling). For instance, his goal to run a marathon was consistent with working out four times a week, which meant he had to quit smoking and eat a healthy diet.

Now things were beginning to make sense. Each objective, large and small, personal or professional, supported the others. To successfully accomplish the large and long-term goals, Scott had to first accomplish the less imposing, short-term goals and maintain them consistently. He had to be a nurturer (who knew?). Happy and healthy children, for instance, require happy and healthy parents who consistently allocate the time to execute the high-payoff activities necessary to care for them. Same thing with goals.

Let's take the parenting analogy a step further. The short-term objective is to regularly spend quality time with one's children;

the long-term goal, of course, is to provide them with a great start in life while helping them to avoid therapy, early wedlock, and jail time. Coming to see these connections was a meaningful awakening, which led immediately to other discoveries.

By applying the parenting angle to his own situation, he realized that his professional objectives could not stand on their own merits. Instead, they needed to directly support his personal goals. He thought of the few positions he had held that required conforming his personal agenda to fit the demands of the job. Although each job had seemed attractive and desirable when he started, none had ever worked out as planned, and all had eventually proved unsatisfactory. Now he knew why.

Whatever we put ahead of our personal objectives will ultimately stand in the way of their accomplishment. Work is indeed important, but only to the degree that it effectively contributes to our larger need for personal satisfaction. If you make your job a higher priority than your family, you will lose a meaningful relationship with your family. When work is more important than your health, you get sick. When the Red Sox are more important than your sanity, well . . . you get the picture. Time away from work should be devoted to our personal agendas—not viewed as an opportunity to slip in even more work.

When our professional lives are synchronized with our personal lives, we are more apt to feel productive and essential. We sense that we are moving toward something meaningful and tangible—that we are working for more than just a paycheck. We have purpose and a sense of progress. We have a life.

> *"Your legacy is your life's work, not your profession. You will not be remembered for how well you did at work, but for how well you did at life. Focus on life."*
>
> —MaryAnne DiCanto

On the other hand, when our professional lives are working against us, either negatively influencing or entirely overwhelming our personal goals, we often feel frustrated, lost and unfulfilled— as if we are merely marking time. We become pessimists—looking at the land of milk and honey and seeing only calories and cholesterol. As pessimists, we drift along toward personal substantiation, but absent of a connection to a living blueprint, we over-indulge in what gratification we can find through our work. Living almost one dimensionally, our identities center on positions, titles, and professional responsibilities. If that's happiness, it's of the artificial variety.

As we move further away from our personal agendas and closer to artificial happiness, superficial measurements of success become confused with fulfilling ones, and we over-identify with "things" measured monetarily or materialistically. Who we are becomes secondary to what we do, what we have, and what we earn. This is the ultimate negation of our humanity.

Creating a blueprint for one's own life includes a number of professional objectives. However, work is supplementary to the plan rather than primary. Making money and achieving professional success are still very important, but they are not all-important.

The idea is to break down the objectives of your plan into daily, weekly, and monthly high-payoff activities that, when accomplished, move you directly toward the achievement of a larger goal. Your action plan will look like any business or sales plan except that it will also contain a calendar of activities that support the numbers, rather than just numbers. It will fit exactly into your calendar and provide balance between your professional and personal lives. All you have to do after creating it is to execute it.

Here's where the plan usually goes south. Sunday's plan becomes Monday's folly, as unforeseen obstacles became all too visible. The harder you try to make the plan work the greater the rebuff. The faster you run, the sooner the obstacles overwhelm you. Your agenda evaporates before your eyes, taking your enthusiasm, confidence, and determination with it.

Defeated and more than slightly humiliated, you look even deeper into your psyche in hope of finding a solution or at least a reasonable explanation—or you blame external circumstances. But the solution, instead, is to take responsibility and to review the entire planning process clinically rather than emotionally.

This approach yields immediate dividends. Upon examination, it's clear your plan is so tightly wound that there is no room for contingencies. Unable to fight a war on two fronts and manage the plan while dealing with issues that you haven't considered, you became imprisoned by your own escape plan.

You believed that discipline and determination would carry the day and neglected to recognize and appreciate the need to remain flexible with your expectations of others. Additionally, you failed to consider the impact of unpredictable interruptions, annoyances, and daily "fires" that consistently disrupt your schedule and sense of well-being.

Now, however, you realize that any expectation of perfection is ridiculous and self-defeating, and you are willing to settle for progress rather than perfection, regrouping and adjusting as circumstances dictate. Days turn to weeks and weeks to months, and you stay the course, gradually recognizing that you are accomplishing high-payoff activities, making progress, and rejoicing at the fact that you are closer to accomplishing your goals than you have ever been before. In time, those months will turn into years and you will never look back.

As a result, you will be able to manage setbacks and false starts with relative ease, viewing them for what they really are—changes that you need to make. You will become much more tolerant and accepting of other people's right to be human and imperfect. You will enjoy the anticipation of the achievement almost as much as the achievement itself.

Before you begin sculpting your plan, consider these thoughts:

**Stuff happens.** Good, bad, and indifferent, it happens. If you are counting on perfect plan execution and your expectations for a successful outcome are connected to a rigid timeline, you are looking at a "DefCon 5"-level plan failure. Effective planning requires flexibility and perspective. Think for a moment about a professional football team preparing for a Sunday game. The coaches, staff, and players spend the entire week creating and practicing a game plan that is based upon all of the available information they have regarding their opponent. What happens the minute the game begins? The plan begins to change and continues to change throughout the game. Adjustments are made based upon new information received and unanticipated circumstances, such as injury, weather, and the score. To enter the game without the initial plan would be folly, as would stubbornly refusing to alter it along the way. An adaptability to change is needed of all plans, including yours. Be patient, look for the unforeseen, and make adjustments as necessary. Treat it as a true work in progress, and you will arrive at your objective—although rarely according to the original plan. Even small changes can reap big results. Think of a sea captain who knows that there are many forces that control the movement of a giant ship in the open seas, especially in bad weather. A sea captain, however, also knows that turning the relatively small rudder only a degree or two can alter the destination of a ship by 1,000 miles.

**Time is not on your side.** Nor is it against you. It just feels that way, because it does not conform to your demands. Time does its own thing; it ticks away at its own pace and pays no attention to your agendas, sales quotas, or deadlines. Be very liberal with your expectations, particularly concerning events or people beyond your direct control. In the end, our objectives are most often achieved when the timing is right. Work diligently toward your objective and focus on the footwork, not on the clock.

**Believe in yourself.** If you anticipate success, you will recognize it when it comes. If you expect failure, you will find more than enough reasons to quit. Although it is natural to second-guess our decisions and doubt our abilities, we must override these insecure moments with heaping portions of self-confidence. You will not get the reassurance you need from any other source but yourself. Others cannot and will not accept ownership for your goals, nor can they ever become emotionally attached to your success. In lieu of a fan club, we must look internally for the support that we need to carry on. When it comes to finding what we want in life, we all walk alone.

**Visualize success.** Surround yourself with tangible evidence of your progress and visual reminders of your objectives. Participants in our programs sometimes create a collage that is a pictorial representation of their individual definitions of success. They hang them in their offices; they tack them up at home; they keep them in their planners, computers, phones, or any other place where they can be reminded on a daily basis of why they do what they do. Many people find it valuable to make a list of their goals and review the list at least once a week to check their progress and to stay on track with their activities. Remember, the larger the objective, the greater the obstacles to achievement. Keeping your objectives in front of you at all times gives you the determination you will need when it is needed the most.

## Four Steps to Developing a Life Plan

In his book, *The Seven Habits of Highly Successful People*, author Stephen Covey suggests that all planning processes should "begin with the end in mind." As we have already reviewed, our "end" is our list of *personal objectives.* Our professional objectives are only a means to that end and are only worth doing if they are directly or indirectly contributing to our personal success. Our first step is to build our list.

## Step One—Identify Some Personal Objectives:

To begin this process, start with a blank sheet of paper and write down *everything* that you have ever considered important or desirable to accomplish, acquire or enjoy. Pay special attention to the things you used to do and no longer do, activities that you presently do, but don't do often enough, and things you always wanted to do, but haven't found the time, the money, or the _____ (fill in the excuse) to get them done. Allow your mind to take you where it wants to go; make no immediate decisions on whether the goal can or cannot be done, or when and how it can be done—just write it all down. There is no need to prioritize at this point, nor do we need to get hung up on evaluating the merits of any one item on your list. Some goals may be as simple as doing laundry twice a week, cleaning the garage, getting to the gym, buying a new suit, being home in time for dinner, etc. Others may be lofty and complex. *All have merit.*

Next, on a separate sheet of paper, describe what your desired life would be like five years from now, both professionally and personally. Pay particular attention to where your time will be allocated, and be sure to note your income level. Record as many details of the vision as possible. Spend some time here, and do not rush the process—short, creative bursts are best. Don't concern yourself with writing style, spelling, or even finishing.

Finally, compare the results of each exercise. Look for similarities and specific objectives that support your vision. These are the things that will add depth and purpose to your life. These are the things that define who you are, where you are, and where you should go. These are the things that you were born to do and should live to do. These are the things that will make you happy. Now you have to determine if you are willing to do all that is necessary to achieve them.

Assuming that you are planning to continue your pursuit of your objectives, let's move onto step two and begin to sketch out your own business plan.

### Step Two—Select Your Annual Income:

The best thing about being in sales is that you are, to a large extent, able to determine how much money you are going to make each year. Of course, you should choose an income amount that is realistic. However, guard against under-financing your personal agenda. After doing the exercises in Step One, you've likely added some additional objectives to your list (i.e. gym membership, tuition, flying lessons) that may not be in the current budget. We usually ask producers with an earnings history in the industry to target a 30 percent increase in production from the prior year. Your figure may be higher or lower depending on what "30 percent" equates to. Either way, challenge yourself to reach a new level.

## Step Three—Identify Income Producing Activities:

What is it going to take to achieve your income goals? Simply stated, if you intend to increase your production by 30 percent, then you must spend 30 percent more time engaged in the activity that will generate the increases. Assuming that you do not presently have three hours (30 percent x 10-hour day) of free time built into your daily schedule to spend on new, high-payoff activities, and understanding that any additional time spent at work will negatively affect your personal agenda, we are left with only one choice—find the efficiencies necessary to create the time required.

As we will discuss in our chapter on Priority Management, deciding what not to do is as important as deciding what should be done. For now, we will limit our topic to determining those strategic, high-payoff activities that will directly contribute to the achievement of our production objective, and we will assume that we will be able to make the time available. It is this planned contribution to the achievement of our goals that earns the "high-payoff activity" the moniker "strategic."

Let's further examine what we mean by income producing activity. In sales,[1] these are the actions that you take to create new business opportunities. They include:

---

1 In a service position, where additional income opportunities may be limited or not exist at all, you will be challenged with creating and presenting a new compensation formula that includes things like referral fees, cross-selling incentives, retention bonuses, and commission splits on new business opportunities that you bring in. Most carriers not only agree to this kind of request, but also welcome it.

- Marketing;
- Prospecting;
- Networking;
- Qualifying/Assessing;
- Referral Harvesting;
- Cross Selling; and
- Client Servicing.

The degree to which *real* opportunity is created and converted into new business correlates directly with your ability to establish integrity-based, producer-client relationships and your capacity to support these relationships with consistent, value-added services.

Unfortunately, most business planning discussions pay too little regard to the proactive, service-oriented selling behaviors found in our model that carefully target and develop quality opportunities. Instead, they prefer to focus on sales strategies that use the conventional "contact, pitch, and close" approach to new business development that targets everybody. They are often inclined to this type of selling activity, because the efforts usually yield short-term results that are generally assumed to be good results.

Additionally, the tactics that support the strategy are easy to quantify and easy to manage: Call quotas are established; contacts are conjectured; appointment hits are calculated; proposal estimates are formulated; and close ratios are determined to define the payoff. One hundred calls yield 50 contacts, which net 16 appointments, which generate eight proposals that convert to one sale. It's all so mathematical. If the results are something less than desirable, increase the number of calls; go bang on doors, and "hit 'em" with direct mail and spam.

Cross-selling, referral-harvesting, networking, and channel-marketing initiatives, if considered at all, are most often perceived as supplemental and too difficult to measure. Building long-term relationships with existing clients is seen as a "service thing," and relationships with prospects are contingent upon timely progress toward a sales event. Proactive risk-management and loss-control programs aren't examined or considered at all. Marketing strategies in this environment are typically impersonal and sporadic, rather than carefully targeted and strategically coordinated. All initiatives tend to be price and product driven, rather than value driven.

Whether or not this price and product formula works is irrelevant. Arguably it does work, and any successful telemarketing or Internet marketing organization is standing evidence to this fact. Does this strategy, however, provide you with the most efficient return for your time and attention, given that it requires up to 20 times more effort, time, and money to court a new client than is required to create a new opportunity from an existing one? Is such a sales-driven, self-serving posture conducive to building lasting client relationships that identify and promote win/win opportunities? We will talk more about this in our chapter on Channel Marketing. For now, the answer to both questions is an unqualified no.

> *"There is no right way to do something wrong."*
> — unknown

If we firmly believe that our existing clients represent more than meat on a hook, and we have faith that through proactive client management we can create a limitless supply of new opportunities, then we must develop a strategy that opens the portals to these more reliable sources for new business development.

We will begin by grouping our business building tactics into four developmental areas that are supported by our high-payoff activities. Our high-payoff activities are defined as the actions that we initiate to build relationships with potential clients or to maintain relationships with existing clients. They include:

**Marketing and Prospecting.** This is the process of identifying, qualifying, and approaching targeted accounts. Our methods are focused on client and market need. Our objective is to establish in the minds of our prospects an awareness of our value and ability to provide proactive risk-management and loss-control services that reduce the cost of insurance over time. Our message is personalized and designed to provide our target clients with enough information to make an educated evaluation of our integrity, value, and trustworthiness. We pick our clients, rather than hoping that they will pick us. We avoid the bidding process altogether. We bring only quality carriers to the table, and we walk away from accounts that are only interested in the lowest price. We are likely to lose this kind of business next year, anyway. Our marketing events are synchronized and consistent, ensuring that each contact builds on the last. Our strategy is designed to attract, not to intrude, and our marketing events are not selling events. We do not make cold calls.

**Presenting.** Maintaining a regular and open dialogue with all clients, potential and existing, is a critical element in establishing confidence in your dependability, integrity, and responsiveness. Because we believe our marketing activities are equally applicable to existing clients and prospective clients (prospects), we often simply refer to them as clients. Only through regular contact will you begin to develop an awareness of your clients' specific needs, and only then will they recognize your value to them. *Every* client contact is relevant to your marketing plan. Clients respect and respond well to producers who are predictably visible, viable, and available. Clients react negatively to hurried and harried producers who, selling the old-fashioned way, have more places to be and more people to see than they can possibly squeeze into a day. Remember that their formula calls for a 1 percent return for their time and attention. They have to move fast, and they have to move often. They have to hear "no" 99 times before they find a "yes." The most important element in any sale, and in establishing any relationship, has always been the rapport and the trust established at the start. The image that you create in the beginning is the one that will be remembered, so it is best to prepare well and listen even better.

**Servicing.** To be considered different and more valuable than other producers, you must actually do things differently and better. This means bypassing traditional insurance selling and servicing practices in favor of activities that prove your commitment to your client and that build your credibility in advance of the sale. Demonstrating how important client relationships are to you at the outset by providing, or offering to provide, value-added services, such as loss-control ideas, risk-management suggestions, current policy evaluations, thorough needs assessments, and forums for client education, allows you to demonstrate your value and your commitment before an insurance decision has to be made. Additionally, you are able to assess your prospect's culture and insurance buying practices prior to investing the time required to find a market and formulate a proposal. By removing the sales event as a precondition for servicing your account, you are immediately established on a different and higher plane than any of your competitors.

**Planning.** Nothing happens unless you make it happen. Suppose you were on a non-stop flight to Tokyo and heard the following announcement: "Ladies and gentlemen, this is your captain speaking. We're traveling west across the Pacific Ocean. In a few hours you will be able to look down and see land. When that happens, we'll start looking for a big city with an airport. If we find one before our fuel runs out, we'll land. Then we'll figure out where we are and decide where we want to go. In the meantime, relax and enjoy your flight." How can you relax when nobody planned ahead? That's why you need a plan, specifically one that works—like this plan. The strategies that we develop will require proactive and consistent delivery over time. Our process is guaranteed to bring you total success, personally and professionally, if you are committed to doing the footwork. Your plan will work if you work it but fail if you don't. True success does not happen accidentally, nor is it a function of good fortune and circumstance. The only way to ensure success is to plan accordingly. Knowing in advance that everything that you wish to do cannot get done, we must create a plan that promises to deliver on the important stuff. What you do and when you do it will be a function of careful planning, rather than on-the-spot reactions. You will do what you need to do when you need to do it, and you will be where you need to be when you need to be there. Hey, as Yogi Berra once said, "If you don't know where you're going you could wind up somewhere else."

Deciding which proactive selling and servicing activities to engage in is a function of preference, experience, and ability. To be effective and credible, your list of sales and service initiatives must only include activities with which you are comfortable, that you believe in, and that fit who you are.

For instance, if you are not good at public speaking, then giving workplace safety seminars should not be on your list. If you shy away from evening social gatherings due to your personal agenda, don't include them either. If you don't believe in direct mail, don't use it. Trying to be something that you are not is awkward and uncomfortable for you and your audience. Forget what other people do or think that you should do. Stick to activities and strategies that are natural and reflect who you are.

Here is a sample list of high-payoff activities developed by other successful producers and account executives. Use it as a thought starter. Notice that each high-payoff activity is proactive, service-driven, quantified, and easy to schedule. See the sample Strategic, High-Payoff Activity List that follows. Again, it is strategic both because of what it does (drives goal attainment) and when it is constructed (when you are thinking strategically vs. operationally).

## Sample Strategic, High-Payoff Activity List

- *"I will ask for two referrals per week from existing clients."*

- *"I will host a series of quarterly workplace safety symposiums."*

- *"I will call three clients per week just to check in."*

- *"I will have two new business appointments per week."*

- *"I will send out 10 pre-approach correspondence per week and call to follow up."*

- *"I will meet with a carrier representative-underwriter each week for lunch."*

- *"I will conduct an on-location visit with each client once per quarter."*

- *"I will attend each safety-committee meeting for my top 10 accounts."*

- *"I will become active with the Chamber of Commerce or Rotary and attend each scheduled meeting."*

- *"I will establish an electronic clipping file for my target market and e-mail copies of pertinent articles with personalized notes to clients and targets once per month."*

- *"I will host an EPLI roundtable for new and existing clients once per quarter."*

- *"I will write two articles per year for an industry trade journal."*

- *"I will create and use a risk-management assessment tool for all new target clients beginning with one per week."*

- *"I will conduct a thorough claims review with my top 10 accounts once per quarter."*

- *"I will have lunch with two clients per week."*

- *"I will develop and distribute via e-mail an electronic risk-management newsletter to my mailing list once per quarter."*

- *"I will attend two target-market industry trade shows this year."*

- *"I will conduct bi-annual needs assessments with existing clients in an effort to locate cross-selling opportunities."*

Take the time right now to create your own list of sales and service activities. Your list does not have to be all-inclusive, nor will it ever be complete. Like fad exercises, ideas come and go. Some are good and will work; some are not feasible and will not work. The trick is to identify which ideas have the best chance for success prior to committing to any course of action. The only way to properly evaluate those ideas is to write them down. Write down *everything* that you would like to do or could do better. Documenting your ideas on a Strategic, High-Payoff Activities List creates a menu from which you will select key, high-pay-off activities for use during your weekly priority-management planning, as described in our chapter on Priority Management. There's no law that's locking you into any one idea at this point, so let the ideas flow.

One final thing—avoid recording activity that is routine or reactive. Answering the phone on the second ring, or conducting pre-renewal meetings 60 days prior to the expiration date is not fascinating, different, or unexpected—unless you do it in a clown suit.

These activities, or others like them, will become the foundation for your business plans. If we wish to increase production by any significant amount, and if we desire consistent, steady growth beyond the short term, we must establish a working action plan that allocates significant time to these high-payoff, new business building activities. Time taken from these activities and given to distractions, interruptions, crises, and other unplanned activities, reduces your production and wastes tremendous amounts of energy.

## Step Four—Developing The Plan:

Starting with your production objective (your sales goal), select the activities that will become the basis of the plan for achieving that goal. Review the Sample Goal Planning Sheet in Figure 2, and use it as a guide while completing your own plan. Later in this chapter, you will create a similar plan for your service objectives and supplemental plans for your marketing initiatives and planning time (yes, you even have to plan time for planning). Let's get started:

## Figure 2: Sample Goal Planning Sheet

| Development Area: Production | | | |
|---|---|---|---|
| Today's Date: | Target Date: *(We suggest this should be an annual target date)* | Measurement: *(Your measurement for stating and tracking your goal can be commissions or personal income (which you already have determined), premium income, or number and quality of new accounts (i.e. $50,000 or more), etc.* | Date Accomplished: |
| June 21, 20XX | June 21, 20XX | Agency Commissions | |
| **Commitment Statement:** | | | |
| I will increase my annual production by 30%, from $310,000 to $403,000 in the next year. *(Create a commitment statement in the space provided that specifically defines the objective. Ensure that the production target is quantitative and realistic.)* | | | |

| Specific Action Steps: | | | |
|---|---|---|---|
| **Activity** | **Start Date** | **Quantity** | **Frequency** |
| 1. Design personalized, pre-approach correspondence to target market hospitality program prospects. Send and follow up. | June 25 | 10 | Weekly |
| 2. Ask for referrals from existing clients. | June 25 | Two | Weekly |
| 3. Identify key associations for target and request membership and publication information. Ask for trade journals and needs-assessment assistance. Write article. | July 1 | One | Quarterly |

| | | | |
|---|---|---|---|
| 4. Develop top 50 prospects list for target market and approach. | August 15 | Five | Weekly |
| 5. Target industry-related networking opportunity with CPAs, lawyers and brokers. Meet for lunch. | August 15 | One | Weekly |
| 6. Host prospect and client Safety-Symposium breakfast for 70 people. | August 25 | One | Quarterly |
| 7. Develop clipping file for client information and send. | August 31 | Top 50 | Monthly |
| 8. Face-to-face meetings with new clients | August 31 | Two | Weekly |

*Benefits from Achieving This Goal:*

1. Vacation to Italy

2. Buy Beach House

3. Increased Job Security

4. Improved Self-Esteem

5. Promotion Opportunities

6. Maximize 401K Contribution

## Examples:

| Poorly stated objectives (Unspecific) | Well-stated Objectives (Specific and Measurable) |
|---|---|
| "Increase New Business" | "Substantially Improve New Business Production by 30 percent in the coming year" |
| "Increase Income from Commissions" | Increase Commission Income this year from $125,000 to $165,000" |

(Our example illustrates a production goal with an increase of 30 percent, going from $310,000 to $403,000 in the next year.)

1) Next, in the section of the Goal Sheet marked "Specific Action Steps," list the steps you will employ that support your objective. You will also state when to initiate the activity and how frequently you will carry out the action. A goals program without this type of detailed action plan to support it is difficult to adhere to and almost impossible to administer consistently. Review your initial list of ideas, and select five or six high-payoff activities with which you would like to start. Remember that an effective plan is composed of specific daily, weekly, monthly, quarterly, and annual action steps that are targeted directly at the objective. When designing your plan, focus on developing new strategies and refining existing approaches to improve consistency and frequency. Make no decisions about whether the desired actions can or cannot be done, or will or will not be done. Focus only on breaking down the large objective into small manageable bites.

2) When selecting the start date for implementing your strategy, try to overestimate the time and attention that can be consistently dedicated to each action item. In most cases, the action items will be new to you and will require more time than you might imagine before they develop into comfortable routines. Spreading out the implementation dates permits this "re-tooling" time and reduces the likelihood that the new strategies will prove too overwhelming to implement systematically. Do nothing in masses. New habits take time to form, and . . . time takes time.

3) List at least six benefits associated with accomplishing your objective. Why do you do what you do and continue to do it? Because it's beneficial for you, that's why. Critical to your success is selecting objectives that you are committed to, rather than just interested in. To succeed, total commitment is needed. Yet sometimes we think we're committed when we're not. A chicken and a pig were talking about commitment. The chicken said, "I'm committed to giving eggs every morning." The pig said "Giving eggs is no commitment—it's participation. Now giving ham—that's total commitment."

A good story and well worth remembering. Why? Because your level of commitment is determined by the degree to which you will benefit from the accomplishment of the goal. The larger the goal, the greater the payoff. If the benefits from achieving the objective out-weigh the inconveniences associated with overcoming the obstacles, then you will be able to muster the compulsory determination, persistence, and creativity—in short, the commitment—to see you through. Reverse the equation, however, and you will falter. Your benefits must be clearly defined before you take any action.

4) Be patient. Most action plans and goal programs don't succeed, because we fail to integrate the desired action steps into our routines. Initially, we may be attempting to hold onto our old habits—going about our business as we always have while trying to add these new activities to an already filled agenda. Eventually, feeling overwhelmed, we drop the plan in favor of familiarity. When properly designed, a good system permits you to progressively inject any necessary new activities into your normal day, where, eventually, they too can become part of your routine. As this transition occurs, non-productive behavior and habits gradually work their way out of your day to make room for the new. Our chapter on Priority Management provides guidance on how to do just that. These changes take time (usually two to three months) to become established, so patience and determination are critical, especially in the first few weeks.

5) Review your Planning Sheet frequently, and make alterations as necessary. When first developed, your action plan is a mere sketch of your intended route of travel, not the well-designed road map we sometimes wish it would be. As unforeseen obstacles develop, you should remain flexible and be willing to adopt a new approach as necessary. No plan is perfect, and no event is entirely predictable. Additionally, new opportunities naturally present themselves as we move along the path. Proceed without blinders, and enjoy the journey.

6) Celebrate your victories. Major accomplishments are the result of chaining together a series of lesser achievements that occur throughout the implementation of an action plan. The simple recognition of these milestones provides the needed incentive, believability, and enthusiasm to help you continue.

> *"The person determined to achieve maximum success learns the principle that progress is made one step at a time.*
>
> *A house is built a brick at a time.*
> *Football games are won a play at a time.*
>
> *Every big accomplishment is a series of little accomplishments"*
>
> —David Joseph Schwartz

## Creating Your Personal Development Plan

Many of us have been taught to separate our personal lives from our professional lives, drawing an imaginary line in the sand that prompts a figurative changing of the guard each time we cross it. In reality, however, such a black and white approach to life is inappropriate and counter-productive to building a solid foundation upon which we can achieve our dreams and aspirations.

Our profession is what we do, not who we are, and we do it to facilitate a standard of living from which we define the meaning of our existence. If you completed the Four Steps to Developing a Life Plan described earlier in this chapter, you identified some desired personal accomplishments, acquisitions, and/or enjoyments. You then focused on the income necessary to achieve them and the high-payoff activities necessary to earn that income. In doing so, you recognized the benefits of integrating personal and professional goals. By working with this interdependency rather than combating it, you will ultimately achieve a sense of balance, perspective, purpose, and direction that will prove more fulfilling than might presently seem possible. You can and will "have it all"—just not all at once.

Creating a personal development plan simply expands on the four-step process used in building a life plan. In other words, we need to take the time to write down our objectives and formulate a personal plan of action.

A few decades back, Yale University conducted a study on a group of recent graduates. After asking who among the group had taken the time to write out their plans for the future, they determined that 3 percent of the graduates had such a written plan, while the remaining 97 percent held only a conceptual idea of what the future should look like. Yale decided to track the group's progress for a 30-year period, and at the end of the study the researchers determined that the 3 percent who had started with a written plan were significantly more financially successful than the other 97 percent combined. This being a scientific study, Yale looked for other contributing factors (such as family wealth, academic achievement, etc.,) and could find no other correlation.

You are no different than these students. What worked for them will work for you and anybody like you who has decided to be more, do more, and have more.

To begin the development of a personal development plan, create two or three Goal Planning Sheets like those in the business planning exercise earlier in this chapter, and follow the same procedure that we used when we developed the business-building strategies related to your life plan. Your development areas may include any of the following, or you may prefer to select others.

## Sample Personal Development Areas:

| | | | |
|---|---|---|---|
| *Health* | *Education* | *Travel* | *Investment* |
| *Time Management* | *Motivation* | *Spirituality* | *Family* |
| *Financial* | *Career* | *Recreation* | *Housing* |
| *Esteem* | *Balance* | *Serenity* | *Love* |

Select only a limited number of crystallized goals to work with at one time to avoid objective overload. Next, identify some specific, high-payoff activities that will move you closer to realizing your goals, and include these with the high-payoff activities listed on your Strategic, High-Payoff Activity List and defined in your Business Plan. You will implement these in our chapter on Priority Management.

Our mutual goal is to understand and implement the process. There will be ample opportunity to expand your personal development program once this is accomplished, so please be patient.

Achieving what you want out of life can be as simple as defining it, believing in it, and disciplining yourself to go and get it. People are successful because at some point in their lives they decided to be successful. You must make the same decision. It is not an easy one, because the road to success is indeed the one less traveled. Ours is not a world filled with people and societies that encourage individual achievement. It is much easier to stick with the herd and adopt a herd mentality.

Our victories are often uncelebrated and our journeys frequently solitary. Successful people are quite different from the norm. And, because you are different, you must do things differently. Your decisions about what to do and what not to do should primarily depend on the degree to which the outcome will propel you toward or away from your objectives. You will not be imprisoned by the fears and limiting beliefs of others. Often you will stand alone, apart from the crowd and shielded from the distractions of life that captivate and entertain the masses. Your focus and intensity will sometimes be perceived as arrogance, intolerance, and social apathy—you will be often be labeled as anti-something. Despite the criticisms, stick to your agenda, and work your plan. Be true to yourself, and enjoy the journey. This is an exciting world—there's a lot to be done. So go and do.

# Chapter Five

# Priority Management

*"Set priorities for your goals.... A major part of successful living lies in the ability to put first things first. Indeed, the reason most major goals are not achieved is that we spend our time doing second things first."*

— Robert J. McKain

The frantic pace at which we live has accustomed us to expect instant gratification and overnight accomplishments. But sooner is not always better. Success is not a competitive sport, and we won't be left out if we don't come in first. The truth is, it just isn't possible to "get it all done yesterday." But you can get the important stuff done—if you prioritize. As Henry David Thoreau said, "Read the best books first, or you may not have a chance to read them at all." More important than speed is choice. Time management always means prioritizing choices; the challenge is to make good ones.

> *"[A]s I formalize my own strategy and start to incorporate it into my every day 'selling,' I know it will keep me headed in the right direction."*
>
> *Catherine T. Daley*
> *Insurance Executive*

Choices. We make them every hour of every day. We have half an hour before lunch, and we ask ourselves: "Should I start to prepare for that important meeting three weeks away or check my e-mail? Should I respond to a recent voice mail or craft a prospect pre-approach letter? Should I take a long lunch hour and surprise my daughter at her high school soccer practice or invite Jack to join me in the cafeteria for lunch?" And on and on it goes. It's helpful to understand why humans make the choices they do. Like all living creatures, we flee from pain and we seek pleasure. It's in our DNA. In the context of how we choose to spend our time, we tend to choose the activities that are quick, easy, fun, and lead to immediate results that we receive recognition for. These are activities that provide us with "pleasure" or immediate satisfaction. Conversely, we often shy away from important activities that focus on goals and take more time than we have available, are difficult and maybe tedious, offer satisfaction down the road rather than right away, and can be put off because no one will notice. Avoidance behaviors such as cleaning our desk or checking e-mail instead of at least starting the research on a prospect by accessing their website or checking social media connections that could lead to a referral often consume our days…and we don't even know it. And then we wonder why we never get to those activities that are necessary to achieve our personal and professional goals—activities we had every intention of completing when we set them as goals but that we somehow never seem to have the time to get to. Understanding our human nature is the first step toward dealing with this in a positive way.

> *"What an immense power over a life is the power of possessing distinct aims. The voice, the dress, the look, the very motions of a person define and alter when he or she begins to live for a reason."*
>
> — Elizabeth Stuart Phelps

In our chapter on Managing Your Objectives, we discussed the benefit of setting personal and professional goals and identifying the strategic, high-payoff activities necessary to achieve them. As might be imagined, many of these high-payoff activities are just the sort of tasks that we consciously or unconsciously defer in favor of the immediate gratification provided by easier, quicker, more enjoyable activities others will notice. We need a system of priority management to help us with our choices as we move through the days, weeks, months, and years of our life.

## Creating Your Priority-Management Plan

It is high time to stake your claim on each day and use what talents and tools you have been given to give your life meaning. You are worth every minute that you spend on making your life meaningful. The following is a priority-management system that, when followed, will prove flexible enough to be realistic yet structured enough to ensure accountability and consistency. It will get you results.

### Step One—Identify Strategic, High-Payoff Activities:

**High-payoff activities are the things that we do or should be doing to advance us in the direction of the achievement of our objectives.** Think of these activities as more "strategic" than other activities in that they truly do represent our strategy for achieving our goals. When you completed your Goal Planning Sheets in the Four Steps to Developing a Life Plan and Creating Your Personal Development Plan portions of our Managing Your Objectives chapter, you listed some of your high-payoff activities in the "Action Steps" section of each form. These are activities that you determined would get you to where you want to be, both professionally and personally. We call this combined list of personal and professional activities a "Strategic, High-Payoff Activities List."

By examining Figure 3, for example, you would be able to hypothesize about the personal and professional goals that the activities contribute to. Whether or not you choose to go through the formality of the Goal Planning Sheets, the priority-management system requires the creation of a Strategic, High-Payoff Activities List.

Ideally, we would all make these high-payoff activities our highest priorities every minute of every day and, in so doing, maximize our ability to achieve our goals in the shortest time possible. If we had nothing else to do, and subsequently had no other conflicting priorities, this scenario would be the only prescription for success that we would ever need.

**Figure 3: Sample Strategic, High-Payoff Activity List**

| Business | Personal |
|---|---|
| Prepare weekly calendar | Set up date night (once a month) |
| Post two business and two personal activities | Attend Mary's soccer game |
| Set up referral-tracking sheet | Attend John's football game |
| Create referral-request list | |
| Ask for two referrals (each week) | Surprise kids at a practice |
| Research top 20 (one hour, twice a week) | One hour treadmill (twice a week) |
| Identify possible associations | Research family financial planners |
| Contact weekly newspaper for column | Check summer rental listings at Salisbury |
| Identify two Centers of Influence (COIs)* | Register for INS 21 |
| Meet with Health and Benefits producer | Volunteer for church blood drive |
| Meet with local banker re partnership | Arrange Carol's birthday party |
| Schedule client/prospect roundtable | Attend Parents Night |
| Create Value-Added Service Menu | |
| Finalize needs-assessment questions | |
| Create cross-sell spreadsheet | |
| Target five cross-sell prospects | |
| Schedule lunch with Harry | |

| Business (continued) | Personal |
|---|---|
| Send five pre-approach correspondence (weekly) | |
| Make five appointments (weekly) | |
| Contact one underwriter (weekly) | |
| Update opportunity pipeline (weekly) | |
| Schedule trial assessment with existing client | |
| Meet with CSR (weekly) | |
| Make a referral to someone else | |
| Conduct three value-added service "calls" (weekly) | |
| Create draft At-a-Glance map | |
| *As discussed in our Channel-Marketing chapter, a COI is an individual or organization with strength of character and recognized leadership in your channel market.* | |

Realistically, however, we are constantly confronted with an overwhelming and always changing list of other priorities that interfere with, and often obliterate, our ability to stay focused on the things that matter most. As the boundary between what we are doing and what we should be doing becomes blurred, it becomes increasingly difficult to distinguish which activities are worthy of our time and which are not. If we permit our instincts and preferences to establish our priorities, we will be drawn immediately to the activities that are easiest to dispense with, those that are late or have an imminent deadline, those that we're afraid of not doing, those that we prefer to do, and those that we are comfortable doing. While all of these activities may seem important, few of them, if any, qualify as true, high-payoff activities. As a result, we tend to establish our priorities and build our "To-Do lists" based on criteria that may not be relevant to the achievement of our objectives. To address this tendency, we find it helpful to categorize the various activities that are likely to make it to our To-Do list, or at least compete for our time and attention every day.

We have already defined strategic, high-payoff activities. In our priority-management system, we refer to these activities as Level 1 activities. **These are proactive rather than reactive.** True "under the radar" operators, they will not "present" themselves the way an emergency or a crisis will. You must do something to make them happen. Unlike the uncontrollable, random, disruptive, and noisy characteristics that are typical of the fires that need to be put out, they are pre-planned and well organized. You have no choice but to deal with your personal and professional fires. High-payoff activities, however, require you to take the initiative and maintain it. Often, this needed drive is difficult to find, because we are so caught up in reactive, pressure-intensive, deadline-driven activities and events. Even when we do find it, this drive is difficult to maintain consistently due to interruptions, fatigue, and other life emergencies. Have you ever enthusiastically developed a new marketing program, a service or prospecting system only to have it evaporate because there is never enough time to devote to the project? More good ideas and well-intended plans go down the drain for lack of follow through than notes in a hymnal. The proactive nature of Level I, strategic, high-payoff activities makes them easy to put aside, while we tend to something more urgent or preferable. After only a few days, weeks, or months of neglect, they will no longer appear on the list of things to do at all. They will instead join the list of things we wish we had done.

## Characteristics of Level 1 High-Payoff Activities

### Level I High-Payoff Activities:

**Level 1 activities prevent rather than address a crisis**. Larry Bird, a former NBA basketball player and coach, once said, "If you don't do your homework, you won't make your free throws."

Translated from "Bird-speak," that simply means to put the time in and do your homework. For instance, an unsolicited service call to an existing client may give rise to a risk-management question that, left unanswered, might have grown into a service crisis. How so? Take your exercise program, which keeps you healthy enough to avoid the heart attack that you otherwise might have had. Or how about regularly scheduled quality time spent with your children that helps prevent the broken family that might have resulted down the road? Rather than fight the daily fires, Level I activities tend to neutralize the arsonists so that the fires never occur. Because we never actually experience the crisis, it is often difficult to associate tangible results with the investment of time and attention. The lack of concrete evidence that the Level I activity is "paying off" will often cause us to doubt the present-day value of our effort and chip away at our resolve. We find it easy to justify postponing these activities so that we may accommodate others that yield a more definitive or timely result. In short, we're not practicing our free throws.

**Level I, high-payoff activities also lack a sense of urgency.** Level I activities are directed at long-term objectives that build or enhance your professional and personal life. Unlike the intense pressure that we feel when we are scrambling to finish an overdue project or responding to a client crisis, Level I activities lack "do or die" deadlines and rarely evoke short-term expectations for results from others. There is no immediate penalty for not executing a Level I activity on schedule. Many of us have a tendency to rank some of our priorities based upon the short-term, known consequences that we feel will result from not accomplishing the task, rather than evaluating the overall contribution and worthiness of the activity. As a result, we will tend toward the activities that are pressing us the hardest and causing the highest degree of anxiety. Our quiet, less worrisome Level I activities become easy to ignore and put off for another day.

**Level I activities do not provide instant gratification for your time and attention.** Like a farmer patiently nurturing his crops, desired results are gradually achieved over a span of time, requiring consistent execution of planned activity. Progress is sometimes difficult to detect during each step in the plan, and we must rely firmly on patience and self-discipline to stay focused and accountable. Generally, we must invest heavily in faith that reinforces the belief that in doing the right things, for the right reasons, with the right people, we will achieve the right result. In this age of instant access to anything, we have grown so accustomed to getting what we want when we want it, that our deliberate, gradual approach to lasting success conflicts with a pre-conditioned expectation of instant gratification. Staying true to your proactive, long-term plan almost always requires you to subdue the instincts that demand a speedy result, while maintaining a consistent focus on the larger, long-term objective. This is not a wrestling match that we win easily.

**Ironically, Level I activities are the most challenging to find time for, yet they yield the greatest returns when you do.** Once accomplished, they leave you feeling exhilarated, more confident, directed, and formidable. Clearly, these are the activities that matter most, and it is our objective to spend more time engaged with them. The time that we need, however, must come from somewhere else, and this inherently means that we must spend less time involved with less productive, inferior activities. We will try to minimize the time spent with activities that are detrimental to our growth. We know what we should be doing. It is now time, therefore, to decide what *not* to do.

> *"In the end we do battle only with ourselves. Once we understand this and focus our energy on what we can do to control our lives . . . we begin to gain important insights into how life works."*
>
> —H. Stanley Judd

## Characteristics of Other Activities (Level II, III, IV):

Before moving to Step Two in our system, it is helpful to recognize that most of what we do every day does not represent Level I activity. This is both acceptable and expected. However, our challenge is to find time to schedule and complete Level I activities, and to do so we must understand the characteristics and impact of completing the Level II, Level III, and Level IV activities we face every day.

## Level II Activities:

**Level II activities are the reactive, in-the-moment responses to the urgent events that occur each day in our personal and professional lives.** Lost car keys, downed computer servers, a sick child, the day of your big client meeting—all are often unforeseen, unplanned, and uncontrollable. These are the reactive, rather than proactive, activities—the crises, emergencies, surprises, and "fire drills" that create chaos, stress, fatigue, and frustration. The list is endless—as are the headaches.

**Many Level II activities are unavoidable and uncontrollable.** Yet they happen and must be dealt with.

**Some Level II activities result from ignored or poorly executed Level I activities that could have eliminated or minimized the need to react.** The claims dispute that you are forced to mediate between the carrier and the client could have been prevented had a proactive, risk-management program been in place. The empty, new business pipeline that your manager is badgering you about would still be flowing with opportunities if you had stuck to your channel-marketing system. You would not be spending the weekend preparing a bid for a client who would not be bidding at all if your value-added service program had stayed in place.

These are just a few examples of common disruptions that could easily be avoided by staying consistently engaged in work-related Level I activities. We could make a similar list for your personal disturbances; however, the point has been made.

You have enough experience with Level II activities to know which are avoidable (therefore self-induced) and which are your job. Although we can never completely eliminate Level II activities, we can definitely reduce the amount of time and composure that we lose to them by devoting consistent time to our Level I activities. We all inherently know this, yet we all struggle with it. Why is this predicament so easy to identify yet so challenging to resolve?

> *"One might as well try to ride two horses moving in different directions, as to try to maintain in equal force two opposing or contradictory sets of desires."*
>
> — Robert Collier

It has become our nature to expect and desire instant and tangible rewards for our time and attention. Level II activities provide these rewards and give us a false sense of accomplishment. When we put out an administrative fire, manage a client crisis or just beat the deadline for a proposal, we take a deep breath and see that we did something. Whether or not it could have been handled more efficiently or avoided might be a secondary consideration. The fact is that we successfully dodged another bullet, and we will live to see another day. The more bullets that we dodge, the better we get at it, and the more conditioned we become to waiting for the gun to go off before we take action.

This gambol can produce gallons of adrenaline and actually feel exhilarating. It also causes damaging levels of stress and emotional fatigue that eventually cause us to burn out. It is a popular way to live; however, it is not the good life.

## Level III Activities:

**Level III activities are nefarious energy drainers that can slow the most promising career**. But if you like putting someone else's agenda ahead of your own, Level III activities are for you. These are the "got-a-minute" requests for your time from co-workers, impromptu phone calls just to chat, spam text messages, meetings that have nothing to do with what's important to you, and social commitments that string you out and hamper your effectiveness. These are the reports you do that nobody really looks at, the little clients that demand large amounts of time, and the assigned projects that help others to achieve their objectives but do nothing for you. These are the countless "sacrificial" occasions that cause us to put aside what is important to us in favor of what is important to somebody else. These are not worth your valuable time. Here's why.

You're a team player, right? So it's only natural to give of yourself to help others and their causes. However, your giving becomes detrimental to you and to the recipient of your charity when your support is unconditional, unrestrained, and unrewarded. They become overly dependent upon your availability, and you come to resent the time and attention that they need. You will eventually realize that you are unfairly taxing yourself and your agenda. You will drop hints the size of manhole covers, suggest that enough is enough and then marvel at their inability to recognize the inequity. Such shallowness, you think, only exists in Hollywood or in Congress. So you likely feel used, pestered, codependent, unappreciated, and taken advantage of by the clients, colleagues, friends, and family who live by the Latin term Ubi Mea" (meaning, "where's mine"). Eventually, when you are forced to come to terms with the imbalance, your frustration will lead to either an uncomfortable confrontation or a disheartening acceptance of the inconvenience. In either case, somebody usually gets hurt.

Effectively managing Level III activities means managing others' expectations regarding your availability and willingness to assist them. Some of these intrusions are unavoidable—they come with the job, or they are a part of life. Many of them, however, can and should be prevented, or at least deferred, by proactively establishing, communicating, and consistently maintaining reasonable boundaries. Most people will respect your boundaries if they understand that you have them. However, nobody can be expected to correctly assume what these are and to know when they are in place. Simple techniques such as moving chairs away from your desk, shifting furniture, or moving plants to minimize opportunities for passerby eye contact, standing and moving toward an interrupter before a long conversation can ensue, meeting outside your office to facilitate a timely departure, periodically forwarding calls to voice mail to execute Level 1, high-payoff activities, and/or using caller ID to screen calls, periodically closing your door to execute Level 1, high-payoff activities, sharing your calendar, and pre-scheduling what would otherwise be drop-in visits will make you accessible without being openly available. These counter measures are absolutely appropriate and necessary. Regardless of the length of each interruption, each time that we are interrupted we lose our momentum and our concentration. It can be extremely difficult to regain this lost ground and get back on track. Experience the dreaded double interruption (those occasions when the initial interruption is interrupted by a second one), and it can be all day before you are able to circle back to the original project. We must learn to hold our ground.

Other activities that qualify under Level III are those things that others could do that we elect to do ourselves—things we could delegate but choose not to because we enjoy them or are bashful about intruding on others' time. Perhaps we are concerned that others won't do them well or on time, or we think that it's faster just to do it ourselves. However, while this may the case, if we don't teach others how to do them, they will be forever ours to do.

## Level IV Activities:

**Level IV activities are the out-and-out time wasters that contribute nothing to support achieving our objectives and that, in many cases, prove detrimental to our growth**. These are our escape behaviors, the things that we do to retreat from the pressure and fatigue of Level II or to get away from the emotional tug-of-war associated with Level III. Simply stated, Level IV activities enable us to tune out reality and take a conscious vacation from our lives and our feelings. Often confused with Level I "recreational" activities, or thought to contain some entertainment value, these behaviors differ in that they lack productive intention and are often practiced to an extreme. For example, taking a quick nap is a Level I activity; sleeping away the day is a Level IV. A fun night out with friends—Level I, a weekend binge—Level IV. Watching a favorite TV show—Level I, watching anything that is on all night, Level IV. Checking social media updates, Level I, Internet surfing for hours, Level IV. While the desired effect may be to deaden emotions and have some quiet time, the physical and psychological consequences of habitual indulgence in Level IV escape can be significant and damaging. These include lethargy, boredom, depression, and isolation—the cornerstones for addiction to alcohol, drugs, and overeating.

> *"If we triumph in the little things of our common hour, we are sure to triumph in our lives."*
>
> —unknown

It is not our intention to be alarmists or purists; we all have our escape activities, and we are all entitled to our downtime. Most of us will never be endangered by it. Our goal is to help you to identify what you do, why you do it, and the effect it has on your ability to manage your objectives. The fact is that we can find the relief and relaxation that we are seeking in our Level IV activities in many of our Level I activities—if we simply look there first before falling into the Level IV trap or habit.

The greatest difference between our Level 1, strategic, high-payoff activities and all of the other things that we do each day is that high-payoff activities are proactive and productive. When you are consistently engaged in these personal and professional activities at the high-payoff level, you establish a balance and rhythm to your day. You live with a sense of purpose and feel more in control, because you are under control. Unavoidable interruptions and unforeseeable intrusions on your schedule cause less friction than they otherwise would, because your perspective is different.

You are able to filter out much of the noise and manage your way through most calamities with a heightened level of detachment. Your method for establishing priorities becomes more analytical than emotional, and you restrain any tendency to plunge directly into the next reactive task. Directed by your internal compass, you move through your day paying attention to your surroundings and reacting when necessary, but you do so without ever losing sight of the horizon.

Figure 4 provides a chart that will help you to qualify and categorize your activities. Keep a copy of this chart on your desk and in your planner to help you get your head straight before you set your priorities.

### Figure 4: Activity Identifiers

## Level I

**Activities:** Strategic, high-payoff, preventive, deliberate steps toward an established objective. Enhancing and enriching. Generally scheduled and controllable.

**Characteristics:** Pre-planned, proactive activities that yield gradual or intangible return, reduce crises and provide a strong sense of freedom and accomplishment.

**Emotional Effect:** Confidence building, competitive stress, exhilarating, motivating, calming, and relieving.

## Level II

**Activities:** Crisis driven, emergencies, missed deadlines, fires, etc. Damaging and unproductive. Generally uncontrolled, random, and haphazard.

**Characteristics:** Unplanned, reactive activities that yield instant results for the time and attention, provide an adrenaline rush and a false sense of accomplishment. Confusing and exhausting.

**Emotional Effect:** Anxiety, negative stress, fatigue, depression, anger, and frustration.

## Level III

**Activities:** Interruptions, others' priorities, favors, unproductive meetings, etc. Things that could be delegated but are not.

**Characteristics:** Unplanned, reactive activities that yield no return. Pressing issues for others that have little or no effect on you.

**Emotional Effect:** Anger, frustration, annoyance, co-dependence, and resentments.

## Level IV

**Activities:** Escape-like behavior used to avoid or distract. Desensitized, solitary, and non-productive. Generally controlled and deliberate.

**Characteristics:** Planned, habit-forming activities that yield no return. Provide relief from stress and deaden emotions.

**Emotional Effect:** Depression, lethargy, boredom, loneliness, isolation, and addictions.

Once activities are categorized in this way, it is much easier to develop a priority-management system that uses logic rather than emotions, personal preferences, or environmental pressures to determine what to do, how much of it to do, and in what order to do it. For instance, if you have an established production objective for the coming year that represents a 30 percent increase over your current level of production, you know that you will need to spend 30 percent more time engaged in the high-payoff activities that will generate the sales—the activities that are categorized as Level I. More production means more time devoted to producing.

Rather than extending your workday by 30 percent and running the risk of interfering with some of your personal objectives, it is more practical to find the time within the confines of your current workday. This inherently means that some things will have to go, and less time will be spent on other, less productive activities. In this instance, we would normally suggest reallocating 10 percent of the time that you spend in each of the other three levels (II, III, and IV) into Level I so that you may accommodate the increase in strategic high-payoff activity. Having categorized your activity as we described, it should be relatively easy to find and eliminate the inferior activity and create the "space" required in Level I. On the other hand, finding these efficiencies and making the appropriate adjustments would be extremely difficult without defining the value of the activities. This kind of approach does not require a radical restructuring of your work habits and routines; it merely calls for some reasonable adjustments and some forethought.

> *"Concentrate; put all your eggs in one basket and watch that basket."*
>
> —Andrew Carnegie

## Step Two—Building your Weekly Activity Menu ("Ta-Da" List):

After completing a Strategic, High-Payoff Activity List containing what we have previously determined to be the Level 1 activities necessary to achieve our personal and business goals, we are in a position to deal with all that faces us from a more operational perspective. We suggest you start each week with a comprehensive "To-Do" list that itemizes *everything* that you can think of that must get done, should get done, and that you want to have done by the end of the week. Experience has taught us that this step is a crucial one and that the more thorough we are here, the better off we are during the week. We actually call it a "Ta-Da" list, as this is what we exclaim when we complete something and cross it off. Please remember, however, that the list is a simmering one—as the week rolls out, you'll be adding unforeseen or forgotten items to your "Activity Menu." The objective is a good start, not a complete forecast.

Starting this Sunday, allow an hour or so to take a good look at your week ahead. First, access your Strategic, High-Payoff Activity List and see if anything on that list should be placed on your Weekly Activity Menu ("Ta-Da" list). Add to the menu everything you hope to do that week, both personally and professionally, regardless of how trivial the activities may seem—pursuits like reading, exercising, shopping, fishing, dancing, painting, etc. These are the activities that rarely make any list. Also, are there any other high-payoff activities that were not on the high-payoff activity list that you might want to add to the menu?

Also include time for your family and friends. List activities that you used to do, but no longer do (activities that you personally enjoyed or found to be professionally effective), things that you presently do but do not do often enough. Most especially, include those things that you always wanted to do but have yet to find the time, or the money, or the energy, or the . . .whatever.

The first few times that you do this, you might struggle and perhaps feel overwhelmed. Your list of activities will be a long one, and it will become quickly apparent that you cannot possibly do everything that shows up on the list. Do not be discouraged; this is not a checklist designed for the purpose of knocking things off. Rather, it is a menu of available options intended to help you see, select, and schedule the most productive activity. Treat it like a menu that you would find at any restaurant. The objective of the menu is to provide you with a complete listing of the available offerings. There, you would not even consider ordering every item that appears but would instead make a selection based upon appeal, appetite or diet. You will select activities from your "menu" based on the degree to which they contribute to achieving your objectives.

## Step Three—Qualify the Activities:

Once your "Ta-Da" list is complete, review it and identify those activities that will most effectively move you in the direction of the achievement of your personal and professional objectives. Almost without exception, these will be Level I, high-payoff activities. As a reminder, most of these activities are proactive, will not seem urgent, and will have no immediate result attached to them. Because these activities are not screaming for immediate attention, they are the ones most often ignored or displaced by life's distractions. These are the many things we promise ourselves we will get to, eventually, someday.

Next, identify the Level II activities on your list, the Level III activities, and the Level IV activities. In the beginning, it is quite common to have more Level II activities than all of the others combined. This is a clear indicator of just how reactive most of our activity is and how much time we actually devote to responding to urgencies and emergencies—doing things that repair but never build.

We are not suggesting that we ignore or delay action on any of the Level II items. To do so would be irresponsible and the consequences extreme. We are suggesting that you give equal credibility to the Level I activities that will inevitably minimize the need to spend so much time on the Level II stuff. The same holds true for the Level III and Level IV activities. We shouldn't become so rigidly disciplined that we don't leave some room for others, and we will never become so orderly that Level IV will completely disappear. We are only aiming for improved coordination and regulation, not complete elimination.

> *"In the last analysis, the individual person is responsible for living his own life and for finding himself. If he persists in shifting his responsibility to somebody else, he fails to find out the meaning of his own existence."*
>
> —Thomas Merton

In Figure 5, you will find a sample of a partial Activity Menu (an actual list would be much longer than this one) that has been rated by levels.

**Figure 5: Weekly Activity Menu**

(for the week ending 9/30/20XX)

| Professional Activity | Frequency | Level | Personal Activity | Frequency | Level |
|---|---|---|---|---|---|
| Clear E-mail Backlog | 28 | II | Run 3.5 miles | 5 Days | I |
| Finish Pipeline Report | 1 | II | Neighbor's Cookout | 1 | II |
| Attend Agency Picnic | 1 | II | Take Daughter to Dance | 1 | I |
| XYZ Corp Sales Call | 1 | I | Wash the Cars | 1 | II |
| Prep for XYZ Corp Call | 1 | II | Review Kids Homework | 5 Days | I |
| Follow-up Calls* | 3 | I | Watch Monday Night Football | 1 | I |
| Follow-up Calls* | 7 | II | Follow-up Calls* | 4 | II |
| Follow-up Calls* | 14 | III | Pay Bills | 1 | II |
| Make Referral Request* | 2 | I | Repair Shower | 1 | II |
| Finish ABC Co. Renewal | 1 | II | Watch TV | 6 Days | IV |
| Make New Bus. "Calls"* | 10 | I | Be Home for Dinner | 3 | I |
| Investigate LMN Co Claim | 1 | II | Next Flying Lessons | 2 | I |
| Send E-Clipping File | 50 | I | Son's Soccer Game | 1 | I |
| Make Service "Calls"* | 5 | I | Writing Workshop | 1 | I |
| Pre-approach Correspondence* | 10 | I | Refrig. Light Bulb | 1 | II |

| Lunch with DEF | 1 | I | Get New CDs | 5 | I |
|---|---|---|---|---|---|
| Attend Service Meeting | 1 | II | Lights out by 11 p.m. | 5 | I |
| Complete Carrier Survey | 1 | II | Breakfast Each Morning | Daily | I |
| Finish QRS Proposal | 1 | II | Study for Flight Exam | 4 | I |
| Online Industry News | Daily | I | Review Stocks Online | 5 | I |
| DEF Claims Review | 1 | II | Send Dad, Sister e-mail | 2 | II |
| Create Football Pool | 1 | IV | Mow the Lawn | 2 | II |

* Use Supplemental Contact Sheet to list names and telephone numbers.

We have also included a sample Weekly Contact Sheet, Figure 6, which we fill out while developing the Weekly Activity Menu. We use a manual sheet; others prefer to use contact-management software or something similar. Regardless of the format, filling out the sheet with the information about your contacts will avoid wasting time looking for numbers and e-mail addresses. It also enables you to be completely portable, and it works well in the car. Like the Activity Menu, it is variable—you can add to it and delete from it throughout each day.

## Figure 6: Weekly Contact Sheet

(For the week ending 9/30/20XX)

| PROSPECT CALLS | | REFERRAL CALLS | | SERVICE "CALLS" | |
|---|---|---|---|---|---|
| Name, Company | Phone #, e-mail Address | Name, Company | Phone #, e-mail Address | Name, Company | Phone #, e-mail Address |
| Name, Company | Phone #, e-mail Address | Name, Company | Phone #, e-mail Address | Name, Company | Phone #, e-mail Address |
| Name, Company | Phone #, e-mail Address | Name, Company | Phone #, e-mail Address | Name, Company | Phone #, e-mail Address |
| FOLLOW-UP CALLS | | PERSONAL CALLS | | SERVICE "CALLS" | |
| Name, Company | Phone #, e-mail Address | Name, Company | Phone #, e-mail Address | Name, Company | e-mail Address |
| Name, Company | Phone #, e-mail Address | Name, Company | Phone #, e-mail Address | Name, Company | e-mail Address |
| Name, Company | Phone #, e-mail Address | Name, Company | Phone #, e-mail Address | Name, Company | e-mail Address |

## Calculating Opportunity Costs

Since the final step of the priority-management system is selecting which items on your weekly "Ta-Da" list to actually schedule on your weekly calendar, it is important to consider the opportunity costs. Opportunity costs are the penalties we pay for choosing one activity over another and/or the cost of inefficiency. Too often, what we do and how we do it are functions of past practice and current habits that limit our ability to identify an alternative course of action. Keep an eye out for activities you presently do that someone else could do better or more efficiently. For example, if you spend a day per weekend mowing your lawn, add up the true cost involved—the gas, the oil, the maintenance of the equipment, etc. You might be able to pay for a professional service and actually save money. Not only that, a professional might also do a better job. The same is true for most large projects around the house. The fact that you're capable of repairing or building almost anything that you need doesn't mean you will save money by doing it yourself. In most cases, you actually come out behind.

Still other examples include working on small accounts rather than large ones, writing correspondence rather than sending e-mails, having lunch with an associate rather than a client, etc. Once the value of your time is correctly calculated into the priority-management process, you will immediately be able to identify the activities that yield the greatest return for your time and attention.

> *"Today, knowledge has power. It controls access to opportunity and advancement."*
>
> — Peter F. Drucker

Figure 7 shows a chart that will help you calculate the value of your time. As you review your Activity Menu, evaluate what you plan to do and how you plan to do it while asking yourself the following question: "Is what I am going to do worth the time I'm going to spend doing it?" The chart shows the value of your time, by the hour and by the minute, based on your annual income, working 240 eight-hour days per year. This assumes a five-day work week, adjusted for normal vacation time and holidays.

**Figure 7: How Much Does Time Cost You Each Day?**

| Your Annual Income Is: | Each Hour You Spend: | Each Minute You Spend: |
| --- | --- | --- |
| $25,000 | 13.02 | .22 |
| 30,000 | 15.62 | .26 |
| 35,000 | 18.23 | .30 |
| 40,000 | 20.83 | .35 |
| 45,000 | 23.44 | .39 |
| 50,000 | 26.04 | .43 |
| 60,000 | 31.25 | .52 |
| 70,000 | 36.46 | .61 |
| 80,000 | 41.67 | .69 |
| 90,000 | 46.88 | .78 |
| 100,000 | 52.08 | .87 |
| 125,000 | 65.10 | 1.09 |
| 150,000 | 78.13 | 1.30 |
| 175,000 | 91.15 | 1.52 |
| 200,000 | 104.17 | 1.74 |
| 250,000 | 130.21 | 2.17 |
| 300,000 | 156.25 | 2.60 |
| 400,000 | 208.33 | 3.47 |
| 500,000 | 260.42 | 4.34 |
| 1,000,000 | 520.83 | 8.68 |

Comparing the Weekly Activity Menu that we displayed earlier in Figure 5 to the Revised Weekly Activity Menu in Figure 8, we can see how some of the activity is re-categorized into other levels based upon our opportunity-cost analysis.

## Figure 8: Revised Weekly Activity Menu

(For the week ending 9/30/20XX)

| Professional Activity | Frequency | Level | Personal Activity | Frequency | Level |
|---|---|---|---|---|---|
| Clear E-mail Backlog | 28 | II, III | Run 3.5 miles | 5 Days | I |
| Finish Pipeline Report | 1 | II | Neighbor's Cookout | 1 | III |
| Attend Agency Picnic | 1 | III | Take Daughter to Dance | 1 | I |
| XYZ Corp Sales Call | 1 | I | Wash the Cars | 1 | IV |
| Prep for XYZ Corp Call | 1 | II | Review Kids Homework | 5 Days | I |
| Follow-up Calls* | 3 | I | Watch Monday Night FB | 1 | IV |
| Follow-up Calls* | 7 | II | Follow-up Calls* | 4 | II |
| Follow-up Calls* | 14 | III | Pay Bills | 1 | II |
| Make Referral Request* | 2 | I | Repair Shower | 1 | II |
| Finish ABC Co. Renewal | 1 | II | Watch TV | 6 Days | IV |
| Make New Bus. Calls* | 10 | I | Be Home for Dinner | 3 | II |
| Investigate LMN Co Claim | 1 | IV | Next Flying Lessons | 2 | I |
| Send E-Clipping File | 50 | I | Son's Soccer Game | 1 | I |
| Make Service "Calls"* | 5 | I | Writing Workshop | 1 | I |
| Pre-approach Correspondence* | 10 | I | Refrig. Light Bulb | 1 | II |

| Lunch with DEF | 1 | III | Get New CDs | 5 | I |
|---|---|---|---|---|---|
| Attend Service Meeting | 1 | III | Lights out by 11:00 P.M. | 5 | I |
| Complete Carrier Survey | 1 | IV | Breakfast Each Morning | Daily | I |
| Finish QRS Proposal | 1 | II | Study for Flight Exam | 4 | I |
| Online Industry News | Daily | I | Review Stocks Online | 5 | I |
| DEF Claims Review | 1 | II | Send Dad, Sister E-mail | 2 | II |
| Create Football Pool | 1 | IV | Mow the Lawn | 2 | IV |

* Use Supplemental Contact Sheet to list names and telephone numbers

**On the professional list:**

- Some of the e-mail responses were moved to Level III because they contributed little.

- The agency picnic was considered nice, politically correct, but not needed.

- Somebody else can handle the claims investigation for a small client.

- The lunch with DEF, another producer, is more social than helpful.

**On the personal list:**

- The neighbor's cookout is really for the kids.

- Washing the cars by hand takes too long; the car wash is better.

- Monday Night Football is not showing a favorite team—why bother?

- Either a service or one of the kids could mow the lawn.

The point to remember is that there are always alternative solutions to getting things done. When reviewing your options, remain as intellectual and analytical as possible. Pretend to be an unbiased advisor to your own schedule. Even if you choose to do things the same way that you always have, you at least know that you are making a choice that you can rationalize. This is why the system is called priority management.

## Step Four—Building A Weekly Calendar:

Having posted our activities, including some from our Strategic, High-Payoff Activity List, categorized them by level, and created a Weekly Contact Sheet, we now know what we want to do and who we want to do it with. All that remains to be done is the construction of a schedule that will tell us when we can accomplish the key activities. Prior to developing our schedule for the week, it is important for us to take a step back and remind ourselves of a few qualifying factors, namely:

**The schedule is not fixed**. Even the most precise plans change as unpredictable circumstances intrude. Rather than fight this fact of life, we are going to build a calendar that is flexible enough to tolerate changes without sending us into a tailspin. Remember that a professional football team spends months preparing a game plan for an opponent, only to have it change the minute the game begins. Rather than abandon the original plan, the coaching staff and players make continual adjustments that improve their chances for a successful outcome. We too will need to adjust.

**What gets done is more important than when it gets done**. Unlike many time-management systems, our focus is on the day and the week, not on the minutes. We will not accomplish every task in the time that we estimate that it will take, nor will we start every initiative on time. Our goal is to end the week with most of our scheduled activities completed.

**You've got rhythm!** Some of us are morning people, and some of us are night owls. Throughout the day, we experience periods when our energy is high and our ability to focus improves, followed by lulls in both. Add to this our normal mood swings that can vary from highly motivated to melancholy, and we can have a frustrating experience if we try to schedule high-performance tasks into blocks of time when we would rather do nothing at all. Conversely, we do not want to waste our peak production hours on trivial tasks. Once you are aware of your own rhythms, you will find them to be fairly consistent, and you can plan accordingly. The point is to do whatever works for you, to work *with* the current of your emotions. Also, don't try to mimic someone else. In an attempt to impress or fit in, too many night people struggle to behave like morning people and visa-versa. Respect yourself and your natural cycles.

**Pay attention to your attention span!** Even when you are operating during peak performance time, the longer you stay engrossed in one task the more difficult it becomes, and the more energy it takes to pay attention to what you are doing. Most healthy adults are unable to sustain focus on one thing for longer than 40 minutes, after which time you hit a wall and begin to require more and more energy to stay focused. Keep working and you will soon be depleted. Know what your attention span is and don't fight it. Take little breaks at appropriate times—get a cup of coffee, a drink of water, check your voice mail, or take a walk around the office to stretch. Then get back to it and see how refreshed you feel.

**Be real.** You will not complete everything on your list. In fact, you may even add more activity than you dispense with as the week rolls out. Even if by some miracle you only had to do Level 1 activities, you would still have to make some tough decisions about what gets done and what doesn't. You will always be dealing with a list of competing priorities; flexibility and practicality are called for.

With these conditions in place, we are ready to develop the calendar. You will need to use a weekly calendar that is formatted, as in Figure 9.

**Figure 9: Calendar**

|  | Mon | Tue | Wed | Thu | Fri | Sat | Sun |
|---|---|---|---|---|---|---|---|
| 7:00-8:00 |  |  |  |  |  |  |  |
| 8:00-9:00 |  |  |  |  |  |  |  |
| 9:00-10:00 |  |  |  |  |  |  |  |
| 10:00-11:00 |  |  |  |  |  |  |  |
| 11:00-12:00 |  |  |  |  |  |  |  |
| 12:00-1:00 |  |  |  |  |  |  |  |
| 1:00-2:00 |  |  |  |  |  |  |  |
| 2:00-3:00 |  |  |  |  |  |  |  |
| 3:00-4:00 |  |  |  |  |  |  |  |
| 4:00-5:00 |  |  |  |  |  |  |  |
| 5:00-6:00 |  |  |  |  |  |  |  |
| 6:00-7:00 |  |  |  |  |  |  |  |
| 7:00-8:00 |  |  |  |  |  |  |  |
| 8:00-9:00 |  |  |  |  |  |  |  |
| 9:00-10:00 |  |  |  |  |  |  |  |
| 10:00-11:00 |  |  |  |  |  |  |  |

We suggest that you use an online calendar and activity planner that you can access at the office as well as at home and on the road. If you have a laptop, a smartphone, or an iPad, you can also use any one of a number of contact-management/activity-planner software products that are available. At the very least, use a manual calendar that opens to display an entire week. For ease of illustration, we will demonstrate using a manual calendar, but we encourage use of technology you are comfortable with.

With the Activity Menu, or "Ta-Da" list, and Weekly Contact Sheet in front of us, we are going to select a limited number of Level I activities and schedule them into the week ahead. Knowing that you will not be able to commit to every Level I activity that you have recorded, let alone every activity on the menu, it would be counter-productive to fill up every time-slot on the calendar without any hope of getting it all done. Although it might be aesthetically pleasing, the calendar would be too jammed up to be workable.

It is also important to remember that life is far too unpredictable to schedule everything precisely. To avoid frustration or failure, we accept this reality rather than trying to fight it. I suggest that you begin by scheduling only three to five professional Level I activities per week and two to three personal Level I activities per week in these first few weeks. If you find yourself completing these assignments with ease, you can add more. Conversely, if you struggle, you can limit yourself even further.

The goal is to develop a consistent and determined commitment to these Level 1, high-payoff activities at a pace that is practical and manageable. Your priority-management system is designed to get you to your objectives over time, not overnight. Remember, too, that even if you complete fewer high-payoff, Level I activities than planned in a given week, it is likely that you will complete more than you would have without the discipline of priority management.

So . . . here we go:

Starting with Monday, select your first Level I activity, estimate the time that it will take to accomplish the task, and box out the time on your calendar. Keep in mind that *first thing in the morning may not be the best time to schedule your first Level I activity.* Many of us (non-morning people) need time in the morning to set up the day, meet with staff, return a few calls, etc. If you are in the habit of taking this morning time to settle in, continue to take it.

|  | **Monday** | **Tuesday** |
|---|---|---|
| 7:00-8:00 | | |
| 8:00-9:00 | | |
| 9:00-10:00 | Make 5 Customer Service "Calls" | |
| 10:00-11:00 | | |

According to the example shown on the previous page, at 9 a.m. on Monday, your door (if you have one) will close; you will post a note indicating you are working on Level 1 activity; your Weekly Contact sheet will come out, and you'll start smiling and making connections. You will not permit interruptions, answer your phone when it rings, respond to e-mail, or settle for anything other than completing the assignment. At this point, you don't really know how long it will take. If everybody you're connecting with is in, you could exceed the hour that you have estimated. If you get only voice-mail greetings or out-of-office messages, you'll be done in 15 minutes. Either way, you're only going to focus on the activity you can control. The rest is out of your hands. The objective is to make the connection. In fact, don't worry one bit about leaving proactive customer-service messages on voice mail. The positive client touch is made; the impact is effective, and you finish early. Advantage . . .you.

You can make Level III contacts and many of your "quick-answers-to-questions" Level II calls/e-mails during lunch or after hours with every intention of getting voice mail and avoiding an unnecessary conversation. Never return Level IV correspondence.

Schedule your next Level I activity for later in the morning or early afternoon. Try to schedule your high-payoff time each day by leaving large blocks of time between other activities that will act as buffer zones and allow for flexibility. This way, you'll leave plenty of time to accommodate all of the normal daily activity and, in the event that we do run late with our first Level I, we are not bumping right into another high-payoff time slot. The trick is to chip away at the truly meaningful stuff throughout the day while fencing with all of the other impositions on your time.

|  | Monday | Tuesday |
|---|---|---|
| 7:00-8:00 |  |  |
| 8:00-9:00 |  |  |
| 9:00-10:00 | Make 5 Customer Service "Calls" |  |
| 10:00-11:00 |  |  |
| 11:00-12:00 |  |  |
| 12:00-1:00 |  |  |
| 1:00-2:00 | Send Pre-Approach Correspondence (10) |  |
| 2:00-3:00 |  |  |

Finish scheduling the remainder of the week in the same manner as shown in this chart. Do not put your other activities on the calendar at all. Instead, keep them on your Activity Menu, and complete them as time permits, within the buffer zones that exist between the high-payoff activities. The exception to this rule is those activities you must attend to on a given day at a given time. Since that time is not available for Level I activities, show the activity on the calendar. Your completed calendar will look similar to the one in Figure 10. Please be aware, however, that the Figure 10 sample calendar represents that of someone experienced at priority management. It is likely your early calendars will and should have more buffer-zone space.

**Figure 10: Completed Calendar**

| | Monday | Tuesday | Wednesday | Thursday | Friday | Saturday | Sunday |
|---|---|---|---|---|---|---|---|
| 7:00-8:00 | Breakfast | Breakfast | Breakfast | Breakfast | Breakfast | Breakfast | |
| 8:00-9:00 | | | | | | | Breakfast |
| 9:00-10:00 | Make 5 Customer Service "Calls" | Follow up "Calls" | | Send E-Clipping File (50) | | Soccer | Breakfast |
| 10:00-11:00 | | | XYZ Corp Sales "Call" | | Follow Up "Calls" | Soccer | |
| 11:00-12:00 | | | XYZ Corp Sales "Call" | | | | Flight Lesson |
| 12:00-1:00 | | | XYZ Corp Sales "Call" | | | | |
| 1:00-2:00 | Send Pre-Approach Correspondence (10) | | XYZ Corp Sales "Call" | Check online news; Review Stocks | | Run | |
| 2:00-3:00 | | New Business "Calls" (5) | | | New Business "Calls" (5) | Study for Flight Exam | Run |

|  |  |  |  |  |  |  |  |
|---|---|---|---|---|---|---|---|
| 3:00-4:00 |  |  |  |  |  |  |  |
| 4:00-5:00 |  | Flight Lesson |  |  | Referral Requests (2) |  | Check online news; Review Stocks |
| 5:00-6:00 |  |  | Run |  |  | Run |  |
| 6:00-7:00 | Review Homework | Father / Daughter Dance |  | Run | Check online news; Review Stocks |  |  |
| 7:00-8:00 |  | Father / Daughter Dance | Dinner | Dinner |  |  | Dinner |
| 8:00-9:00 | Review Homework | Father/ Daughter Dance | Check online news; Review Stocks |  |  | Review Homework |  |
| 9:00-10:00 |  | Father/ Daughter Dance |  | Review Homework |  | Check online news; Review Stocks |  |
| 10:00-11:00 |  |  | Study for Flight Exam |  | Study for Flight Exam |  | Study for Flight Exam |

You have completed your calendar, and you now have a reasonable prediction of how the coming week is going to shape up. You have proactively established your priorities to avoid having to make crucial time-management decisions in the heat of the moment, when you are most likely to be impulsive and reactive. This is the reason we refer to the Strategic, High-Payoff Activity List and create the Menu, Weekly Contact Sheet and Calendar on Sunday.

By Monday, or at any other time during the week, we are already fully engaged and will find it too difficult to withdraw, reflect, and reorganize our perspective and our priorities. A pro-active hour on Sunday is the catalyst for an effective and efficient week.

Still, your weekly calendar is only your trail map for the week. It is your game plan that will be adjusted and revised many times as events unfold. The only thing we can predict with absolute certainty is that unpredictable events will occur and upset our preconceived plan for the week. Be ready to move your Level I activities up and back and from side to side. Work your calendar like a game of chess—strategically and logically. If you keep it in front of you and follow it with determination, focusing on what gets done while being flexible with when, you will feel a great sense of satisfaction by week's end. As weeks turn into months and months into years, you will realize that, in spite of all that did not get done, what did get done made a difference.

## Additional Priority-Management Tips

### Get Clean and Stay Clean:

Every now and again someone will try to convince you that a cluttered office is a sign of a real worker. They will go on to say that a clean desk signifies that a person doesn't have enough to do. Ah, no. If you wish to stay mentally organized, you must also be physically organized. Don't listen to all the alibis and justifications for maintaining a sloppy work area: "I know where everything is;" "I'm afraid I'll forget it;" "I'm afraid that I'll lose it;" and the ever popular "I'll clean it up tomorrow."

## Don't Buy Any of Them:

It is much more difficult to stay focused on what you are doing when you are surrounded by reminders of other things that need doing as well. Consciously, you may think that you are paying attention to what you are working on, but, subconsciously, your "mind's eye" is constantly scanning your work environment and keeping track of everything else it sees and hears. Unable to prioritize on its own, your subconscious will flood you with reminders, worries, concerns, and doubts about what you are and are not doing. All of this noise interferes with your ability to concentrate.

So . . .clean your office and your work area. Move your "in-box" out of sight to keep it out of mind. An in-box on your desk is an invitation for people to interrupt you while they put stuff in it. File your piles, and toss the stuff that you've been meaning to read but haven't gotten to yet if it is more than a week or two old. If you must keep certain pending files out, keep them behind you and out of scanning range. Turn your "e-mail notifier" function off, so that you are not interrupted every time you get a new e-mail. It is better to scan your e-mail and your voice mail when you decide to. Keep your desktop as vacant as possible—reserving your workspace for work in progress. The fewer distractions, the easier it is to focus. And *no music*. Background noise of any kind, pleasant as it may sound, is nothing short of disruptive to your ability to concentrate. Be clean and be quiet.

## Schedule your Appointments in Clusters, Months in Advance:

The more proactive you are with your schedule, the easier it is to control your time. Because you initiate Level I appointments, you can schedule them well in advance, and you can group them together by geographic proximity to avoid excessive or redundant travel. When you schedule these appointments, your client or prospect instantly recognizes you as a person that is busy, patient, and well organized. They will appreciate the proactive nature of your approach, and their availability to meet with you is dramatically increased, because they are usually not scheduled that far in advance. In the event that they are busy, be prepared to offer an alternative date when you plan to be in the area that is even further out. This again sends the right message and helps you to stay in control of your strategy.

When we leave it up to the client or prospect to pick the appointment date and time, or we try to schedule our appointments in the current week, we sound too available, too unorganized, and sometimes too desperate. A proactive appointment is as good next month as it is today, so . . .think and plan ahead. Now, on Sunday, when we sit down to build our weekly calendar, we can schedule our activity around our appointments, rather than trying to squeeze our appointments into the midst of our activity.

Two final suggestions about in-person appointments: If your position requires you to schedule four appointments per week or more, pre-select consistent days in the week that will be your "appointment" days. For instance, try to fit all new business and service "calls" into either Tuesday or Thursday. As the week begins, use Monday to prepare for your Tuesday calls, Wednesday to follow up from Tuesday and to prepare for Thursday, and Friday to follow up from Thursday. On appointment days, start from home; end at home, and never go near the office. This allows you to focus entirely on clients and prospects without distraction.

Finally, create adequate buffer zones between each scheduled appointment. Allocate enough time to permit each appointment to run long and to get to and prepare for the next call without being rushed. There is nothing worse than arriving late, leaving early, and being unprepared for a client or prospect. If you do not need the time, use it to follow-up calls, get the car washed, etc.

## Make Productive Use of Time in the Car:

Just because you are on the road doesn't mean you can't be knocking items off of your "Ta-Da" list. In fact, sometimes the least productive place to be is in a chair behind a desk. Opportunity is most always found outside the office and meeting rooms. For

CHAPTER FIVE: PRIORITY MANAGEMENT

that reason, remain perfectly portable. When you can safely do so, return most of your phone calls from the car. Carry your laptop/ smartphone/ iPad wherever you go, and keep all vital information with you in your brief case. You can work from anywhere at any time. The time you spend in the car doesn't have to be wasted.

What used to be Level IV time can be usable time, so get portable!

## Get E-Smart:

It's good to be cyber savvy. Use your e-mail as often as possible, and train your clients and colleagues to do the same. Using e-mail permits you to organize your thoughts and communicate efficiently and effectively. It also provides you with an electronic record of all correspondence.

Reduce the paper, the time spent shuffling paper, the time spent on the phone, the time spent sorting through messages and chasing down information. Get e-smart.

## Managing the System

There are only a few things that are mandatory for participants in our Performance Development Programs, because we prefer to have each participant select what to use and what not to use from the available options. This priority-management system is one of them. Of course, there is plenty of room for interpretation and customization according to individual needs.

Our demands for adhering to the process are justified. Having worked with thousands of sales professionals over the years, we can say with complete confidence that those who embrace priority management will succeed, while those who don't won't do as well. It is the foundation that supports the entire process.

If you work this simple little exercise into a habit and stay with it for a few months, you will feel better and accomplish more than ever before. If you do not in fact feel better, we will refund the price you paid for this book, and you may return to your old system with our blessing.

We did not develop this priority-management system from anything we read or discovered in a classroom. It is the product of countless experiments with time-management systems that never proved appropriate or effective. It is the result of trial and error, of learning on the job what really works and what does not. It is the finished product that can only come from an honest self-evaluation.

When you finally give up the need to have absolute control of time and accept the natural order of the world around you, you will discover an instinctive tempo to follow—a cadence that keeps you in step with the way life should unfold. You still won't be capable of planning with enough perfection to fulfill every wish, but you will be wise enough to embrace imperfection and to work with it.

You will hear your own drummer as time goes by, and you will develop a rhythm that is natural for you. As you make progress toward your objectives, you will realize that personal and professional success in life has much less to do with luck and intellect than you thought. You will see that the right combination of determination, discipline, honesty, flexibility, creativity, and hard work will take you anywhere you wish to go and permit you to convert your wildest dreams into reality.

Figure 11 summarizes the steps in our process for quick reference:

## Figure 11: Priority-Management System

| Step 1 | Step 2 | Step 3 | Step 4 |
|---|---|---|---|
| Identify Level I Strategic, HPA Activity List | Create a "Ta-Da" List | Qualify the Activities | Build a Weekly Calendar |
| **Level I's are:** Proactive Preventative Not urgent No instant results **Examples:** Ask for two referrals a week Create a referral tracking sheet Create an at-a-glance business plan Run four times a week | Start on Sunday List all potential **personal** activities List all potential **professional** activities Create a Supplemental Contact Sheet Include it all Know that it will grow Accept that you will not get it all completed | Find the Level I stuff Find the Level II stuff - grimace Find the Level III stuff - think of boundaries Find the Level IV stuff - don't do it | Select 3-5 Personal, Level I, activities per week Select 3-5 Business, Level I activities per week Schedule only Level I activity on weekly calendar, leaving buffer zones Revise and reschedule activity as necessary during the week. Move it, don't lose it! |

# Chapter Six

# Pipeline Management

*"As always, there [are] a couple of things in the pipeline—
but that pipeline is a strange and ambiguous place."*

—Hugh Dancy

As producers, you often get so caught up in "doing" that you forget to ask *how* you're doing. You are always *somewhere* relative to your annual production goal—but where? If you look at the business you've closed and add it to the opportunities you're working on, you'll get a sense for what your annual new business production will be. But that calculation could be misleading at best, and it will be meaningless if you haven't set specific production goals.

> "I now have clear goals, channel markets, a personal marketing plan, plus a Priority-Management Process."
>
> *Jeff O'Connor*
> *Insurance Agency Executive*

There are a number of factors that influence the accuracy of your end-of-year results projection. They include your routine close rate, the probability of closing a particular account, and the size of the accounts targeted.

Think of your sales pipeline as a *funnel,* through which you pour all qualified prospects. Those that stream from the funnel's end, however, are new clients. Since not all opportunities result in a sale, it is naïve to assume you will achieve your goals simply because you have identified a sufficient number of qualified prospects. Success demands that you manage your pipeline effectively.

Here are some rules of the road to help you quantify where you stand throughout the year.

## Rules of the Road for Pipeline Management

### Know Your Monthly New Business Goal:

Any premium (or revenue-based) pipeline-management process begins with an annual new business-production goal. However, an annual goal is only a starting point. On a monthly basis, assess how your new business stacks up against your annual production goals. Then determine how many prospects you need in your monthly pipeline to achieve those goals. The required number of very active prospects in your pipeline each month is a function of your monthly closed business goal, your average account size, and your close ratio.

Calculate the required number of very active prospects in your pipeline each month by using a Determination of New Business Flow Worksheet, as shown in Figure 12.

**Figure 12: Determination of New Business Flow Worksheet**

---

**Determination of New Business Flow Worksheet**

1. Establish annual new business premium or revenue objective = <u>$250,000</u>

2. Divide objective by 12 to determine average monthly premium or revenue = <u>$20,833</u> per Month

3. Estimate average account size in premium or revenue = <u>$5,000</u>

4. Divide average monthly premium or revenue ($20,833) by average prospect size ($5,000) to determine average sales per month = 4.166 Sales per Month

5. Estimate close ratio = .50 (i.e. .50 = 50%)

6. Divide average account sales per month (4.166) by close ratio (50%) to determine number of very active prospects needed per month to achieve premium or revenue objective = 8.33

**This number (8.33) represents how many <u>very active accounts</u> must be in the pipeline at all times.**

---

## Know Where Business Comes From:

Another key piece of the pipeline-management process is knowing the source of your business. A healthy pipeline contains qualified prospects from many sources, including:

- Key targeted accounts that represent the size and characteristics you aspire to add to your book (top 20);

- Referrals from others that you proactively seek, and others that come your way unsolicited (referral harvesting);

- Selling new coverages (as opposed to lines of business) (account rounding);

- Selling new lines of business to an existing client (cross selling);

- Opportunities that surface as a result of your personal marketing activities (network); and

- Business that comes to you from unexpected sources (other).

By identifying your sources, you can pinpoint where your pipeline is strong and where you have some work to do. Figure 13 is a tool you can use to identify sources of business, and where there are holes developing. It is also valuable in determining where you might make some cross-selling and account-rounding quick hits late in the production cycle to achieve your goals.

For example, you would hope to generate a high percentage of your business over time by referral harvesting, cross selling, and account rounding. However, as Figure 13 indicates, only one prospect is identified in each of these categories.

> *"The barriers are not erected which can say to aspiring talents and industry, 'thus far and no further'."*
>
> —Ludwig Van Beethoven

**Figure 13: Opportunity Pipeline**

## Opportunity Pipeline

| Rating and Effort | Top 20 | Referrals | Cross Sell | Account Round | Network | Other |
|---|---|---|---|---|---|---|
| **Excellent** 3-6 Months (Very Active) | Prospect A $20,000 | | Prospect C $10,000 | | | Prospect H $18,000 |
| **Good** 6-12 Months (Active) | | Prospect B $62,000 | | | Prospect G $12,500 | |
| **Fair** 12-24 Months (Passive) | | | | Prospect E $12,000 | | |
| **Other** Who Can Say (Drip) | Prospect F $85,000 | | | | | |

Note that the Rating category indicates the "likelihood of close," while the Effort category indicates "how active you will likely be" with this prospect based on the proximity of closing the sale. In the last row of Figure 13, the *Drip* effort level reflects that Account F (a highly desirable Top 20 prospect) has an unlikely near-term probability of close. However, check in, or "touch," this prospect, as the day will come when its rating will improve, and you will want to be there when it does.

## Know Where You Stand:

Now that you've determined new business flow and created an opportunity pipeline, you get to project how likely you are to end the year at any point in time. It is necessary to know with some degree of certainty where you stand relative to your annual production goal; otherwise, you run the risk of falling short—especially if you realize you're not in a good position when it is already too late in the production cycle to do much about it. Use the Pipeline-Management Worksheet to record your annual goal, your year-to-date progress (YTD) toward that goal at any point in time, and the projected end-of-year and running 12-month production results, considering known, qualified prospects and their probability of close.

Figure 14 displays production results through the first quarter (June) of the financial year 20XX. With an annual premium goal of $600,000 and YTD results (through June) of $45,000, another $555,000 remains to be closed. The good news is that there is $1,220,000 in the pipeline. The bad news is that, considering the realistic probabilities of close, only $378,500 is likely to close by financial year end, leading to a shortfall of $176,500.

## Figure 14: Pipeline-Management Worksheet

|  |  | Key |  |
| --- | --- | --- | --- |
| (Year) Premium Goal | $600,000 | Source | Probability |
| YTD | $45,000 | Top 20 | E=Excellent |
| (Year) Pipeline | $1,220,000 | Referrals | G=Good |
| Reflecting Probability | $378,500 | Cross Selling | F=Fair |
| Current View | $423,500 | Account Rounding | O=Who can say |
| 12-month Pipeline | $1,460,000 | Networking |  |
| Reflecting Probability | $498,500 | Other |  |

# Figure 14: Pipeline-Management Worksheet (Part 2)

| Prospect | (Year) | | | | | | | | | (Year) | | |
|---|---|---|---|---|---|---|---|---|---|---|---|---|
| | A | M | J | J | A | S | O | N | D | J | F | M |
| A | | | | $150,000 | | | | | | | | |
| | | | | 30% | | | | | | | | |
| | | | | 5 | | | | | | | | |
| | | | | F | | | | | | | | |
| B | | | | | $150,000 | | | | | | | |
| | | | | | 40% | | | | | | | |
| | | | | | 2 | | | | | | | |
| | | | | | G | | | | | | | |
| C | | | | | | | $300,000 | | | | | |
| | | | | | | | 30% | | | | | |
| | | | | | | | 5 | | | | | |
| | | | | | | | G | | | | | |
| D | | | | | | $120,000 | | | | | | |
| | | | | | | 50% | | | | | | |
| | | | | | | 1 | | | | | | |
| | | | | | | E | | | | | | |

| Prospect | A | M | J | J | A | S | O | N | D | J | F | M |
|---|---|---|---|---|---|---|---|---|---|---|---|---|
| E |  |  |  |  |  |  | $150,000<br>20%<br>1<br>O |  |  |  |  |  |
| F |  |  |  |  |  |  |  |  |  | $240,000<br>50%<br>1<br>E |  |  |
| G |  |  |  |  | $150,000<br>20%<br>2<br>0 |  |  |  |  |  |  |  |
| H |  |  | $80,000<br>40%<br>2<br>G |  |  |  |  |  |  |  |  |  |
| I |  |  |  |  |  |  |  |  | $120,000<br>20%<br>1<br>F |  |  |  |

By maintaining and referring to the Pipeline-Management Worksheet, you know how you are doing soon enough to act, and you are not deluded by the size of the opportunities as yet unclosed.

## Know How to Adjust:

Faced with the prospect of falling short of your goal, you have a number of steps you can take to compensate for the shortfall. These include:

- Search out similar qualified prospects, and apply your personal marketing techniques to close those businesses.

- Improve your close ratio by seeking more referrals for already posted accounts and accounts not yet included.

- Examine your existing accounts, and identify some cross-selling and/or account-rounding opportunities that could close before year end.

Although pipeline management may appear to be a relatively detailed part of sales and business development, it is an integral aspect of the process, and cultivating the discipline necessary to do it is equally important as sales and servicing.

---

### Key Points: Pipeline Management

**Steps to include:**

- ○ Determine monthly new business flow requirements

- ○ Know and track business opportunity sources

- ○ Post annual new business goal and YTD results

- ○ Post business in pipeline, including $ value and probability of close

- ○ Adjust based on pipeline "story"

---

# Chapter Seven

# Discovering Opportunity

*"[A successful person] always has a number of projects planned, to which he looks forward. Any one of them could change the course of his life overnight."*

—Mark Caine

It is said that opportunity doesn't knock twice. Our experience indicates that it doesn't knock at all. Opportunity *is* everywhere—all around us, all of the time, but it never just comes "knocking." We must go to it, identify it, take some initiative, and make something of it.

> "I just wanted to drop you a fast line and let you know that right now I'm on track to increase my commissions by 42% over last year. Since my goal was 45%, I only have a little ways to go to break that! The ... program is working!"
>
> *Michael J. Lloyd*
> *Agent/Producer*

## Recognizing Opportunity

Why is opportunity so difficult for us to find? Because real opportunities are often the by-products of problem solving and trouble shooting, they are frequently camouflaged as dilemmas or service issues. Because they do not command our immediate attention, mesmerizing busy work and established routines often obscure them. Genuine opportunities are oddities. They are created in the realm of the unknown, developed in uncertainty, and refined beyond the confines of conventional wisdom. In our industry, new opportunities (such as new markets, new products and programs, and especially new services) spawn from new perspectives, new ideologies, and untested circumstances. Therefore, harvesting opportunities requires us to disengage from current assumptions, activities, and habits, so that we are free to create and apply new ideas and behaviors to a new set of standards and conditions. Creatures of habit that we are, this is not easily done.

Comfort is a big opportunity killer. We are programmed to prefer the comfort of established routines and perspectives to anything foreign and mysterious. Our need to be comfortable is a survival impulse that causes us to be fearful of anything new and untested. It is responsible for an automatic rejection of new opinions, perspectives, and suggestions for behavior modification. Because change is difficult for people, because we succumb to change only when the pain of not changing becomes too much to bear or if we have no choice and are forced to change, genuine opportunities are often discovered on the tail end of crisis or catastrophe. Some of our greatest opportunities are sparked from the charred remains of ideas or circumstances gone bad, simply because, smarting from a defeat, we are finally ready to see them.

> *"Difficulties mastered are opportunities won."*
> —Sir Winston Churchill

Complacency is the shrewdest of all opportunity killers. Complacency lures us into believing that we need not change because who we are and what we are doing has worked and will continue to work. Complacency says "if it's not broken, don't fix it," almost always sacrificing genuine opportunities for familiar plays. Complacency convinces us that old routines can be successfully applied to new conditions, and that we can continue to do what we do the way that we do it and fully expect to get different results. In reality, genuine opportunities are only developed when

we are developing—when we are growing beyond our precon-
ceptions and comfort zones.

A notable difference between average and top producers is the
level of complacency apparent in their approach to work and to
life. While each type of producer is equally capable of identifying
a potential opportunity, top producers seize the initiative, apply
some ingenuity, break through the commotion and clutter of
business as usual—and cash in on the opportunity. Witnessing
the success of top producers, average producers will often attri-
bute their own lack of success to bad luck or unfair advantage,
never realizing that if they would simply lift their head up from
time to time, they could be just as successful.

---

## Key Points: Recognizing Opportunity

### Opportunities are:

- Frequently camouflaged as dilemmas or service issues

- Oddities

- Developed in uncertainty and beyond convention-al wisdom

- Often discovered at the end of a crisis, catastro-phe or idea/circumstance gone wrong

---

## Converting Opportunity

We are witnessing the beginning of a whole new Insurance
Market. We are incredibly fortunate to be participants in this
transformation, because we are being given the chance to create
something new and better, rather than merely experiencing the
legacy. The opportunities to come are as limitless as the stars, and
our generation will be the first to explore them. Standing, as we
are, on the cusp of what was and what will be, there has never

been a better time to work in our industry. The price of entry is a willingness to look at what hasn't been looked at, try what hasn't been tried, and change when change is needed.

It should be obvious that new ideas require new initiatives to support them. To make room for the new endeavor, old behaviors must be altered or discarded all together, and priorities reestablished in favor of new objectives. The greater the opportunity, the more radical the change that is required. The larger the opportunity, the more time and effort we have to invest to realize it. Ultimately, the price that we pay for our success is measured in energy, flexibility, and elbow grease.

Provided that they take the time to do it, most producers and service professionals can easily make a list of new and creative ideas that will launch them toward a new opportunity. Most of them can also take the next step and advance their ideas into a master plan. However, too few of them regularly muster enough sustained concentration to stick to their plan and convert opportunity into long-term prosperity. They simply lack the patience, discipline, and resolve to push beyond their need for immediate results and to remain unaffected by passing distractions.

This inability to create and adhere to a long-term vision imprisons people and organizations in an overly animated environment. Decisions are made and strategies are launched based upon temporary situations and transient information that is falsely interpreted to be permanent and fixed. Constantly reacting to the moment, in the moment, producers and their staff are unable to prioritize activity, synchronize it, and direct it at truly monumental opportunities.

Within companies that operate this way, it is rare to find business plans that stretch beyond the scope of convention to identify new and blatantly different market opportunities. Seldom do we see tactical marketing plans, sales plans, and service plans that are synchronized to ensure that every contact builds new opportunity upon the last. Infrequently do we find producers and service staff focused on anything other than the crisis of the moment, the work of the day, and the sale of the week. If these companies ever replaced their mission statements with reality statements, they would look something like this:

> *"As a traditional provider of insurance products to a vague and volatile market, we believe that we know all that we need to know about most things. What we know to be true today will always be true, and what is working today will always work. We seek growth, but not at the expense of change. And we are firm believers in selling what we can, when we can, to whomever we can get to buy it. You can count on us to do the same thing in the same way, regardless of shifting needs or special circumstances."*

Harsh? Maybe. But it's painfully true. Overcoming a company culture or personal selling process governed by conditioned responses and reactive thinking requires a more disciplined and systematic approach to attracting and retaining the right clients.

We must recognize that "selling" is a process that does not begin and end with "the transaction." As producers, we love to focus on the sale—the actual exchange—the conversion of prospects into clients. Even on our best days we have a tendency to rush, or to want to rush through the preliminaries—the "courtship"—and get to the sale. It is after all, our just reward, our redemption, and . . . our nature. Sometimes in our haste to harvest, we forget that each sales opportunity is unique with respect to the people involved, the process it must follow, and the time required for the relationship to develop.

Traditionally, we do a very good job with the perfunctory components of the sale. We collect the loss runs, review the policies, audit the reserves, design and shop the program, secure the best available price, and present our work like a technician. Focused as we are on product and price, we can easily forget that the most important, most dynamic, most unpredictable, and certainly the most fascinating attributes of the selling process are the relationships—the relationships between people who sell insurance and people who buy insurance. We are perhaps ordinary looking at first glance, but if you dig below the surface a bit you will find an extraordinary glossary of experiences, motives, values, behaviors, habits, beliefs, ambitions, fears, emotions, likes, and dislikes that all combine to form a unique selling environment. Serving as a trusted advisor will go a long way to develop and cement these relationships. Remember, our job is not to sell insurance, but rather to help people buy it, by providing consultative services, choices, and solutions that reflect this glossary.

Now, what happens when we pay lip service to the "nature" of the sale and focus instead on the facts and figures? We inadvertently signal that our primary interest is completion of the deal and that the relationship will develop within the confines of the timeline that we have placed on the deal. We treat every client like every other client and incorrectly assume that because we know our trade, we know our traders. Sensing our lack of awareness and sensitivity, our clients treat us like a common peddler and their insurance program like a commodity.

Now let's put some pressure on the whole thing. Unlike every other financial advisor (attorney, accountant, banker, etc.), our relationship is up for grabs at every expiration date. Our clients would never consider shopping for legal services each year, nor would they regularly bid out their corporate tax contract. Yet every year we are faced with the very real risk of losing our clients to a competitor and, conversely, we are presented with the opportunity to gain clients from a competitor. Consumed as we can be with life's preoccupations and interruptions, the time that we can actually devote to selling and client-service activities never seems to be enough. We are equally overwhelmed by the need to retain our existing book and by the need to add new clients whenever and wherever possible.

As we get increasingly anxious about adding new business, we get more "demanding" about binding business or getting a broker of record letter. The need for instant gratification (in the form of a sale) for the time and attention devoted to a prospect overwhelms the long-term advantages of patient and deliberate client acquisition. Urgency and emergency replace proactive client development, and we set our sights on what appear to be easy targets—prospects that are nearing their expiration date and those that regularly bid. Following the herd of other producers during this, our harvesting season, we struggle to differentiate, collect the policies and claims data, grab whatever market that we can, hastily prepare a proposal, and hope that ours is the one with the lowest price. We do it all in a flurry of activity, and we do it all without ever truly getting to know our prospective client. Sometimes we win, but most of the time . . .we lose.

Another prospect gone bad.

Now hurry along to the next one.

Quickly now, before somebody else gets there first.

Hurry!

Quick!

Fast!

Move!

Gooooo!

Yuck.

And we do it all the time. Even if we win the business, we often lose. Clients that come by bid will eventually go by bid. Clients in motion tend to stay in motion due to service issues, financial difficulties, poor claims performance, and less than credible insurance buying practices.

No wonder we have earned such a poor reputation for integrity and sincerity. Frankly, our behavior validates the stereotype. We don't want to sell this way; none of us has to sell this way, but all of us, at one time or another, have been convinced that this is the right way. We are in dire need of a fresh perspective.

Shortcuts, quick pick-ups, and overnight successes are for package delivery companies and Hollywood starlets, not for insurance producers. Our success will be determined by our ability to identify lasting opportunity, establish a plan to capitalize on the opportunity, and discipline ourselves to carry out the plan. To avoid corruption, we must allow the opportunities to evolve naturally, patiently, and consistently. Our plan will be called a "marketing plan;" however, it will be unlike any marketing initiative that we have undertaken before and it will be dramatically different from the banal marketing tactics used by hit-and-run producers. Your plan will be custom-developed to communicate your message of integrity to a limited audience that is pre-selected to appreciate who you are and what you can do for them.

Insurance marketing programs go wrong because they start wrong. They correctly assume that opportunity is everywhere, yet they incorrectly suppose that everyone is a potential opportunity.

Everyone is not qualified to be our client. One of the greatest challenges that we encounter as producers is learning how to distinguish the genuine opportunities from the multitude of vagabonds. Traditional marketing gimmicks actually exacerbate this problem by indiscriminately reaching out to saints and sinners alike.

Take for instance the "cold call." Most producers dislike them, and few prospects enjoy receiving them. Yet many of us rely on this traditional technique to mine for opportunity in the marketplace. It is intrusive, inefficient, and discomfiting for peddler and prospect alike.

Most of us have long since abandoned this intrusive practice in favor of a more palatable one. That said, a cold-call *mentality* still dominates in a majority of producer marketing and prospecting systems. The premise of this strategy is that selling is a numbers game. Cast a wide net (through spam, mass-mailers, telemarketers, advertisements, radio, etc.); reel it in; sort it out, and work frantically to find a keeper. Although this process generates an impressive amount of work, it does so at the cost of efficiency, and it creates a selling environment that reeks of urgency and desperation. This numbers game does not and will not provide enough quality return for the time and attention invested. It simply creates too many unqualified exposures that are hastily and fruitlessly pursued as if they were real.

---

## Key Points: Converting Opportunity

### *Converting Opportunity Requires:*

- ○ Using new and creative ideas

- ○ Advancing ideas into a master plan

- ○ Developing a disciplined and systematic approach to attracting and retaining the right clients

- ○ Focusing on relationships instead of transactions

- ○ Selecting only qualified prospective clients

---

We are much better served by a calmer, more manageable system. We feel less pressure; client selection improves, and integrity is established as a way of doing business. Recognizing that there is a more appropriate way to conduct ourselves is a vital first step toward truly making the transition. Following up the change-of-heart with a determined effort to replace the old behaviors, however, is where the work and the real challenge begin.

Yet while breaking established habits is one thing, doing so while trying to immediately adopt an entirely new set of behaviors is quite another. It is similar to swearing off a native language prior to learning a foreign one.

Developing fresh ideas and creating an innovative marketing strategy are fairly simple—consistently executing the strategy can seem impossible. Rather than synchronizing and simplifying activity, the new plan can seem as cumbersome and inefficient as the old. The results you expect don't materialize, and your distress is as high as ever before. You send out correspondence, host roundtables, conduct workshops, write articles, give speeches, shake hands, and kiss babies. Nothing materializes—it all seems like a huge waste of time and effort.

Don't give up! Instead, consider that your expectations may be out of whack.

## Author Snapshot: Scott Primiano

"I am so grateful to my wife for her insight, bravery and for the verbal kick-in-the butt she gave me when I almost gave up on a career in the insurance industry. *'The only thing I see that isn't working is you,'* she said. *'Your expectations are way out of whack, and you are trying to apply old thinking to a new set of circumstances. You're always running. Never do you pause, sit still, and wait, for anything. Have you ever wondered what you are running from? Have you ever really considered what it is that you are running so hard to catch?'* My wife's point was that it makes no sense to expect instant results when you develop a marketing plan that requires organized, systematic, pause-reflect-adjust thinking and execution in order for it to prove effective. And it isn't effective to chase after any and all clients. Gradually, I came to understand that fear was motivating me to rush the process and act out of desperation. I had to recognize that my fears of losing out, not measuring up, not getting what I wanted, and not keeping what I had were controlling me; I was using all my energy running and grasping at anything I could. *'The cure for your fear is faith,'* my wife said. *'Faith that doing the right thing in the right way with the right people for the right reasons will yield the right result. Faith in your ability, faith in your integrity, faith in your plan, and faith in those of us who support you'.*

Recognizing the wisdom of my wife's words, I decided to change. Of course, it took years of wrestling with bad habits to master better ones. But as I learned to accept the *process* (and life itself) on its own terms, things improved. It wasn't that life got better—*I* got better, because once my faith grew, my fear quieted. I could hear the signals that my soul was sending and act accordingly. I came to understand that a *right* opportunity is not fleeting; it is forever, so I don't have to chase it. And I learned to work systematically and deliberately, focusing my attention and directing my energies, rather than being consumed by the expected result. Instead of running after clients, I began identifying a manageable population of carefully profiled prospective clients who are worthy and wanting of the time and attention that I devote to them. My wife's words were the catalyst for a new way of life and a vastly better way of doing business."

Giving up is not the solution. The solution is to abandon the "fetch and close" mentality and replace it with an earnest desire to consistently provide your clients with enough information to make an educated decision, regardless of the time it will take. Your approach to the market will be careful, considerate, credible, unique, and highly personalized, because you are building relationships, rather than pushing product or price. You will feel better about *who* you are, *what* you do, and *how* you do it, because you are treating people the way you wish to be treated. You will learn to accept the way things are, rather than constantly struggling to have them your way. You will redefine the meaning of success in terms that you can't even imagine exist today, and you will accomplish more than you have ever dreamed possible.

We promise that if you are fearless and thorough about this process, you will be amazed before you are halfway through. We're thrilled to share this approach with you, and we hope that you will one day share your own success story with us. The marketing concepts that follow are all a product of what we have learned. Prior to moving on, please consider the following:

**Desperation is sinister.** It causes us to behave in ways that we would not even consider when our confidence is intact. Worse yet, it is hard to hide and is usually apparent to all who come into contact with it, particularly prospective clients. The movie "Glengarry Glen Ross," is a chilling example of how desperation taints our relationships. Desperation doesn't stand a chance against hope and progress, both of which result from working an established plan in a meaningful way.

**The easiest people to talk to and meet with are usually those who waste your time.** The problem with cold calls and other intrusive marketing schemes is that you attract people who respond to these tactics. You have to wonder what is inspiring them.

**Timing really is everything.** However, finding the right place to be is a necessary first step to being there at the right time. Successful marketing plans begin with detailed market research and an accurate cost/benefit analysis. It's usually boring, time consuming, and often expensive. It sometimes yields results that contradict our initial assumptions and inform us that our good idea isn't so good after all. Good research can be a spoiler, but it can also save time and resources in the long term. Although most producers avoid it due to the downside, those that deliberately quantify and qualify the real opportunity are able to draw a direct line to it, efficiently retrieve it, and be home before dark—while everyone else is still wandering around.

**Opportunity is a moving target that must be tracked and captured.** Any guide will tell you that each hunt brings new opportunity and new challenges along with it; no two are ever the same. Successful hunters rely on their previous experience and wisdom to overcome the challenges that they face and seize the opportunity that results. You are no different. Enjoy the safari.

> *"You, yourself, have got to see that there is no just interpretation of life except in terms of life's best things. No pleasure philosophy, no sensuality, no place nor power, no material success can for a moment give such inner satisfaction as the sense of living for good purposes, for maintenance of integrity, for the preservation of self-approval."*
>
> —Minot Simons, D.D.

# Chapter Eight

# Channel Marketing—Gaining Visibility and Viability

*"When an archer misses the mark, he turns and looks for the fault within himself. Failure to hit the bull's-eye is never the fault of the target. To improve your aim, improve yourself."*

—Gilbert Arland

A wise person once said that the success of a business doesn't depend on its size. It depends on filling a void in the marketplace. Consider 7-Eleven, the convenience store chain known for its accessibility and piping hot coffee. Sure, 7-Eleven isn't going to usurp market share from Kroger, Safeway, Save-A-Lot, or any other national grocery store chain. Then again, neither will the big grocery stores compete successfully with 7-Eleven. Each serves different needs.

> "You have given me a refreshing perspective on what it is we do, and I am relieved to know there are people like you operating in the world and elevating our profession to the highest possible standard with dignity and class."
>
> *Brian Gruber*
> *Agent/Producer*

After all, serving customers' specific needs is what business is all about. Sometimes it's best done in multimillion-dollar marketing campaigns, as Apple did with its iMac computers in 1998, and its iPad in 2010. Other times, it can be as simple as selling yourself on a one-on-one basis, much like financial planner Fritz Brauner did some years ago at a conference he was attending. Frustrated by weak response from potential customers, Brauner changed his nametag from "Financial Planner" to "Money Planner" and soon found himself surrounded by new customer opportunities.

7-Eleven, Apple, and Brauner succeeded because they knew their customers. As Peter Drucker once said: "The aim of marketing is to know and understand the customer so well the product or service fits him and sells itself." Effectively communicating a message that is attractive enough to draw clients to you, ahead of all others, is, by far, the greatest challenge you'll ever face in your sales career.

Are we being overly dramatic? Hardly. There's so much marketing clutter out there it's difficult to know what to do. Here's what we do know: We know that the insurance industry constantly bombards prospects with presumptuous marketing litter. We also know that despite their claims, agents all sound, act, and even look alike.

## The Trouble with Legacy Marketing

This commonality of message and behavior is one of our industry's greatest deficiencies. What does that mean to us? Plenty, as it turns out. Our system is designed to expose this opening and exploit it by debunking conventional marketing practices and creating new ways to position you properly in the marketplace.

As mentioned already, our industry needs a fresh message and a new approach to marketing, especially when it comes to promoting its greatest asset—you. Impersonal, broad-based, traditional approaches to "getting things sold" are usually designed to announce a special program, price, product, or service. Generally categorized as mass marketing, these methods inadvertently portray insurance as a commodity and, by default, promote insurance buying practices that are price and product focused.

Unable or unwilling to distinguish one producer from another in a seemingly unlimited pool of providers, clients establish a buying process that mirrors the selling characteristics of the industry. They create a proposal package for each bidder, make it available 90 days ahead of the expiration date, cover the markets, and hunt for the lowest cost provider. That means you, the producer, are considered an intermediary, a necessary middleman whose only function is to complete the transaction.

It's not that clients wish producers entirely out of the picture. They just don't truly know the importance of having a really good one. Consequently, beyond securing a desirable market, little consideration is given to the potential impact of the producer/agency/client relationship. Clients have learned to expect limited or no post-sale producer contact and to resign themselves to reactive, problem-based, administrative service from carriers and agency personnel whom they have never met.

## Mass and Spam Marketing

Consider for a moment the junk snail and e-mail that clutters up your mailbox. How much do you get, and how much do you actually read? Probably plenty and none, respectively. To trick you into opening their junk snail mail, direct mail houses have actually started concealing their mailings in blank envelopes, while e-mail marketers attempt to create catchy subject lines. What is your state of mind when you open or receive junk mail?" It's probably closed. Most likely you are skeptical, slightly annoyed, and looking for "the catch." If and when you do respond, what is your motivation for doing so? In most instances it's a special deal, a discount, or a novelty—in essence price and/or product might cause you to respond. Do you expect anything more? Usually not. The same can be said for the people who respond to our mailings and cold calls.

Let's keep things civil and say that these prospective customers are not exactly the pick of the litter. The majority of them are shopping for a bargain, not a buddy. Quite often they are on the verge of being non-renewed or canceled for one reason or another, frequently due to a poor loss history or for failure to pay their premiums. Either way, these clients are transients. Be wary when they contact you, and keep your guard up. Chances are such clients won't be with you for long—regardless of what you do or don't do.

Unfortunately, in our industry, mass marketing usually nets only squandered resources, fruitless follow up, and wasted exposure to people and organizations that may or may not be good prospects. Under normal circumstances, mass marketing usually gets us in front of people we don't want or who don't want us. That's a recipe for disaster.

## Legacy Marketing

- All things to everybody
- An inch deep and a mile wide
- Random and haphazard
- Product/Price focused
- Nearly impossible to differentiate
- Reactive, hit and run approach

## Anti-Mass and Spam Marketing

In an age of hard to find premium dollars and stiff competition, the average agency or broker is better served by a more deliberate, less expensive, carefully targeted marketing effort that sells you to the people you want to be sold to and affords you the time to service your current clients. Remember that a good marketing campaign allows you to keep what you have and get you what you don't have. That's the objective of a personalized marketing system—to reach out and captivate a limited group of carefully selected clients who recognize and value what you have to offer and are worthy of your time and attention.

When implemented, your marketing strategy represents a significant split from what your clients consider to be normal and expected behavior. Historically, sales objectives and marketing strategies evolve from a preoccupation with converting clients to cash in the shortest time possible. In this scenario, the selling process is a game of ratios. The motive is self-serving, the approach is intrusive, and the clients are not fooled by the vanity. They know the game.

By concentrating on yourself and how *you* can help the clients you're targeting, your strategy starts different and stays different. Eventually, your clients will recognize that you are truly sincere and come to appreciate the value, integrity, and trust that you provide. However, it will take time to break through the layers of presumption and skepticism that defend against the pretenders. The key, as you'll soon see, is putting that time to good use.

## Introducing Channel Marketing

Channel marketing has nothing to do with your TV clicker! In the insurance industry, channel marketing occurs when agencies, producers, and sometimes carriers strategically identify a niche or market, develop an expertise in that market, and specialize in satisfying the risk-management, loss-control, and specialty needs of that market.

Such "specialization" causes a "snowball effect." As proficiency and exposure to the industry evolve, so too will a reputation. Alliances within the market will grow to such a degree that they create a virtual monopoly and own that niche. For the agency, carriers scramble to assemble special programs; potential clients are referred in, and trade journals and associations want to know more. Integrity and expertise become the calling card. Those who are successful and who have consistently out-performed all others have done so by employing this strategy earnestly, honestly, systematically, and thoroughly.

---

**Channel Marketing**

- Focused on unique needs of segment

- Value based on visibility and viability

- Heavily networked and referred

- Easily differentiated

- True partnerships with carriers and clients

- Selective and proactive

---

## Why is Channel Marketing so Effective?

Call it the herd mentality. Just as individuals within a specific group exhibit common tendencies, organizations engaged concurrently in an industry or association will also demonstrate group characteristics.

These market characteristics lead customers to act similarly in their affiliations, buying habits, opinions, and methods of operation. A customer will be more comfortable and receptive to you, above all others, if you demonstrate an unmistakable awareness of who they are, what they do, how they do it, and how you can help them do it better.

Having established your visibility, viability, and credibility in a myriad of industry venues, customers will seek you out based upon your expertise and the recommendation of others within the industry. Your competitors, usually perceived as generalists, will be pressured out of the market or not permitted entry because of your value and proficiency as an industry specialist—someone customers perceive as being able to solve particular problems better than anyone else.

## How do you Select a Market?

It's time for a look in the mirror. That's because your initial step in determining which market to approach should be an informal self-evaluation. Remember how skeptical potential customers can be—many suspect that, given a choice, your interests will outweigh theirs every time. As a result, your success in the market that you select will be rooted in your sincere desire to help and advise, not to exploit and manipulate. Your motive must be service oriented, steeped in an honest desire to make the industry better for your presence. It's not your words that matter; it's your deeds. Also, remember what you are marketing—your expertise and ingenuity. Then there's your ability to reduce a client's long-term insurance cost by designing and implementing custom-developed, proactive, risk-management, loss-control, and specialty programs. You are not marketing insurance or your ability to sell it. The relationships that you establish within the market will be based upon these differences, and these are preconditions that cannot be simulated.

Plenty of sharks swim in these deep waters. It's hardly a secret that the market is full of marauders and specialists of the month whose motive is simply to make a sale. The shallow interest that they exhibit in the market is clearly apparent to most customers, who find their presence offensive and intrusive, thus making your job that much more difficult. In the end, your honesty and strong ethics will make the difference. Because potential customers will perceive you as different only if you honestly are, your selection of a "specialty" should be based upon who you are and where your interests lie, and the knowledge you have of the industry or group.

> *"First say to yourself what you would be; and then do what you have to do."*
>
> —Epictetus

Also, try to find a market that is not excessively prospected by others looking to specialize. You'll recall the example in the beginning of this chapter—the small convenience store and the big grocery chains. "Specialization" explains how a big supermarket and a small, quick-stop store can survive and thrive on the same block. Both generate profits in separate ways. The giant grocer offers variety at low prices. The convenience store provides constant access to highly sought-after goods, like milk and bread, at high prices. While both exist on the same block, they prosper because they each fill different needs. In the insurance sector, some of the most "attractive" markets are big targets with an abundance of snipers. Why take on that much competition? Instead, be creative in selecting your niche, and choose a market that is stable, proven, growing, populated, and/or undiscovered. If a geographic or demographic territory limits you, the target population within the given boundaries must be significant; otherwise, it could be a waste of valuable time, energy, and resources.

Selecting the niche that works for you is easier said than done, right? It's difficult to find fertile ground these days. Insurance companies have long understood the inherent value in targeting industry specific clients with specialty programs. As a result, you might find it difficult to gain prominence in a market segment that has been inundated with similar claims to fame. If this is the case, select instead a non-industry specific segment of the middle market that will value your initiatives.

As you consider what niche or niches to select, consider the following. What life experiences have you had that have shaped your knowledge of and experience with that niche? What are the general characteristics of the individuals operating in that niche... and are you comfortable with that type?

And remember, the more specific the niche, the more your expertise will matter. "Contractors" is a specialty many select. Why not narrow the selection to artisans, painters, framers (or some such sub-set of contractors) and learn all you can about their world?

Once you have narrowed your choice, be sure it measures up to the *P.A.S. test:* Do you have a *Passion* for the niche? Does working in that specialty with the type of people found in that group excite you?

Is there enough new business opportunity *Available* to allow you to achieve your goals? If not, maybe you need another niche (or two), or something different. Sometimes your territory may dictate geographic constraints. If so, your goal is to become so active in the community that everyone, regardless of their discipline, seeks you out because of your visibility and viability in the community.

Finally, from an agency perspective, is there a market/carrier (or markets) that will *Support* your choice in a manner that is consistent with the value-added service approach you rely on to differentiate yourself and your agency? Is there agency management and service backing?

When selecting your niche(s), remember that your first pick may not be your best or final choice. Keep an open mind as you develop and execute your personal channel-marketing plan. It is likely that a new and even more viable specialty may emerge over time.

Once you are comfortable with your choice, it's time to consider how to become visible and viable in that industry.

## How do you Approach the Market?

Marketing yourself as an expert requires more than grabbing a bullhorn and mounting a soapbox. You can try it, but self-promotion isn't enough to claim fame as an industry expert or risk-management specialist. It's better to be known for your expertise by demonstrating to the members of the market your ability to creatively develop new solutions to existing problems and identify future opportunities and potential hazards. "I fix cars" is one thing. But "I fix cars affordably and deliver them to your home," or "I fix Ferrari's better than anyone else," is something else altogether. Take a deep breath and recognize that this is a process and not an event—a process that begins with your education. The general regimen to follow is this: Having identified your channel market, go where they go; do what they do; read what they read, and listen when they talk. Listen really well.

Also, get used to the notion that up is down and down is up—it's what helps split you from the herd. The traditional approach to selling is to attempt the sale first and then build a relationship with those who buy. In channel marketing this process is reversed, so that our motive is better served. We seek first to build a relationship with selected prospects and maintain the relationship with service initiatives normally reserved for post-sale account management. Sales opportunities will naturally develop and occur as our value to the industry becomes more entrenched. Our value to the market will be correlated with our understanding of the specific needs and concerns faced by the industry and our ability to respond.

Be careful how you frame those needs. Client needs must be defined from the client's point of view. Again, some due diligence is the key. The needs of your market can be determined by reading trade journals and risk-management reports, conducting informational interviews with market members, studying industry trends, reviewing claims data and regulatory rulings, attending association meetings, and by surveying centers of influence (COIs) within the market. (Simply stated, a COI is an individual or organization with strength of character and recognized leadership in your channel market.)

Your initial contact with the channel market should be systematic, professional, and consistent. Do nothing in big volumes—a bad idea for those who are efficiency oriented. Understand that any attempt to overwhelm the market with glossy marketing materials will be perceived as stereotypical and prove counter-productive. Your motive must be to support, service, and provide information to the industry. Every contact with the industry should bolster this effort. In essence, you are treating your potential clients as if they were already clients by providing consistent demonstrations of your value and commitment.

In this successful and unique marketing strategy, you are investing in your clients before asking them to invest in you and thus proving yourself to be legitimate.

Here is your objective—to create a system for providing service that is manageable and unique. No worries, we'll help you do it. Just review and use the ideas in this book; adjust them to match up with you and your market, and design your own plan. Remember that the key to success in any channel-marketing system is consistent exposure to organizations and individuals that need and want what you have to offer. Take the time to plan a deliberate and disciplined approach.

We can't emphasize the point enough. Successful marketing to a target industry takes time, patience, diligence, and an honest desire to help. You will be successful if your approach is focused on building and maintaining long-term client relationships by consistently and measurably providing solutions to the market and by establishing your role in this accomplishment. Once installed as the agent of choice for your professional, consultative, and informed approach to the industry, you are untouchable.

## Beginning at the Beginning:

A thorough channel-marketing system consists of at least three non-selling approaches (see Approach Methods for Channel Marketing later in this chapter) that are implemented simultaneously and consistently. Prior to starting any marketing effort, make sure that you have adequately addressed the following:

### Selecting Your Market:

a) Select your market on the basis of your prior knowledge and your ability to help and inform.

b) Select a market that is not excessively prospected by other producers.

c) Select a market that is present and populated in your geographic nest.

d) Select a market that respects and values proactive risk-management practices.

**Researching the Market:**

a) Analyze existing and historical trends, habits, and needs.

b) Determine what markets and carrier programs are available.

c) Identify your competitors and what they bring (or don't bring) to the marketplace.

d) Estimate average premium to ensure targets are large enough.

e) Review online and hardcopy trade, industry, and association publications, newsletters, and risk-management articles.

f) Identify key prospects and COIs

**Marketing Plan Design:**

a) Design your marketing plan to target a small, select group of prospects.

b) Design your marketing plan for low-volume, consistent monthly touches.

c) Your marketing plan must be professional, highly personalized, and service-based.

d) Your marketing plan should be easy to administer.

## Researching Your Market:

1) Determine your market, and select a sales objective indicated by number of accounts, value of premium, or revenue.

2) Create a top 15-50 prospect list for your market, with key contact information, which is readily available from:

   a) Existing clients;

   b) Association membership rosters;

c) Chambers of Commerce;

d) Better Business Bureau;

e) Social media and online groups;

f) Online and on-site public library business directories;

g) Trade journals and industry publications.

We strongly encourage you to invest in some type of contact-management system. Doing so will help manage your data and your activity efficiently and consistently.

3) Obtain a list of trade journals and industry associations and visit their websites.

a) Request subscription information.

b) Request a sample copy, or sign up online.

c) Request publishing guidelines for articles and blogs.

d) Build a database noting publication information and the editor.

4) Interview current clients within your target market, and conduct a detailed assessment of industry needs and common risk-management and industry concerns. Also review trade journals, risk-management articles, web articles, association publications, and related social media. For commercial lines, you are looking for new and developing issues that encompass all lines of coverage, including employment practices, general and product liability, workers' compensation, group and voluntary benefits, insurance buying practices, etc. Plan regular calendar time to record each issue and trend.

5) Find out which agencies and carriers are currently insuring the market, what programs are available, and what services are being provided. Ask specifically about the risk characteristics of the industry, claims history, underwriting criteria, and specific industry challenges. What makes for a good risk and why?

6) Based on the industry assessment, brainstorm for potential solutions to each identifiable need. Indicate the source of the solution, action required, and the positive effect of implementing the resolution. Seek the input of carriers, industry specialists, and COIs. Don't forget to include the savings associated with the "soft effect" of your solutions. Remember, you are about preventing bad things from happening, not just covering losses after they do. Often, these "soft costs" represent the real benefits of your value-added service. Soft cost examples include:

a) Reduced employee turnover;

b) Improved morale;

c) Increased productivity;

d) Improved quality;

e) Enhanced customer service.

7) Establish an industry "clipping file" to hold pertinent information about the market and its members. There are numerous tools online to search and manage data, stay in touch with COIs, and sweep the trade journals. If your channel market is geographically based rather than industry specific, keep a careful watch for news regarding the companies that appear on your prospect list. This includes both good and bad news.

Your research does not end here. In fact, it never ends. You can never, ever know enough about your market. As the industry expert, you must have a firm foundation to cement your expertise. Your ongoing education is the cornerstone of this foundation.

## Approaching the Market:

Having selected and properly researched your targeted niche, it is now appropriate to professionally approach the market from the perspective of an industry observer and partner. You have in hand all that you will need to effectively differentiate. Your research has provided you with your market's specific needs, and now it is time to gradually and systematically convert such needs into your opportunity. Your method for doing so is informative rather than intrusive, solution based rather than sales driven.

The objective of your marketing effort is to provide your prospects with enough information to make an educated decision about who you are and what you do. Remember, your message should convey professionalism, specialization, and your desire to provide a service—not to sell a product.

Your system is designed to ensure consistent exposure to the market over time, and your method for doing so will be personalized, honorable, and manageable. Try employing three or more of the following approach methods:

## Approach Methods for Channel Marketing:

1) Pre-Approach Correspondence

2) Newsletters (paper and electronic)

3) Roundtables

4) Associations

5) Networking

6) Referrals

7) Articles

8) COIs

9) Focus Groups

10) Seminars, Webinars, and Risk-Management Workshops

11) Speeches

12) Clipping Files (paper and electronic)

13) Social Media and Online Groups

Each of these approaches has its own part to play in your channel-marketing strategy.

**Pre-Approach Correspondence**

Cold calls are like root canals. Dentists don't like doing them, and patients don't like getting them. Even so, producers continue to waste time trying to get through to prospects who have no known need for their service, hoping to grab lightning in a bottle and catch them at the precise moment they may be feeling the need for a change and are ready to listen to another agent. The success rate for this approach is slow and inefficient at best and tedious at worst, due to the intrusive nature of the contact. As we have already discussed, your time is better served by talking with those who already know who you are and what you do.

Instead, plant a few seeds first, and watch them yield bountiful results. Using personalized, pre-approach correspondence in advance of a telephone call to convey your message, mention your expertise or specialization, and inform the prospect that you will be calling to follow up. This removes the element of surprise and creates a warmer reception. Now, when you do call, you're no longer the stranger, the intrusive maker of cold calls. Instead, you're the familiar—or at least recognizable—maker of follow-up calls. Here, prospects are aware that you will be calling. They also know why you're calling, and they can make an educated decision whether or not to accept or return your call. Not only is this approach less intrusive and far more professional, the time spent chasing prospects who would rather avoid you is greatly diminished.

Not everyone is a fan of laying the groundwork before calling. Opponents of pre-approach correspondence and follow-up systems often base their opinion on past mailings that have met with little or no success. However, after reviewing samples of such correspondence, we often find that the message, not the messenger, was to blame. Here is a short list of the most common errors found in failed pre-approach systems:

**Motive:** The objective of any pre-approach correspondence should only be to introduce you, your agency, your specialty, and the fact that you will be calling in a few days to follow up. It is not intended to get an appointment, make a sale, or to have the potential client call you.

**Length:** Studies conducted on what gets read all indicate that the most effective business correspondence is concise, direct, personalized, and bulleted. We often find that producers have attempted to convey far too much technical information about a product, rather than focus on the specific benefits of a service. Remember that this correspondence is only intended to be a preliminary introduction. We suggest limiting it to one or two simple and direct paragraphs. There will be plenty of opportunities later on to get specific.

**Follow up:** Perhaps the greatest stumbling block of them all is the tendency to try and do too much too soon. Remember, these are personalized introductions that must be followed up with a phone call in a timely manner. For that reason, we should stagger the mailings and limit the volume to ensure proper follow up.

Try these suggestions for designing your pre-approach correspondence and delivery system so it works.

**Your correspondence should be:**

- Personalized and sent directly to the decision maker. Don't start with the gate guard by addressing it to "Attn: CEO." That's just a guarantee that it won't make it to the CEO.

- Brief (one page maximum!) and easy to read. Hemingway was on to something: Brevity *is* key. Use bullets to highlight key points. Leave out any reference to competitive pricing or claims of superior service. You cannot accurately establish your value for the client until you have asked the client to define value.

- Crystal clear in purpose. Your intention is only to introduce who you are, what you do, and to inform the recipient that you will be calling to follow up.

- "Signed" by you.

- Include a few testimonials, references, or benefits.

**Your system should be:**

- Manageable and consistent. This is not a mass-mailing or marketing effort. You will need to follow up on every correspondence sent. Prepare a fixed number of "mailings" per day or per week, and schedule your phone calls for a specific time and day.

- Structured for contingencies in advance. Each contact that you make will lead to an appointment, a request for additional information, a continuance, an advance, or a no. Regardless of the result, each contact should trigger more correspondence. Remember that we are building relationships based upon our ability to respond, and you should be prepared to respond to every call or attempt.

- Written out on a Goal Planning Sheet and known by your service and support team. Set a weekly objective for "mailings" and follow-up phone calls.

The following pre-approach correspondence samples effectively cut against the grain of legacy marketing systems.

## Pre-Approach Correspondence I (Anti-Marketing Theme)

Dear Contact:

This correspondence is only one of many that you will receive during the year from a variety of insurance agencies requesting a look at your policies. Most will trumpet competitive rates, good service, and a dedicated staff. Few, if any, will actually deliver, and none will dare to proactively venture beyond the issues of policies and rates to thoroughly understand your organizational culture and unique needs. To do so requires an honest demonstration of an agency's commitment and capability in advance of selling you insurance.

Our method of protecting you and the financial health of your company does not begin and end with the purchase of insurance. At [*Agency*], we refuse to use the old models and outdated techniques that are designed to generalize a business, feed it standard insurance, and then vanish until renewal time. We know that you deserve more, and we are prepared to give it . . . up front and without reservation.

Attached you will please find a brief description of our agency and our process. Our record proves that this value-driven approach leads to enhanced program design, reduced premiums, and satisfied clients.

In the near future, we will call you to formally introduce ourselves, and we will do so with the knowledge that our process is not for everybody. On the other hand, if you are weary and leery of conventional agency limitations, ours would be a good call to take. In the interim, please feel free to call me directly at [*Phone Number*] with any questions or comments.

Sincerely,

## Pre-Approach Correspondence II (Article Enclosed)

Dear Contact:

Getting our message through to you is a tremendous challenge for our agency. I know that you are constantly targeted by insurance "salespeople" professing to be bigger, better, faster, or cheaper. I know that their marketing tactics are often intrusive, rarely unique, and very impersonal. I also know that despite their affirmations, they are largely interested in what you can do for them. I am as offended by their lack of sincerity as you are, and I can certainly appreciate why you might be skeptical of our approach. I only hope that you might take a moment to consider our ideas before you make up your mind.

During the past year, we have witnessed significant rate increases across all lines of business. Next year, we anticipate this pricing action to continue. Feeling powerless, many people begrudgingly consent to the increased cost of insurance without first inspecting all available alternatives. I want to make sure that this oversight is corrected and not repeated.

We use a unique method with our existing clients to avoid this issue, and I am offering our services to you without cost. Our agency has developed a comprehensive assessment tool that we use to evaluate every component of your health, safety, and risk-management concerns, as well as your organizational development and corporate cultural issues. Our onsite team of specialists conducts this process free of charge and provides us with the knowledge necessary to make qualified recommendations regarding your risk-management, loss-control, and insurance programs. Our record proves that, far from being a gimmick, this bold approach leads to enhanced program design, reduced premiums, and stabilized insurance costs—even in a rising market.

The enclosed article from [*Leading Industry Publication*], does a good job of explaining how our proactive philosophy and unique approach benefit our clients. I know that you are skeptical; however, if you are even marginally curious, I encourage you to investigate us further. Please call me directly at (*Phone Number*), with any questions, comments, or for additional information.

Sincerely,

## Newsletters

Newsletters are a magnificent way to establish credibility and market awareness, but only if they are written well and published consistently. Since we live in an e-world, the easiest and most reliable method for creating and consistently sending newsletters is e-mail.

Your newsletter can serve the dual purpose of staying in touch with existing clients and, with the addition of customized pre-approach correspondence, provide you with another avenue for introducing yourself to new prospects. Some suggestions for publication are as follow:

- Clients will read your newsletter if the selected topic is pertinent, and the layout is attractive. Both printed and electronic newsletters should be designed well. Review your list of market needs for topical information. This is an ideal forum to present your ideas. Focus on the challenges and solutions specific to the market or industry. Claims stories and investigation techniques are always interesting. However, avoid stories about happenings at your organization, as no one cares. Your goal is to educate, and if you do not have suitable software or are limited in your graphic design ability, "canned" newsletter services are available for a fee.

- Contact COIs and request an interview to include in the newsletter. Inform them that the interview will be published in your newsletter, and permit them to discuss any topic of interest to the market—regardless of whether or not the discussion is insurance related. Ask them to both identify future topics and other potential interviewees. Permit them to review a draft copy prior to publication. Also, ask for contact information for organizations and individuals that should receive a copy.

- The newsletter is written for the specific industry and should be about that industry. Avoid the urge to sell or introduce new services. You can, however, designate space to welcome new clients, announce workshops, and introduce new employees. Also, feel free to highlight any meaningful testimonials or success stories that clients pass along, providing you obtain permission to do so prior to publishing.

- Design pre-approach correspondence for prospects, and personally contact them for feedback. Request an appointment to discuss your specialization in the market, how you service your clients, and to conduct an interview for a future newsletter.

- As mentioned, your newsletter provides an efficient method of keeping in contact with your current clients, COIs, and top prospects. You can also use the newsletter to conduct a survey of your clients.

- You must plan your newsletter proactively. Plan out each step in detail on a Goal Planning Sheet, and ensure all contributors and support people are familiar with the importance of the deadline. Once the first newsletter is done, you must keep on planning. It is always best to be working one issue ahead of the current edition.

### Roundtables

Camelot it's not, but the idea is the same. A roundtable brings members and observers of the market together to discuss issues, events, problems, and ideas that are risk-management related.

Your motive in hosting a roundtable is relationship-centered and not sales-related. Though attending members are very often competitors, your roundtable represents one of the few times that they may gather in a non-competitive, informal environment to discuss mutual threats, opportunities, issues, and solutions. For this reason, roundtables are viewed by most participants as invaluable, productive, and revitalizing.

Your roundtable satisfies their need to associate with a knowledgeable peer group and to indulge in a topic they know and live. Your role, as the facilitator, gives you instant credibility and permits you to build rapport with your market. The key elements of an effective roundtable are as follow:

- The discussion should focus on a single, pertinent topic that changes with each roundtable. You must know the market, the topic, and the impact it has on the industry.

- Two or more market COIs should be in attendance. COIs give you and your roundtable credibility and attract other members to the discussion. An excellent method to ensure that COIs attend is to invite them to be guest speakers, select the topic, invite other associates, etc.

- Limit the time that you speak to the introduction of the topic and/or the guest speaker. Your objective is to listen and listen well. The needs of the market will develop as the discussion unfolds.

- If onsite, you don't have to rent out Madison Square Garden for your roundtable. And if online, there are many low-cost "meeting" options that will facilitate roundtable discussions. Keep the group small to facilitate an open discussion; large groups are impersonal and prohibitive. Experience indicates an ideal size is 10-15 participants. A rule of thumb to use in determining the quantity of invitations to send out is four to one, or 40 to 60 invitations to net 10-15 participants.

- Always diversify. The targeted participant population should be a mixture of existing clients, key prospects, and other market supporters.

- Keep the invitations simple. Like pre-approach correspondence, invitations should be limited to the date, time, location, topic, etc. All must be personalized and should be sent one to two months in advance of the gathering.

- You may wish to serve a simple lunch or breakfast to provide an additional incentive to attending on-site roundtables.

- Follow up each invitation with a phone call to confirm attendance, or use an electronic confirmation process. If people are unable to confirm, use the phone contact to set up another appointment to service, interview, or present. Never waste a phone contact.

- Schedule two follow-up calls, one two weeks in advance and another, two days in advance of the gathering.

- Prior to ending the session, have the group select the topic for the next session, and inform them of the date, time, and location of the next gathering.

- Follow up with a personal note to each participant within one week of the meeting and another to those who could not attend in the same week.

- Once again, be consistent and proactive. Your system must be clear to all involved, and your events must be scheduled regularly throughout the year.

## Association and Group Memberships (online and in-person)

Be a contributing part of a group—it will give you a hefty dose of credibility. Adding your name to the channel market's membership organization as an associate or full member is a logical step toward building credibility, contacts, and opportunities within the market. Your regular affiliation with these groups and your active participation in their interests, issues, and activities establishes you as an industry insider. Initially your role will be that of an active observer, carefully listening for the needs of the association's members while identifying COIs.

Eventually, your relationship with the group will blossom, and your advice, opinion, and participation will be requested. This will happen only if you remain an active member of the association, and if you consistently donate your time and energy to the association members' projects. If, on-the-other-hand, you approach the membership with the sole purpose of drumming up business, you will be viewed as a parasite, and you will be avoided.

Like everything else that we have reviewed, regular demonstrations of integrity, trust, and value must precede the development of real opportunity. It is not uncommon for eager producers to approach associations and groups looking to market a discounted specialty program to members. From the beginning, you must make them aware of just how different you are. Eventually, you may wish to design a hybrid product for the group, but not until you know the issues and players and have earned their trust. The following is a suggested plan of action:

• Create a list of all market-related trade associations and groups; include those of major suppliers and other potential market influences and affiliates. If you are marketing to a diverse population in a defined geographic area, your target associations will include chambers of commerce, rotary clubs, and civic organizations.

• Contact each with adapted pre-approach correspondence. Request information on membership demographics, guidelines, dues, association publications, meeting schedules, etc.

• Review your list with existing COIs and other market contacts to determine which associations are most popular and credible. Select three target associations based upon your research, and request a referral or introduction from existing client members or COIs to the appropriate contact within the organization.

• Contact the presidents of each association to inform them of your experience in the market and of your desire to affiliate with the organization. Probe for specific association or member needs. Request newsletter publication information and possible topics of interest.

- Having determined the needs of the association and its membership, re-establish your contact and review what direction your involvement with the association can take. Options will include writing for the newsletter, blog, or trade journal, hosting seminars, webinars, and giving speeches, etc. Also request a copy of the membership roster.

- Join the association, and stay in contact with the group's decision makers by attending all association meetings and hosting your own business and social functions regularly.

- Service the association as you would service your best client, regardless of the initial return on your investment. Your success will evolve from your determination and persistence to make the association better for having met you. This must be your objective.

## Networking

James F. Lewin, a former executive at Security Pacific National Bank, once said, "Activity is the life blood of a successful selling process. Networking is probably the most effective way of creative activity." It is an appropriate line. We can all agree that some of your best prospects may never actually buy from you. However, if you build the relationship correctly, they can and will lead you to others who need your help, usually people with an immediate and well-defined requirement, who under normal circumstances may have proven elusive. Additionally, other vendors and industry observers may know who best in the market to approach, and when it is a good time to do so. Chief among this group, and perhaps the most influential, are the financial advisors—bankers, CPA's, lawyers, brokers, etc. These professionals, in one capacity or another, have an impact on every investment decision made by their clients, and they are often the first to become aware of a developing need. One way to network with this group is to sponsor or conduct workshops. For instance, an EPLI workshop for attorneys or a session on alternative markets for CPAs will draw the crowd that you are looking for.

We strongly recommend that you take the time and the initiative to build a relationship with this secondary market. To approach this targeted group, employ the same strategy we outlined in the preceding section on association membership, but once again, you must clearly communicate your ability to help their clients.

## Referrals

Asking for referrals demands what we like to call a "decent boldness"—it's not arrogant, unprofessional or untoward to ask for a referral from a client to whom you have demonstrated value, integrity, and trust. In fact, such clients often jump at the opportunity to reward such service. So don't be intimidated by asking for referrals. You will rarely hear anything but a resounding, "I'd be more than happy to." Read more in our chapter on the Magic of Referral Harvesting.

## Articles and Blogs

Here's a choice. You can dazzle a dinner party with your thoughts on banks merging with agencies, or you can put those thoughts down on paper, have them published, be read by target-market readers, get extra copies, and send them out to prospects. Voila, you're immortalized as a credible source on the topic. The credibility and exposure that is created by having an article appear in a trade journal, newspaper, or in an association newsletter is tremendous. "Getting Published" is relatively easy, providing that you have something of value to offer that is timely, well written, and meets with publishers' specifications. These will vary depending on the nature of the publication and its purpose. Presenting your article or blog for publication is best done systematically. Here are the steps to follow:

1) Set a quarterly goal for article submissions, and use a Goal Planning Sheet to help you stay on track.

2) From your research and market surveys, develop three or four topics that are pertinent to your market. New twists on old topics are good; new strategies that address new issues are better. And don't worry about whether the topic is related to insurance—you are about solving industry problems. Also, you may wish to submit an article that profiles an industry member, an existing client, or a COI.

3) Create a prospect list of all publications you desire to approach, and request from each their publishing guidelines. Inform them of your desire to submit an article for publication, and review with them the proposed topic or topics that you intend to write about. Ask publishers for their thoughts and assistance to design the article to match the format of the magazine. Request specific information on desired article length, measured in number of words.

4) On the basis of this information and your market research, write your article and run it past a few "critics" prior to submitting it. Submit it in its final form, as most editors prefer not to edit (and they hate to rewrite).

5) After a peer or client review, submit the article to the targeted publications, one at a time. Include a cover letter that briefly summarizes the topic and the impact to the market. Specifically answer this question: "Why would somebody want to read it?"

6) Follow up each submission with a phone call. Be willing to re-submit the "draft" after making any suggested changes, and be sure to indicate that you are not requesting any compensation. Even so, you could very well be paid.

7) You might be asked to send a picture of yourself that will be published with the article. If you are serious about regularly publishing articles, get your press shot done in advance of your submission. Use only a studio shot. Portrait shops know how to shoot these press shots, and they offer them very economically. Do not try this at home. Color is always preferable to black and white.

8) Continue this process with each article written and with every publication that you have targeted. When you are published, request electronic and hard copies from the magazine to use in the future. You may have to pay a nominal amount for these magazine-quality copies.

9) You can apply the same approach you used for one-time articles or blogs to create a recurring column. Often, the repetitive nature of a column establishes your credibility as someone who has something worthwhile to offer.

Those who have published routinely share stories with us about how they became the "go-to" professionals in their industry or community as a result of their activity. In many cases, industry publications and weekly local newspapers are hungry for content. Why not feed that hunger and establish your visibility and viability at the same time?

If a customer's decision comes down to the industry expert whose face appeared in the business section of the local newspaper or the insurance professional without the photo and the byline, the "expert" wins most every time.

**Centers of Influence**

As stated earlier in this chapter, a COI is an individual or organization with strength of character and recognized leadership in your channel market. COI's tend to be more progressive and profitable than most others within their industry. The mention of a COI's name will elicit a positive response from most prospects within their market, because success is respected, and people want to be identified with success.

Our travels throughout the U.S. reveal an interesting truth about success. Go to New York and you'll see a lot of Yankee fans. No surprise there. But go to Salt Lake City, Toledo, or Sacramento and you'll find a lot of Yankee fans there, too. Why? Because, historically, they're winners. Their wins are not isolated occurrences. During Michael Jordan's reign with the Chicago Bulls, it was not uncommon to walk down the streets of Tokyo or Milan and see those familiar red jerseys with the number "23" on the back and the word "Bulls" on the front. People of all nationalities saw Jordan as a winner and, hence, wanted to "Be Like Mike."

The thinking goes like this: If you are affiliated with success, you too will enjoy others' respect. Consequently, industry members and market observers hold COIs' opinions in high regard. Your relationship with COIs in your market will ultimately determine your level of acceptance and influence others' perception of your integrity within the industry.

COIs are the decision makers for the industry. They are also community leaders, elected officials, and board members. Their buying habits, strategies, programs, and policies are closely monitored and usually mimicked by others within a channel market or the community. A simple nod of approval from a COI establishes instant credibility, to say nothing for what a referral from one can do.

Your objective in approaching a COI should only be to establish a relationship and to learn more about the market. Any attempt to "sell" to the COI will result in an abrupt dismissal. You will fall into the same pit of rejection those who preceded you with such an approach are in. Please understand, eager producers looking for the "one big hit" are constantly barraging COIs. They will not waste time with you or anyone else if they feel at all cajoled. In order to be perceived as different, you must be different. This requires a polished, professional, and practiced approach, as follows:

- From your research, identify the COIs in your market or geographic boundaries. List all known affiliations, associations, and potential referral sources. The best way to meet a COI is to be introduced by a friend in common.

- Contact each COI to request an informal meeting. Some prefer this via phone; others prefer e-mail, and some prefer online introductions or social networking. Make an extra effort to let them know that the meeting is only for an interview, and that you are not attempting to sell anything. Indicate your desire to learn as much about the target market as possible, so that you may service it effectively. Mention that you consider the COI to be highly informed and extremely influential within the industry and, as such, an excellent resource for the information that you need. Follow up every contact, including this initial one, with a thank you note.

- Offer to meet with the COI on his or her terms, wherever and whenever they wish. You must be extremely flexible.

- To keep the conversation focused, develop a questionnaire to use at the interview.

- Plan to review your existing approaches to the market, and invite any new ideas on different approaches. Probe for specific needs and, if appropriate, ask the COI for an interview or to speak on a particular topic at a roundtable or other client gathering.

- Do not ask for referrals at this early stage in the relationship; however, certainly accept them if they come. You can ask for a recommendation to others who can assist in a further evaluation of your ideas or add further insight. These referrals will usually be to other COIs.

- Whether an appointment is made or not, design a system that will ensure that you are making contact with each COI monthly. Your system may include updates on your progress, newsletters, e-mails, invitations to roundtables and focus groups, handwritten notes, phone calls, etc. Staying consistently visible and viable at all levels of the market is critical.

- Remember: Send a thank you note after every contact. Some might call it "killing them with kindness," but it will be appreciated—and remembered.

## Focus Groups

Similar to a roundtable, the concept behind a focus group is to bring together members of a market to share their experience and develop solutions to industry-related risk-management and loss-control issues. A focus group differs from a roundtable discussion in structure and facilitation.

Typically, a focus group discusses one or two specific items at a session that participants choose in advance. The group is usually made up of high-level decision makers and COIs, and the meetings generally run longer than a roundtable discussion. It is generally a good idea to limit the size of the group to 10 participants.

For an in-person focus group, facilitate the session at an aesthetically pleasing location that is free from interruptions, such as a hotel conference room or a restaurant's banquet area, which is usually set aside from the main dining room (but close enough to the food). When conducted online, be sure that the chosen technology is easy to use, and ensure participants receive guidance on how best to engage in the conversation. The group should pick a topic with the objective of problem solving. As with the roundtables, your role is to facilitate and provide a forum for discussion, nothing more. Follow the same guidelines listed under "Roundtables" to design your system, with the following exceptions:

- Participants should be limited to decision makers and COIs. This protects the integrity of the discussion.

- Focus group meetings should be scheduled well in advance and held consistently throughout the year. A once-per-quarter format is the most popular.

- Membership in a high-level industry focus group is both an honor and a privilege. Do not invite members who do not clearly see a value in participating or are unwilling to commit to attending all scheduled sessions.

- Make it nice. Your short-term investment in making the setting relaxing, luxurious, and completely compatible will make the experience pleasurable for everyone and keep them coming back.

- If conducted in-person, consider hosting the focus group at a country club or retreat center. This will enable you to combine your formal session with some informal recreation. Participants will usually pay for the privilege and certainly welcome the release.

**Seminars, Webinars, and Workshops**

More teaching-oriented than roundtables or focus groups, seminars, webinars, and workshops are ideal presentation formats to use when the market needs to be educated. They are also used to efficiently showcase a new product or service to a large segment of the market. Though interactive, the intent of these sessions is to disseminate new information. Consequently, they must be formally facilitated. The idea is to educate participants by guiding them down an information path that leads to you as the solution to the problem. The key is to keep it useful. As simple as it may sound, the greatest danger in hosting a seminar, webinar, or workshop is not having anything worthwhile to present.

The topic must provide a solution to a need, and the benefits of attending must be clearly apparent and lasting. For the commercial insurance market, stick to new and evolving risk-management and human-resources issues and solutions. Your goal is to provide value for the time spent, not to entertain or socialize. Your credibility and value to the market will correlate with the caliber of the presentation. You may wish to use a guest speaker or professional workshop facilitator to present the information. Human-resources specialists, risk-management professionals, underwriters, claims attorneys, OSHA officials, and other industry experts will line up to assist you, usually at little or no cost. Be sure, however, to have personal knowledge of the intended speaker's presentation skills. The following steps will assist you in planning for a successful seminar or workshop:

- When selecting your topic, clearly identify what needs the information that you intend to present will satisfy. Make a list of these benefits, and ensure that they are numerous and tangible. What impact will your presentation have on the market, and how will that impact be measured?

- Consider letting your audience pick the topic for you (or carry an idea over from a recent focus group or roundtable). Send out a survey with a list of potential topics, along with a cover letter detailing your objective. Not only will you get a response that will help to ensure a popular topic; you will also generate a lot of preliminary interest.

- Remember that this is NOT a sales presentation. Your goal is to inform and serve the market.

- Review your ideas with selected members of the market and COIs. Gauge their level of interest by asking them if they will attend. If they hesitate or balk, your topic is not pertinent, or you have not clearly communicated the benefits.

- Keep the presentation to a maximum of three to four hours, with breaks scheduled on the hour. Most workshops and seminars are best scheduled in the morning. Webinars are most effective when they are 45-60 minutes in length.

- Unlike roundtables and focus groups, you will want to have as large an audience as possible. Establish a list of potential participants from your existing client base, prospect lists, and other industry providers, making sure that each will benefit from attending. Set an enrollment objective, and use a Goal Planning Sheet.

- Do not proceed unless your list numbers at least 60 potential participants.

- Establish the location, time, and agenda two to three months in advance. If guest speakers are to be used, make sure they participate in this phase of planning.

- Send out invitations to all prospective participants two months in advance. Your invitations should be personalized, identify the need, highlight your solution, and summarize the benefits to be derived from attending. You may want to start even earlier with a simple, save-the-date notice. Include a simple, "register for the event" process.

- Gauge registrations, and divide your responses into three categories—"Yes," "No," and "Undecided." Next to each no, make a notation of why. If there are too many "no interest" notations, revisit the topic. Depending on the venue and whether it's online or in-person, if you are unable to confirm a minimum of 15 to 30 participants, consider canceling or postponing the event.

- Confirm two days in advance of the event to finalize your list of participants.

- For in-person events, prepare a participant list to hand out at the event. Your clients will want to know with whom they are associating. Personalize as much of your presentation material as possible, particularly the handouts or workbooks. Nametags are requisite.

- Prepare an evaluation form to be collected at the end of the presentation, or when online, use polling questions. These will be used to measure your impact and identify follow-up opportunities and future topics.

- Following the event, send a personalized note or e-mail to each participant within one week of the meeting and another to those who could not or did not attend in the same week.

## Speeches

Just as a seminar, webinar, or workshop can solidify your reputation as an industry expert with potential customers, so too can a speech. Any opportunity to address an association or a gathering of your market provides additional exposure and further establishes you as the industry insurance specialist. Good speakers with insightful information are always in demand, and they are considered welcome additions to conventions, dinners, seminars, etc. The fact that you come free of charge provides an added incentive for your market to utilize your talents. However, in order to take advantage of these opportunities, you must have something of value to offer, and you must be a polished presenter.

Regardless of the message, your audience will focus on you, the messenger, first and foremost. Do not enter this arena unless you are confident in your public speaking abilities. This is not a safe testing ground. To receive an unbiased opinion about your skill as a presenter, ask those who have witnessed you in action before, and demand an honest evaluation. If the reviews are unfavorable or neutral, try to determine if it's a matter of content or delivery, or combination of both. If your presentation lacks content, probe reviewers for additional guidance and ideas. If the problem is with your delivery, there are groups such as Toastmasters International that teach public speaking skills. Once you're confident in your ability to address an audience, the following suggestions will improve your channel-market opportunities.

- From your research, develop a prospect list of association conventions, trade shows, and other industry gatherings. If you are already an active member in one or more of these groups, start with the home team.

- You should be aware of which clients are active in these associations, if any. A referral to the speaker selection committee is better than a cold introduction. If you do not have a home team or you cannot find a referral source, please continue to the next step.

- Create pre-approach correspondence that identifies you as a potential speaker, your area of expertise, your message, and why it is pertinent.

- Identify the event planner or decision maker, and send out your correspondence. Follow up each with a phone call, probing for needs and desired topics.

- Follow up each call with correspondence that summarizes the discussion and indicates your ability to offer a valuable presentation where appropriate. Enclose a copy of past speeches and a list of your references.

- Speeches are not sales presentations. If perceived as such, you will immediately offend your audience and your host.

- You may wish to record your speech. However, ensure that you request permission from your host prior to doing so, and be willing to make copies available to your audience. At a minimum, prepare a text copy of your speech.

- Request in advance, a list of participants for follow up and to better qualify your comments.

- Visit the venue where you are speaking at least an hour before your presentation to get a feel for the room. Talk to the person who will introduce you, if possible. Rehearse/review your speech at that time as well. If speaking via webinar, conduct a dry run in advance to ensure that audio, visuals, and technology are in sync. To confirm all technology is still functioning properly, on the day of the event, login at least 30 to 45 minutes in advance.

- Those old saws about envisioning the audience in their underwear or focusing on a point in the room? Forget them. Instead, rehearse your speech, and know your subject cold. Preparation is critical when delivering speeches. For webinars, fight the desire to read from your script. Do envision an audience, and elicit feedback via polling questions to keep a connection and engagement.

## Clipping Files

A simple way to stay in front of prospects and clients is the clipping file. Your clipping file is used to collect information on the market and its members, personalize it, and disperse it when appropriate. Contained within your clipping file are articles on the industry, trends within the market, organizational and personal announcements, etc.

If your market is geographic, screen the local newspapers that usually contain significant announcements, such as promotions, births, deaths, weddings, contract signings, expansions, court rulings, etc. (Prior to the Internet, clipping files were hard copy and stored in file drawers, binders, and notebooks. Today, most people use online methods to collect and store clipping file information.) Once collected, send an appropriate note or card with the original article or announcement whenever possible.

This level of attention sends a clear message to clients and prospects alike. It tells them that you are informed, observant, and responsive. You care about what they care about, and they know it. Setting up your system involves only a few simple steps, as follow:

- Make a list of all publications and websites that may contain news about the channel market, organizations, and individuals within the market. Include in your list trade journals, association newsletters, local business digests, newspapers, etc.

- Develop a strategy to consistently review the information collected, and team with others within your organization or on your partnership team who may wish to employ the same strategy.

- Create a designated in-house or digital file folder to hold all selected clippings. Review the file weekly for time sensitivity, and send out pertinent information as appropriate.

- Do not send jokes, chain letters, or cute quips, and don't forward information from another group or outside source. This stuff is always annoying, sometimes offensive, and if sent electronically may contain viruses and malware.

In addition to your group e-mails, personal e-mail and other forms of virtual communication (chat, social media, etc.) can and should be used to reach out and connect with clients individually. Personal e-mails and virtual communication are less intrusive and more efficient than calls or face-to-face meetings with your clients. This is not to suggest that e-mail and virtual communication should be used to the exclusion of the face-to-face meeting or the proactive call. Only use these communication methods with clients who prefer them and to augment your other client-communication initiatives.

## Social Media

At the time of publication, using social media—LinkedIn, Facebook, Twitter—as part of your channel-marketing strategy is essential to attracting and retaining clients and prospects. Both expect you to be visible online, and developing an online presence provides instant credibility. It also gives prospective and existing clients access to information about who you are, what you do, how you do it, and why you do it. Social media enables clients to see at a glance who you are already providing services for, what valuable industry information you have to share, and what strategies, tactics, tools, and/or problem-solving tips you offer. It's important to remember, however, that, as befits our overall approach, social media should be viewed as a tool to educate and help—not to sell or market.

The list of approaches that we have suggested should not be viewed as all-inclusive. Our goal is to help you start developing an organized, process-driven, personalized marketing program that aligns all content with your primary purpose, and utilizes new and creative methods to approach, inform, and serve a channel market. It is, however, only a start.

Effective marketing programs take months to hit their rhythm, and channel markets take years to develop. You must give your ideas the patience and discipline they require. When you use channel marketing to attract and retain desirable, qualified prospects rather than casting your net as wide as it will stretch, when you define value-added services that are beyond the mainstream and develop them as specialties, when you demonstrate your expertise by educating instead of selling, you are differentiating yourself with integrity—not just offering a sales pitch. Combined with your non-traditional, prevention-based, needs assessment process, you create a value proposition that will serve your clients over the longterm. Our plan fundamentally changes the "sales and marketing" process and makes room for distinctive new levels of value, integrity, and trust.

## Key Points: Channel Marketing

*Objective:* *To create a focused, niche-specific marketing system that reaches out and captivates a group of carefully selected prospects who recognize and value what you have to offer… and are worthy of your time and attention.*

- Select niche(s) that P.A.S. the test

- Craft marketing strategies that demonstrate your visibility and viability

- Know yourself, your market, and your buyer

- Differentiate with integrity to earn trust

# Chapter Nine

# Carrier Connection—Searching for the "Sweet Spot"

*"Alone we can do so little; together we can do so much."*

—Helen Keller

Without a willing and appropriate carrier marketplace, producers are often left to scramble—"deals of the day," inferior carriers, and/or price become dominant factors. This is why time spent building a positive, collaborative relationship with carriers is worthwhile. Working as hard at carrier relationships as with clients and prospects inevitably leads to carrier trust—a trust that translates into pricing flexibility, resource availability, and meaningful partnerships.

> "[T]he most beneficial aspect of [this] program has been not only how to work more efficiently, but also how to identify myself as a more competent business partner to potential and existing clients."
>
> *Marco Constantino*
> *Agent/Producer*

## Different Perspectives

Such trust must be earned, because carriers and producers have differing perspectives: Underwriters and carriers look at the big picture, and book profitability is their primary motivation. Service-oriented producers and agencies, however, will focus on one account at a time, building relationships with prospects and clients, understanding their needs and expectations, and developing risk-management plans.

These differing perspectives often create potential points of contention that producers must anticipate and deal with proactively if the relationship is to be collaborative. Such potential points of contention include:

- Mismatched expectations and intentions;

- Different definitions of value and service;

- Lack of accountability;

- Over focus on reaping, rather than building;

- Joint business plans based on "understandings" that don't exist;

- Cultural incompatibility;

- Lack of co-development opportunities;

- Price, price, price;

- Poor communication; and

- Little proactive engagement.

When any one of these factors interferes with establishing the trust and respect necessary to enable collaboration, price drives the process. When price is the dominant factor, you have what's called a "traditional industry alignment," which is especially unfavorable for producers.

> *"Everything you put in your way is just a method of putting off the hour when you could actually be doing your dream. You don't need endless time and perfect conditions. Do it now. Do it today. Do it for 20 minutes and watch your heart start beating."*
>
> —Barbara Sher

**Figure 15: Traditional Industry Alignment**

As shown in Figure 15, in a traditional industry alignment, when insurance premium prices are high (hard market), carriers are satisfied; clients are unsatisfied, and you, as agents, are "caught in the middle." When premiums are low (soft market), clients are satisfied; carriers are unsatisfied, and you are again "caught in the middle." In either case, you are left, as the Peter Yarrow song goes, "torn between two lovers, feeling like a fool," because price is king, and other factors are often not considered. In such a situation, producers don't have the opportunity to fully describe a prospect's culture and commitment or loss-control efforts. Therefore, underwriters are unwilling to share carrier resources and support, resulting in pricing by the book.

## Searching for the Sweet Spot

In an ideal carrier/client/agency alignment, underwriters share information about carrier appetite, resources, and prospects that might be jointly produced. Carrier marketing representatives become thoroughly familiar with the agency's sales and risk-management philosophy. Underwriter preferences for submissions are clear and complete, and communication is ongoing. In such an environment, you have an ideal relationship, and all entities share the benefits of operating where the circles converge—in the "Sweet Spot."

**Figure 16: Ideal Carrier/Client/Agency Alignment**

As shown in Figure 16, in this ideal carrier/client/agency alignment, agents and carriers work *together* to address clients' needs. Price is not the dominant factor. You as a producer understand underwriter preferences. Underwriters know, trust, and respect you, and they are willing to co-produce selected desirable business. They have relevant facts about your prospects and clients, including your plans for risk management. Therefore, they will exercise pricing flexibility. When operating in the Sweet Spot, everyone wins.

---

### Opportunities to Experience the Sweet Spot

- Proactively and routinely reach out to underwriters

  - Explain your process (value-added service, niche preference, etc.)
  - Determine carrier and underwriter appetite and cover letter preferences
  - Seek co-production opportunities
  - Schedule routine contacts as Level 1, high-payoff activities

- Submit complete and timely applications

## Agency Segmentation

Carriers differentiate agencies within their agency distribution system, sometimes by volume, but mostly by profitability, growth, and potential. Carriers routinely allocate resources to a limited group of preferred agencies, as reflected in Figure 17, the Agency-Segmentation Matrix.

**Figure 17: Agency-Segmentation Matrix**

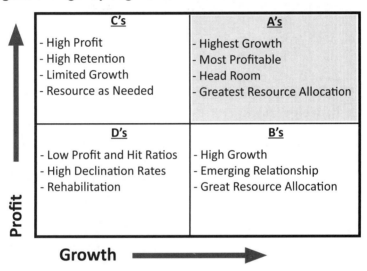

Agencies in the "A" segment have the highest growth, are the most profitable, and have the head room to grow significantly. Consequently, "A" agencies are considered to be premier agencies, with access to the greatest carrier resources. Agencies in the "B" segment have high growth but lower profitability. "B" agencies have an emerging relationship with the carrier and receive significant resources to strengthen the relationship—with the expectation that profitability will improve. "C" category agencies are highly profitable, retaining the business they have but enjoying limited growth. They receive resources as needed. Finally, agencies in the "D" category have low growth, poor hit ratios, and high declination rates. "D" agencies run the risk of losing a particular carrier if growth, efficiency, and profitability don't improve.

In short, segmentation is *not* about volume with carriers; it's about *potential*. If an agency has viable niches, focuses on building business through referrals and cross selling with correspondingly high close ratios, if it targets qualified accounts with personal vs. mass-marketing activities and follows an assessment-based, value-added service approach to sales, it will likely be in or moving toward the "A" segment.

## Establishing a Solid Carrier Connection

If you are a producer in the "C" or "D" category, should you give up? No! Luckily, every sale is dependent on producers who are willing to do what it takes to *connect* with underwriters and other carrier representatives, even if your agency is positioned in a less than desirable segment.

Producers who forge ideal carrier/client/agency alignments and follow the "Winning Model" enjoy strong, lasting, carrier connections. Some Level 1, high-payoff activities that will help differentiate you from those practicing traditional industry alignment include:

- Talk about/sell your process to your carrier representatives.

- Establish clear objectives regarding target niches/accounts, submission guidelines, cover-letter expectations, etc.

- Create an activity-driven sales plan, including co-production opportunities as appropriate.

- Prioritize all planned activities.

- Evaluate effectiveness and efficiency quarterly, and react accordingly.

Remember to work as hard at connecting with your carriers as you do with your clients and prospects, and you will be well on your way to meeting carriers and clients in the sweet spot.

# Chapter Ten

# Cross-Selling and Account-Rounding Strategies

*"If you want to be creative in your company, your career, your life, all it takes is one easy step…the extra one. When you encounter a familiar plan, you just ask one question: 'What ELSE could we do?'"*

—Dale Dauten

One of the fundamental tenets of our sales and service model is that new business is most efficiently generated by cross selling, account rounding, and referral harvesting. In organizations where there is a focused and effective cross-selling and account-rounding strategy, new revenue and client retention dramatically improve. Clients benefit from cross selling and account rounding too, because they don't need to spend time with multiple

> "The very first client [who] walked into the office this morning was here to write a new policy, and when we were done we had upsold her two extra policies and asked her for some referrals. She gave us four, and she called two of them while here in the office and told them they need to come see us ASAP."
>
> *Mike Richie*
> *Agent/Producer*

agents, suffer from too much insurance coverage, or forgo benefit from discounts. Essentially, cross selling and account rounding are valued services you should routinely and proactively offer your clients.

## Cross Selling Versus Account Rounding

We are frequently asked about the difference between cross selling and account rounding. While there is a subtle difference, it's important to remember one thing: It doesn't matter to your customers. They don't care. Nor should they. What does matter to clients is proactive service, and that you meet their expectation of being properly insured for *all* of their needs. For the record, however, cross selling refers to selling new lines of business to an existing client, such as selling personal-lines coverage to an existing commercial client (as highlighted in the 55 Plan, further on in this chapter). Account rounding refers to selling new coverages (as opposed to lines of business). One example is adding umbrella coverage to a personal-lines account.We use these terms interchangeably.

## Covering Your Bases

### Creating Opportunity:

Having a cross-selling, account-rounding strategy in place is vital, because if your client holds any part of their insurance coverage with another agency, it invites business migration. For example: You have a sizeable commercial client, and you do not provide personal-lines coverage for key executives (nor have you referred them to a trusted personal-lines partner who could). Think about it. Why not take the opportunity? Doing so will prevent the clients' existing personal-lines agent, who may be closer to the client due to the nature of their relationship, from possibly appropriating your commercial business.

## Errors and Omissions Protection:

In addition to cross selling being a proactive service that protects you, it also limits errors and omissions (E&O) exposures. There are numerous sad stories about successful law suits brought by customers who claim their agents didn't ask them about something they feel they should have been informed of. "Why didn't my agent ask me about (fill in the blank)," is a common complaint among clients who expect that, as a licensed expert, you will anticipate their need for any and all coverage. Not only are you expected to cross sell, you are required to do so. Further, you need to document it when you do.

## The 55 Plan

Take this simple test:

1) Review five of your larger commercial clients.

2) In each, develop a list of the top five employees from that company—likely the CEO, CFO, COO ("C-suite" individuals), etc. (You'll now have a list of 25 names.)

3) Next, determine how many of those 25 you write personal-lines insurance for. (You'll be surprised; it's probably fewer than 10.)

If you're not writing at least 75 percent of these (nor proposed coverage), there's a terrific opportunity here. And given that these potential personal customers are likely to be more affluent, the revenue generated will be significant too. If you don't have such relationships, at least have a meaningful discussion. If you don't, you risk not only losing the opportunity to write the personal-lines coverage but also losing the commercial account you worked so hard to secure.

Note also that the 55 Plan can work in reverse. That is, examine your top personal-lines clients to determine if they own, or have a major role in some commercial business. Don't leave revenue on the table by failing to provide "total solutions" for your clients.

## When to Cross Sell

So when is the best time to talk with clients about additional insurance needs? The answer is simple—any time, assuming you have a trusted relationship in place. Of course, there are opportunities that might arise during the policy term that provide an easier lead-in to have that discussion, such as after a positive claims experience, or when entering a new product line with a different manufacturing and distribution process, or after a life-changing event (marriage, having children, relocation), or after the purchase of a newly insurable asset (car, valuables, etc), or simply prior to renewal. The point is, if you are providing a rich, all-encompassing, value-added service program for your clients, you should already have all their needs properly handled. If you're not already enjoying such a relationship, the time to ask is "any time."

## Tracking Results

As with pipeline management, having a tracking mechanism is integral to the success of your cross-selling program. Whether accomplished within your agency-management system or manually, a disciplined way to track results adds dramatically to your success. However, with many lines of coverage to track, for all types of customers (commercial, personal, benefits, life), tracking can be an unwieldy and daunting task. Frankly, because it's so burdensome, agents often revert to relying on happenstance to generate cross-selling opportunities—which is precisely why many cross-selling strategies fail.

Consequently, in Figure 18, we offer the following matrices to track your cross-selling and account-rounding activities, both for commercial and personal lines. Whatever way you choose, however, the key is to follow, monitor, and measure regularly. We suggest starting small. Just select a few accounts, and add them to your spreadsheet. You'll see the result—in increased revenue and retention, in additional referrals, and in reducing your E&O exposure.

CHAPTER TEN: CROSS-SELLING AND ACCOUNT-ROUNDING STRATEGIES

## Figure 18: Sample Cross-Selling Matrices

### Commercial Lines

| 1 | We have the business. |
|---|---|
| 2 | We have offered the product and are waiting for a decision. |
| 3 | We have offered the product. The client has declined, or there is no application at this client. |
| 4 | We need to approach. |

| Company | Package | Auto | WC | Umb | Exec Ben | Grp Ben | Retire | EPLI | Pers Ins | Other (Specify) |
|---|---|---|---|---|---|---|---|---|---|---|
| 1 | 1 | 1 | 1 | 1 | 4 | 2 | 4 | 3 | 3 | 1 |
| 2 | 2 | 2 | 2 | 2 | 1 | 1 | 1 | 1 | 1 | 4 |
| 3 | 1 | 3 | 1 | 2 | 4 | 4 | 4 | 4 | 4 | 4 |
| 4 | 2 | 3 | 1 | 2 | 4 | 4 | 4 | 2 | 4 | |

### Personal Lines

| 1 | We have the business. |
|---|---|
| 2 | We have offered the product and are waiting for a decision. |
| 3 | We have offered the product. The client has declined, or there is no application at this client. |
| 4 | We need to approach. |

| Name | Home | Auto | Umbrella | Itemized | Life | Financial Planning |
|---|---|---|---|---|---|---|
| Personal Lines 1 | 1 | 1 | 1 | 2 | 3 | 4 |
| Personal Lines 2 | 1 | 2 | 2 | 4 | 4 | 4 |
| Personal Lines 3 | 1 | 1 | 1 | 3 | 3 | 4 |
| Personal Lines 4 | 1 | 2 | 2 | 4 | 4 | 4 |

## Campaigns and Recognition

Up to this point, we've described how you can use cross selling and account rounding to increase your revenue and retain clients. Advancing cross selling in an agency environment, campaigns, contests, and rewards may help everyone in your agency engage in the cross-selling process. Rewards and recognition for cross-selling efforts could be financial, such as sharing in a portion of the new revenue, or just a simple acknowledgment of performance. Regardless of the reward, campaigns and recognition may be just the right motivation for a comprehensive, agency-wide, cross-selling program.

*"The darkest hour of a man's life is when he sits down to plan how to get money without earning it."*

— Horace Greeley

## Key Points: Cross Selling and Account Rounding

*Objective: Generate new lines of business and coverage, secure client retention, and pro-actively provide clients with comprehensive protection for their commercial and personal insurance needs.*

- Believe that cross selling is in your clients' best interests, because they won't need to spend time with multiple agents or suffer from too much insurance coverage, and they may be able to benefit from discounts.

- Believe that cross selling strengthens your role as a valued, trusted advisor.

- Make cross selling a regular, disciplined practice.

- Track your cross-selling and account-rounding activities.

- Consider campaigns, contests, and rewards.

- Remember that your current clients offer additional revenue opportunities.

- Successful cross selling leads to additional referrals.

- Develop a cross-selling and account-rounding strategy; implement and track it.

# Chapter Eleven

# The Magic of Referral Harvesting

*"The way to gain a good reputation is to endeavor to be what you desire to appear."*

—Socrates

There's an old Chinese proverb that says it takes two wings for a bird to fly. Loosely translated, that means you'll travel much farther in life if you build relationships with people you can help—and who can help you.

In our line of work, that means getting referrals (introductions). And to get referrals, you must build a reputation as a sincere and consistent creator and as a provider of insurance programs that truly make a difference for your clients—a difference that is measurable, visible,

"Referrals were something that I just did not request in the past. My mentality [was] that I thought it was inconsiderate to ask my clients, let alone prospects, for a referral. Knowing what I know now, I was missing the boat big time. I have begun my referral tracking program, and so far it has gained me a $15,000 new business account this year and several other opportunities for me to continue to develop as the year progresses."

*Brooke Fisher*

*Agent/Producer*

and viable. The trick is not only to build those relationships, but to do so in a manner such that your clients will understand your value, respect your integrity, and trust your ability. Once this is done, you will discover that they will have an inherent desire to do more for you—to go beyond the commission to reward you for your professional friendship and loyalty to their cause—which satisfies this desire. Consequently, requesting a referral is indeed a service as well as the greatest method of building business that you have at your disposal.

In fact, referral harvesting is also the most efficient and cost-effective prospecting strategy that you can engage. Referrals from clients, COIs, and industry friends are the most expedient route to meeting prospects who have an established need and are looking for a trustworthy solution.

How? For starters, think of your professional network as a "referral garden." It's a clear way to visualize that you have to plant the seeds (build relationships), pull the weeds (eliminate the time wasters), nurture your business contacts (grow the relationships), and harvest them when the time is right (ask for referrals)—just as you would working in your backyard garden. Your referral garden is actually your most valuable business asset. It is your most reliable source for new business development and serves as a major source for renewal and cross-selling premium. As is true of any garden, however, you can only reap what you sow.

What's the key to a thriving referral garden? At the top of the list is the caliber of your relationships with existing clients, COIs, and professional friends. That, more than most factors, will determine the quality and quantity of the available referrals. If you have nurtured your contacts and clients well by consistently and proactively delivering value, integrity and trust, you will have an unlimited supply of qualified referrals to harvest. If you haven't, you won't.

### Author Snapshot: Scott Primiano

"Long before I was able to capitalize on the simple tenet of asking for referrals, I did recognize that the few that came my way were much more accommodating than the introductions I was creating on my own. In most cases, the referred prospects were willing to at least let me quote their account, and in all cases I was granted an audience. Occasionally, I even sold something. Compared against the dismal results generated by my traditional marketing programs, referral harvesting was, even then, the most tolerable and effective of all selling methods."

Imagine a selling system where the business comes to you, pre-qualified and ready to start the courtship. Imagine relying on referrals as the sole source of supply for new business opportunities. This isn't wishful thinking. It can be a reality, if you steadfastly invest time and attention in your clients. They will embrace you as a partner and "share" you with others. This will increase your viability among a pool of businesses and others that have already established good relationships with each other and therefore enjoy a reputation for credibility. Consequently, being referred by such businesses (for commercial business) and individuals (for personal lines) will, in effect, make you hyper visible and hyper viable. Of course, you have to first plan a deliberate system for harvesting referrals—meaning you'll have to ask for them.

But asking for referrals is challenging for most of us. Mark Twain once said, "Man is the only animal that blushes—or needs to." This means, of course, that we are naturally self-conscious, fear embarrassment and rejection, and are capable at any moment of committing a social blunder that will validate the reasoning for our fear. Even when we know that our relationships are healthy and sound, even when we are sure that we have made a significant contribution, even when we have invested countless hours and significant money in marketing programs designed to attract the same potential clients that we could be introduced to directly, we are still uncomfortable asking for a referral.

We are in good company, however: Fewer than 10 percent of producers around the country respond in the affirmative when asked whether they routinely and proactively ask for referrals. They know referral business is the best business and the easiest to close, but their discomfort at asking prevents them from doing so. Instead of admitting this discomfort and fighting through it, however, they concoct excuses. Some of the more common are as follow:

- *"I don't want to appear needy or pushy."*

- *"I always forget to ask."*

- *"They will not send me to their competitors."*

- *"It feels unprofessional."*

- *"It violates the nature of our relationship."*

- *"I get them without asking."*

- *"It's not the right time."*

- *"They don't know anybody."*

- *"I'm too busy as it is."*

- *"I'll feel indebted to the client."*

As George Constanza, of "Seinfeld," once said, "yadda, yadda, yadda." The real reason is that we're mortified at the thought of being rejected. We may also fear that we have not done *everything* we could do for the client and worry that we might not be entitled to a recommendation. Real or imagined as such fears are, producers who decide to push through them find a whole new world of business opportunity awaits them.

Ultimately, you'll learn that these anxieties are born out of a misunderstanding of the true nature of a referral, insufficient experience with a professional referral-harvesting system, and a lack of exposure to the psychological benefits a client receives when he or she is asked for a referral. Once you are able to see the referral-harvesting process for what it really is—a valid service technique and prospecting strategy—you will instantly became more comfortable with the idea and learn to counteract the anxiety with a rational approach.

The remainder of this chapter will help you to effectively eliminate these unnecessary encumbrances and provide you with a foundation to build your own personalized referral-harvesting program.

## Referral Magic

Why will new clients do business with you instead of somebody else? As we reviewed in our chapter on Channel Marketing, their decision is based on your ability to communicate and demonstrate a level of value, integrity, and trust that outshines your competition.

Allow us to provide an example. You may not know the name Cyrus McCormick, but he helped invent the reaper. It wasn't the first such tool ever patented, but McCormick made sure to offer customers an installment plan and a money-back guarantee, which made a big name for him and swept away his competition. Pretty soon, word got around that if you were in the market for a reaper, Cyrus was the man to see. Old Cyrus's marketing system was designed specifically—just like yours is—for this purpose by providing his prospects with gradual exposure to his message and consistent evidence of his sincerity. The major drawback to any marketing effort, including our own, is the time required to establish the credibility necessary to convince the prospect that you are for real.

Enter the referral. Here, the key is being viewed by prospective clients as a "known commodity," like Cyrus McCormick. Known commodities jump right to the front of the line when clients begin making decisions as to who receives their business. The fact that you are being recommended verifies to the new contact that you are reliable and proven—allowing you to avoid most, if not all, of the credibility-building steps in the relationship-development process. Being a known commodity helps in other time-saving ways as well. Referral contacts are typically decision makers, so you do not waste valuable time working your way through layers of bureaucracy. This elevator goes straight to the top. As a known commodity, you are talking with people whose interest you have attracted. They want to hear what you have to say and see what you can do. You are projected directly into the heart of the needs-development stage of the relationship—no marketing chicken dance, no serenading, no bidding, and no nonsense.

Why are these recommendations held in such high regard by your prospects? Unlike all of the untried and untested claims of your competitors, somebody that they know has tested you. If the prospect values the referral provider's opinion and trusts that his or her judgment is sound, the prospect will extend that trust and value to you as well. As has been said many times before, people buy from those whom they trust and respect, and the referral provides just that.

## Referrals that Service:

How do you feel after you see an inspiring movie, dine at a sensational restaurant, or read an extraordinary book? Are you quiet about your experience, or do you like to talk about it? How do you react when you are asked for a recommendation regarding the movie, restaurant, or book? Are you non-committal, or do you enthusiastically give your opinion? Most of us are excited to share our positive experiences, and we actively encourage others to accept our endorsements. We do this to be helpful, and we do this as a way to validate our opinion. Without any particular allegiance to the producer of the movie, the chef at the restaurant, or the author of the book, we make recommendations and actively seek feedback. If the feedback is positive, we will feel even better about our initial experience. This phenomenon plays a large role in counteracting buyer remorse, and it is why most of your clients will give you a referral if you ask them.

The fact is, we all have a need to share our opinions and positive experiences with others. This is true of your clients and their experiences with you as well. We asked 3,000 commercial-insurance purchasers what their response would be if approached for a referral. Here is what they told us:

- 86 percent would give a referral if asked.

- 40 percent would give more than one referral.

- *Only 4 percent* had ever been asked for a referral.

Of the 14 percent that would not give a referral . . .

- 85 percent indicated that they could not think of anyone at the time.

- 10 percent said that they did not give referrals.

- 5 percent said that the service could not be recommended.

So . . .why the hesitation? Your clients are waiting for you to ask them, and they are eager to help. Sounds like a no-brainer, right? But obviously it isn't—and that calls for a closer look.

Knowing what we know now, let's review the most common justifications that we use for not asking for referrals and respond to each one.

**"I don't want to appear needy or pushy."** Okay, fine. The reality is that your clients are the ones who are needy. To paraphrase the Jack Nicholson character, Colonel Nathan Jessup, in "A Few Good Men," they *want* you to ask them; they *need* you to ask them, and they would push you to do so if you provide them with the opportunity. They need to know that their opinion matters to you and to others, and they need to reinforce their decision to do business with you. You will actually improve your relationship by asking for their recommendation, because it enables them to give back and help you.

**"I always forget to ask."** Sorry, but this is a cop out. The remainder of this section will detail a referral-harvesting system that is easy to use and easy to remember to use.

**"They won't send me to their competitors."** This is one we hear a lot. The fact is, you don't know who they know, and you don't know where they will send you. Clients share referral information with each other on a regular basis. In fact, it is what they talk about the most.

**"It feels unprofessional."** That depends on how you ask, when you ask, and what you do after you ask. Referral requests can be handled unprofessionally—usually by those who don't belong in our profession. The difference will become clear as we describe our system.

**"It violates the nature of our relationship."** Yes it does—for the better. Nobody has ever lost a client as a result of asking for a referral.

**"I get them without asking."** Excellent. This is a good indicator of sound and healthy client relationships. How many more would you get if you asked for them, rather than waiting for them?

**"It's not the right time."** This answer only works if you have no clients and no network. Otherwise, it is always the right time. And remember also that procrastination is the thief of time.

**"They don't know anybody."** You'll be amazed at who they know. They can also tell you who not to work with. Don't pre-judge the answer to your referral request.

**"I'm too busy as it is."** Too busy doing what? Referral harvesting is the fast and efficient track to new business development.

**"I'll feel indebted to my client."** Remember that you can offer to refer your client to others, too. It works both ways. That uncomfortable feeling that there's a debt owed can be alleviated by offering to share your new "partner's" name with others.

## How Not to Request a Referral:

One of our first facilitations of our sales training program was with a group of whole-life producers from a giant mutual insurance company. When we inquired about their volume of referral requests, the response was that they were required to ask for a minimum of three referrals at every appointment with every prospect and client. They had been trained not to leave the appointment until they had secured the referrals and developed an elaborate script that was intentionally designed to pressure the client or prospect into coughing up the names. Additionally, they each sent out quarterly mailings, disguised as customer-service surveys, containing yet further referral solicitations.

Not surprisingly, this producer group was required to make 100 cold calls per day, push to close all prospects on the first meeting, and only schedule appointments to get a check and an application. Service "calls" were out of the question; relationships were non-existent, and anybody with a checkbook who was not at death's door was considered a potential client.

We had landed in producer hell. The entire sales process had to be retooled, and the existing sales culture completely abandoned. One of our primary objectives was to transform the referral-bludgeoning process into a referral-harvesting system.

As we have already reviewed, clients provide qualified referrals for two primary reasons:

1)  They feel that they have received something extraordinary, something special, and they wish to reinforce this belief by sharing it with others and receiving validation.

2)  The producer has demonstrated a unique level of value, integrity, and trust that is often considered to be above and beyond the call of duty. The relationship is personal—a professional friendship—and the client wishes to help the producer become more successful.

In the case of this insurance company, neither condition was present. When we asked for impressions of the referral program, the company labeled it unprofessional and intrusive—rightfully so. They also found it to be terribly unproductive due to a high frequency of unqualified referrals. One of them had even been referred to a prospect's paperboy, another to an estranged ex-wife, and more than a few mentioned referrals to the deceased. Talk about dead ends.

There is a right way and a wrong way to ask for a referral, and clearly this is the wrong way. However, let's not throw the baby out with the bath water.

## Who to Ask, When to Ask, and How to Ask:

The cornerstone of any referral program is the strength of the relationship that you have forged with the referral provider. No relationship, no referral. Therefore, we do not ask for a referral until we have successfully, sincerely, and consistently demonstrated a value-added commitment to the referral provider, and he or she has acknowledged our effort. We'll share more on this in a moment.

An effective referral-harvesting system is set up and managed in the same way as the other prospecting systems that we have reviewed. Start by making a list of all existing clients, COIs, and other market-service providers that you have developed a relationship with. This is your target market within a target market.

Next, set a weekly referral request objective. Of course your objective will depend on the number of names on your list; however, a minimum of one request per week is your goal. Don't worry about a lack of referral candidates—you haven't made it this far in either sales or life without accumulating a stack of business cards from networking contacts. If you do not have at least 20 potential referral sources listed, it can only mean that you are new to the industry and the agency. Your list can begin with internal referral sources—friends and colleagues who are willing to introduce you to industry contacts and potential clients.

With referrals, your timing counts. The most obvious time to make the request is during a service-review conference with the client or during a pre-renewal meeting. These events are usually retrospective in nature and present a wonderful opportunity to acknowledge the value and goodwill that you have brought to the relationship. Additionally, you are face to face with the referral provider, which adds credibility and professionalism to your request, enables you to better qualify or define who you would like to meet, and allows you to help your client think through the introduction. Finally, your clients will often feel compelled to pick up the phone and make the introduction for you then and there. Like we said, people want to help you.

Don't ignore any opportunity to earn a referral. Often, referral-request opportunities occur during normal conversations with your client or with a COI. Whether or not you are talking on the telephone or face to face, any time the topic of discussion is about the service that you provide, the value that you have established, or the positive impact that you've made, circumstances are right for you to find out who else might benefit from your capability. We find that even when a sale is not made for reasons beyond the producer's control, if you handled the sale *process* well and the prospect was impressed with you, your referral request will meet with favorable response.

Be direct about it. Schedule a client meeting where the primary agenda is requesting a referral. Call the client or COI; request some time over breakfast or lunch, and clearly state that the reason for meeting is to discuss new opportunities that they can recommend. Prior to the meeting, send a list of prospective new accounts, along with a profile of a typical client. This premeditated approach alerts the client to your intention, allows each of you to prepare, and sets the stage for a positive outcome.

As already mentioned, the act of "popping the question" is what many producers find most vexing. Tedious as it may seem, scripting the question and preparing to field the response is a great way to relieve some of this self-imposed pressure. Additionally, scripting the request will help you to qualify the referral and remind the referral provider that it is your value, integrity, and trust that is the foundation of your relationship. The recommendation is for you—not an insurance product.

A typical request contains five or six key components that vary according to your circumstances and personal style. When preparing to script your referral request, you must plan to either ask in person or over the phone. If you are meeting or calling specifically to ask for a referral, your script begins by disclosing your intention (Step 1). If your request will fit into another meeting or conversation, your script begins with the relationship reminder (Step 2). The remaining steps can be inserted in any order that feels comfortable to you, with the exception of Step 6. Regardless of circumstances, never solicit referrals through the mail or via e-mail. Mailed requests are impersonal and unprofessional.

Your referral-request script should contain the following elements:

**Step 1—A disclosure of your intention:**

Indicate clearly that you are calling or wish to meet about referrals.

**Step 2—A relationship reminder:**

Reinforce the importance of the existing relationship.

**Step 3—A professional request:**

Don't beat around the bush or hint at the question.

**Step 4—A qualifying statement:**

"Who do you know like yourself?" or "Who could you recommend in the industry?"

**Step 5—Reassurance and assistance:**

Take the pressure off and help them think.

**Step 6—A professional thank you and a commitment to follow up.**

Here is an example of a telephone request:

**(Producer)**

*"Hi Bob, this is [your name]. Do you have a moment?"*

**(Client)**

*"Yes"*

**(Producer)**

*"The reason I called, Bob, is to ask for your help. I truly respect your opinion, and I was hoping you could recommend another organization like your own that would benefit from the same level of service I have provided to you over the past few years. My intent, Bob, is to continue to develop my business, but I would not do so at the expense of our relationship. So if you don't feel comfortable, this is not critical."*

Before we proceed any further, let's spend some time reviewing Bob's potential responses to your request. As indicated earlier, 80 percent of the time you will be given a referral. If this were to occur with Bob, you would immediately move into a "thank you and follow-up" strategy that appropriately acknowledges the goodwill Bob has extended.

However, what if the answer is not the one you were hoping for? In fact, what if Bob's response is the answer that we feared the most—a rejection? Do you:

a)  Run away and stay away?

b)  Never ask for a referral again?

c)  Pretend that you were joking?

d)  All of the above?

e)  None of the above?

The correct answer is, of course, "none of the above." The truth is that *any* answer to a referral request can be a positive one, providing that we respond appropriately by doing something constructive with the information that we have been given. For example, Bob says:

*"I can't think of anybody" or "I really don't know anybody."*

Your first reaction is likely to be "Uh-Oh." Your instincts tell you that something bad has happened. You will interpret Bob's message to be a polite "no," and you will feel the urge to mumble "goodbye" and hang up—or change the topic and pretend it never happened ("Say Bob, how 'bout dem Red Sox?"). In the time it takes for your body to process its "fight or flight" response—a second or so—you will be flooded with negative impressions of Bob's response that will be, at best, uncomfortable. Worse yet, if the moment is allowed to awkwardly hang where it is, Bob will sense your reaction and immediately become uncomfortable as well. So . . . you need to act.

First, you must realize that Bob's answer is perfectly legitimate. You called him out of the blue and asked him a very important, thought-provoking question. You also know that Bob was hardly hanging by the phone, wringing his hands in despair because you hadn't called and asked him for a referral yet. So what on earth would lead you to expect that he would be able to offer a quality recommendation on the spot?

Second, you have to ignore your initial reaction. Your feelings of rejection and disappointment are conditioned responses to an unrealized expectation. However natural they may be, they are inappropriate for this situation and of absolutely no help to you.

Third, you need to help Bob think. He wants to help you. He's feeling awkward about not being able to, and he needs you to help him do so. Therefore, your response to Bob must be supportive rather than evasive. You are obligated to clarify your question by providing him with enough information to make an educated decision about where to refer you. This may take time and involve tactful follow up.

For example, your response to Bob's answer, *"I would love to help; however, I can't think of anyone,"* may be:

> *"That's understandable. I called out of the blue. Many of my clients refer me to indirect competitors, industry associates, vendors and/or their clients. "Why don't I give you some time to think about it and follow up with you next week?"*

Alternatively, you might say:

> *"Many of my clients refer me to indirect competitors, industry associates, vendors and/or their clients. I have a list of organizations that I think meet my client profile and that I would like to be introduced to. Perhaps we can we review it together and see who you might recognize—or I can e-mail it to you and we can talk over the phone? I welcome your thoughts regarding who is on my list that shouldn't be, who is not on my list that should be, and who, if anyone, you would be comfortable referring me to."*

Such replies are specifically designed to take the temperature gauge down a notch, remove any pressure that Bob might be feeling, and to move beyond an immediate "yes" or "no" answer.

It's a good idea to brace yourself for some variation of direct rejection. For example, a client will occasionally immediately answer a request for a referral with "I don't give referrals." Your reaction to this type of answer is apt to be even more negative and defensive than it was in the previous scenario, and you will definitely feel like it's a brush off. As before, however, you must override your instinctive urge to run away and consider more carefully why your client has closed the door on referral requests. Chances are very good that the client, Bob in this case, has had a bad experience with a referral before and is reluctant to stick his neck out again. Perhaps Bob is friendly with other agents and prefers not to give special treatment to any one of us. Maybe he is just not comfortable with the idea and really would prefer to keep you a secret. Whatever the reason, you need to find out.

With this in mind, your follow up to this response is a simple question: *"Oh, I wasn't aware of that. Why don't you give referrals?"*

Inevitably, you will learn the reasons for his resistance and, instead of combating them, you will support them. The idea here is to remove any hint of tension. You don't want to be in a position that requires you to justify why you're worthy of his recommendation. Nor do you ever want to "sell" him into giving you a referral. Regardless of his rationale, this is Bob's decision. You must respect his position, rather than argue against it. Your reply to his explanation will be an empathetic one, such as: *"Oh, that makes sense, I understand completely."*

Once again, you have taken the pressure off of the situation and allowed Bob to stay within his comfort zone. However, your work is not done. Bob is going to have some guilt. At some level, he'll feel inadequate because he will believe that he let you down. You're going to remove this burden by describing other ways that he can help. For example:

> *"Oh, that makes sense, I understand completely. Would it be okay if I used you for a reference instead? New clients often ask me who I'm working with, and I prefer to give them names of people and organizations that they will recognize and respect."*

Alternatively, you might say:

> *"Oh, that makes sense, I understand completely. How about this instead—the marketing company that develops my material is constantly after me to provide client testimonials. I prefer to give them the names of people and organizations that are recognized as industry leaders and respected for their leadership. If they were to call you, would you be willing to offer a testimonial or an endorsement?"*

Clients rarely say "no" to this request. They usually smile, feel flattered, and are more than willing to help. Everybody wins.

But what if Bob's answer to your original referral request is, in fact, the one that you feared the most? What if Bob says:

*"I cannot recommend you to anybody."*

Okay, now it is time to run away. Just kidding. This is actually the best answer that you can get. Something has obviously gone terribly wrong with your relationship—certainly it is not what you thought it was, or you never would have asked for a referral in the first place. Bob is not pleased—of that you can be sure. In fact he is so displeased that you were about to lose him as a client, and you weren't even aware that the relationship was in jeopardy. You can respond to this turn of events with much wailing and gnashing of teeth. Or, you can see it for what it really is—a gift. You have been granted the gift of a second chance—an opportunity to discover what is broken, to fix it, and to replenish the value, integrity, and trust that has dissolved. In service-program parlance, this is what is known as a "moment of truth"—a chance to repair a broken relationship if handled properly. And, often, a repaired relationship will become even stronger than it was before it was broken. You may not be successful; Bob may be too far gone. But if you're going to lose him, you're going to lose him while trying to keep him.

Why are you willing to invest so much time and energy into a relationship that may have been soured forever? For a number of reasons:

- Chances are very good that the wound is fresh; otherwise, you'd already be aware of it. If you work quickly and earnestly, it probably isn't fatal. If the wound is not fresh, you can presume that it was not painful enough for Bob to mention previously (unless he is just a silent sufferer, not prone to complaining but needing to be heard). In either case, you've opened a door, and you're going to encourage Bob to walk through it. You want to hear everything that is troubling him, get it all out on the table, remain non-defensive, and convince him that you're going to try and repair the damage.

- Customer-service statistics show that your most loyal clients (your best source for references) are those that have experienced a breakdown in service with which you've worked to fix the problem. Those that have never had a service problem with their account will usually tell one to two people about your good service, while those who have had a service issue that you at least tried to correct will recommend you to five or six people. "Problems" are really opportunities waiting to evolve. After you discover what Bob's problem is, you're going to provide him with a detailed action plan that will specify exactly what you are going to do and when you're going to do it. You will also forecast the probable outcome and double check that it matches his expectations. You will keep him updated every step of the way and, when you're done, you're coming back to Bob for a referral.

- Remember, time is money. You will spend up to 20 times more money, time, and effort trying to replace Bob's account with a new client than you will if you try to keep him. Plus, you have worked very hard to get and to keep Bob's account. Obviously you did not fully understand every expectation that Bob may have had, and there is certainly cause for concern—but not for surrender.

- You have a reputation to protect. You know that you will never be able to fulfill every client's expectation, all of the time. However, you should be aware of every client's expectation all of the time. If one gets by you, own it, and do what you can to repair the damage. If they continue to get by, the damage will be permanent. Statistics tell us that dissatisfied clients will tell 10-12 others about the poor service they received. Your world is too small to have that kind of message on the street.

There's more about this in our chapter on value-added service. The point is: Always attempt to correct the problem. An ounce of prevention is definitely worth a pound of cure . . ., but a pound of cure is still worth the time.

We have demonstrated that a referral request is clearly not a simple "yes" or "no" proposition for either you or for your client. If we approach the question intellectually rather than emotionally, structure our request in a clear and deliberate format, relax our expectations, and simply listen to the response, something good will develop. On the other hand, if we stumble into it, stumble through it, and stumble out of it, we will never be quite sure of what the result will be.

## After the Answer . . . Giving Thanks and Following Up

Okay, you have asked for a referral and received a response. Now it's time to move on to the next step. Starting with the most probable response, let's assume that your referral request harvested two referrals, one that hits pay dirt and one that leads to an undesirable account.

You will likely be tempted to immediately start chasing the qualified opportunity, and you'll want to ignore the other. Considering the value of your time, this behavior would seem perfectly compatible with your need to be highly selective when allocating your time and when choosing which opportunities to pursue. Under normal circumstances, when you are the only one making the decision, this would be appropriate. In this scenario, however, the decision about which opportunity to pursue has been made for you. Your client, colleague, or COI has decided that both opportunities are worthy of your time and, out of respect for the referral provider, you are obligated to connect with both.

Let's remember what's at stake here. The referral provider has put his or her name on your marquee. He or she is framing the value, integrity, and trust that you have delivered along with his or her own story and allowing you to use it elsewhere. Yes, it feels great giving referrals, but they aren't given casually or without concern for the outcomes. Rest assured that the next time the referral provider speaks with the person to whom he or she referred you, your name will come up. Imagine how embarrassed your friend will be if the other party has never heard of you.

Professional and consistent follow up with both the referral provider and the new contact will guarantee a steady stream of new opportunities. Random and haphazard follow up will close the door on them forever. So (no surprise), we need a proactive system to manage the referral-harvesting process. Now for Step 6: a professional thank you and a commitment to follow up.

Acknowledging the fact that you received a referral, any referral, or that you are being considered for one is the first thing you must do. A hand-written note or a formal letter is best for this purpose. You may also e-mail a card if you wish; however, make sure that the referral provider is a "fan" of electronic mail. You might also want to consider using a card from a non-profit corporation to send your thank you. This adds a touch of "paying it forward" to your message of gratitude. Many such organizations provide free e-cards from their websites that you can use.

Here are four sample referral-thank you correspondences, letters that address the contingencies that we covered with "Bob." These are for you to use as a template for your own notes or letters.

**Referral-Thank You Correspondence:**

Dear Referral Provider:

I would like to take this opportunity to express my appreciation for the referral to John Warren of Clayton Widget Manufacturing.

I am honored that you're comfortable enough with my agency and the level of service that I provide to recommend us to others. There is no better feeling than the one that comes from having a satisfied client who refers you to their trusted friends and business associates.

**In the next few days, I will be sending John a letter of introduction and following up with a phone call. I will cc you on the letter, so John knows we have spoken, and I'll be sure to keep you informed as things develop.** In the interim, please feel free to call me if you have any questions, or if there is anything I can do for you. Once again, thank you very much.

Sincerely,

**Thank You for Considering a Referral Correspondence:**

Dear Referral Provider:

I would like to take this opportunity to thank you for considering me for a referral. I am honored that you're comfortable enough with my agency and the level of service that I provide to recommend us to others. There is no better feeling than the one that comes from having a satisfied client who refers you to their trusted friends and business associates.

**I will call you next week to discuss any contacts that you think I should make and to review a list of potential clients that I would like to meet.** In the interim, please feel free to call me if you have any questions or if there is anything I can do for you. Once again, thank you very much.

Sincerely,

**Thank You for Being a Reference/Testimonial Correspondence:**

Dear Client:

I would like to take this opportunity to express my appreciation for allowing me to use your name as a personal reference and as a testimonial for the work that we have done for your organization.

I am honored that you're comfortable enough with my agency and the level of service that I provide to recommend us to others. There is no better feeling than the one that comes from having a satisfied client who is willing to endorse our performance both publicly and privately.

**When the opportunity to use your name as a reference arises, I will be in the habit of calling to brief you on the prospect and the opportunity. I'll also keep you in the loop as things develop.** In the interim, please feel free to call me if you have any questions, or if there is anything I can do for you. Once again, thank you very much.

Sincerely,

---

**Thank You for Being Honest Correspondence:**

Dear Client:

Words cannot express how sorry I am that your account was not being serviced in a fashion that met with your expectations. Nor can they appropriately describe the embarrassment that I feel for being surprised by the news that we have disappointed you.

Needless to say, I am going to do whatever is within my power to do, so that I may regain your trust and reestablish our value as your Broker of Record. **Enclosed you will please find a preliminary action plan that outlines the steps I will take to remedy the service gaps that you described.**

Make no mistake about it, this work is my highest priority and it will remain so until you are once again satisfied. I will plan to follow up with you on a weekly basis, by telephone and through e-mail, to keep you updated and informed of our progress.

Thank you for giving us a second chance. I assure you that we will not need a third.

Sincerely,

---

Notice that each correspondence contains a brief description of the next continuation step on your agenda. (We've set this in bold type to show you what this looks like; however, your correspondence should of course not do so.) This description keeps the referral provider aware of what is being done and informs him or her of what to expect in the future. You do not want the referral provider to develop "referral remorse" or to feel left behind. You should send such correspondence as soon as possible—certainly no later than the day after the conversation takes place and preferably the day of the conversation.

Having done this, it is now time to approach the new contact(s), if you received a referral. If you did not receive a referral, comply with the continuation plan that you described in your correspondence. Be absolutely certain to proactively calendar all these Level 1, follow-up activities, as described in our chapter on Priority Management. There is no margin for error.

## Making the Introduction

Hallelujah! Like General Patton rolling through a liberated Paris on a Sherman tank, you're flush with victory and excited about the new opportunity. In fact, you're hardly out of the building before you reach for your cell phone to make the call to set things in motion. Then . . . you get voice-mailed or stonewalled by a gatekeeper. You dutifully leave a message, wait a few days for a response, try again, leave another message, wait some more, and . . . nothing. Your "referral missile" is looking more and more like a dud, and you're feeling less and less positive about the efficacy of the whole exercise. Your calls seem like cold calls, and the lack of response reminds you of the old days. Talk about disappointment.

What happened? Although you perceived your call to be credible enough to be accepted, the contact registered it as just another cold call and treated it accordingly. Simply dropping the name of the referral provider was not enough to get you through the door, because your call had all of the elements found in a traditional cold call. It was unexpected; you were most likely excited, and it appeared intrusive—just another slick producer peddling product.

As you might expect, we suggest a more polished approach. First, take a deep breath and get a grip. There is no need to rush into the contact. Haste makes waste. When you apply urgency, you bring unwanted pressure on a potential opportunity that will not tolerate it. Give yourself, the referral provider, and the new contact time to develop a level of comfort and understanding (there's that nurturing garden again). The referral is as good next week or, for that matter, next month and next year, as it is today. Now, with sound mind and body, we move on.

In our chapter on Channel Marketing, we reviewed using pre-approach correspondence to introduce who you are and why you are making the contact. Our method for presenting yourself to a referral contact is quite similar, with the added benefit of notifying the referral provider that contact has been initiated. For example, you send the following introductory letter to the referral contact:

---

**Sample Referral-Approach Correspondence:**

Dear Contact:

Your name recently came up in a conversation I was having with [*Insert Name*] of Nice Premium, Inc. [*He/She*] suggested that you and I make contact to review the risk-management program that we have custom developed for Nice Premium and to explore the potential for doing the same for you.

I have enclosed some information about our company and the program. I will call you next week to formally introduce myself and to review this packet with you in greater detail. In the interim, please feel free to call me directly at [*Insert Number*], with any questions or comments.

Sincerely,

CC: [*Insert Name of Nice Premium Contact*]

---

What do you think might happen when your contact at Nice Premium and the referral contact receive your correspondence? Usually, one will contact the other and discuss who you are and what you are about. In the normal course of that conversation, your client contact at Nice Premium will explain the reasons for the recommendation, review the program you provide, and firmly establish your credibility and value. But wait, it gets better. Your contact will then call you to summarize the conversation and provide you with greater insight and vital information. *Now* when you make your introductory call, you can expect that your call will be returned.

As an additional enhancement to this growing sense of cama-raderie between the referral provider, the new contact, and yourself, we suggest that the first meeting with the new contact take place over breakfast or lunch, if possible, and include the referral provider. This technique makes the introduction much more comfortable and relaxed for everybody, affords you the opportunity to keep the referral provider active in the process, and actually allows you to witness somebody else selling you. Not only is it flattering, it is incredibly effective.

Wait, there's more. We cannot count the number of times that, during the walk or ride back from lunch, the referral provider starts enthusiastically discussing the next introduction that he or she is going to make for us. This is producer heaven.

Of course, on the heels of these meetings, everybody gets a thank you note. In fact every contact made during this process requires that follow-up correspondence, a letter, note, card, phone call, or e-mail is sent to all parties. No exceptions. Here is another sample of referral-approach correspondence—this one specifical-ly designed for a channel market (the YMCA).

---

### Referral-Approach Correspondence: Channel Market

Mr. Stephen Wayne
Your Town YMCA
2500 Main Street
Your Town, PA 18901

Dear Stephen:

Liz Louise of the Any Town YMCA provided your name to us. Liz suggested that we contact you to review the risk-man-agement audit process that we have just completed at the Any Town YMCA, and to discuss the feasibility of conducting a similar program for the Your Town YMCA.

Our extensive experience with non-profit organizations, combined with this unique risk-management assessment

---

tool, provided Liz with an unbiased, comprehensive analysis of the facilities, staff, culture, and insurance program currently in place at the Any Town YMCA. Our final report contained a concise explanation of our findings, along with a series of recommendations to enhance each location's risk-management and loss-control program. Working with select insurance providers, including the National YMCA Mutual Program, we were able to custom develop a comprehensive strategy that is tailored to address the specific needs of the Any Town YMCA.

Attached you will please find a brief description of our agency and our process. Our record proves that this value-driven approach leads to enhanced program design, reduced premiums, and satisfied clients.

In the near future, I will call you to formally introduce myself and to review our program in greater detail. In the interim, please feel free to call me directly at [*Insert number*] with any questions or comments.

Sincerely,

CC: Liz Louise, Any Town YMCA

## After a Sale

Next, let's review what to do when your referral turns into a sale.

You are triumphant. Having patiently worked your referral-harvesting system and enlisted the help of your trusted client, you have successfully developed another trusted client. You have created the ultimate Win-Win-Win. Everybody involved is feeling validated. You know what to do next with your new relationship—stay close, stay proactive and stay involved. You know how important it is to remain visible and viable, especially during the first few months following the transaction. But what about the referral provider? Now that the circle has closed, what happens next in that arena?

Certainly you need to express your gratitude; however, sending yet more correspondence of thanks would be, at best, redundant. What can you do to adequately demonstrate your gratitude? Well, a gift would be nice—but not just any gift. You wish to give something special, something tangible and something permanent. It must be something appropriate that will remind the referral provider of this wonderful episode in your relationship and also reinforce the goodwill that you have established.

Here is our list of "Do's and Don'ts" for referral gift giving:

**Do give something personal; don't give a tacky trinket from the company store.** Although your office closets may be overflowing with logo golf shirts, logo pens, and logo coffee mugs, this is not a marketing event. Save that stuff for the new accounts. Your gift should be selected based upon your personal relationship, not your professional one. If you know the referral provider's taste in music, give a CD. If you know his or her taste in clothing, give a tie or a scarf. If you are aware of a relevant business book that your referrer would appreciate, deliver it in person. If you see plants in the office, give an interesting plant (just make sure it isn't one that will die without inordinate attention, as this will send the wrong message).

**Do give something nice; don't give something lavish.** There are laws in most states that place a specific dollar value limitation on non-taxable gifts. Additionally, many companies do not allow their employees to accept gifts from vendors. Tactfully find out what is appropriate for your referral provider. In the event that he or she is not permitted to accept a gift, a small donation to a charity of his or her choice is usually acceptable.

**Do give something permanent; don't ever give anything edible or anything alcoholic.** Edibles are perishable; you never know what allergies people have, and the booze-giving days of yesteryear are behind us forever. There could be a nightmare, or a car wreck, an embarrassment, or a lawsuit in giving a bottle, so don't take a chance. Instead, give a non-consumable gift that will serve as a permanent reminder of the experience. Flowers are nice, but they die. Food is nice, but it gets eaten up. Tickets are nice, but the show ends. These gifts will be forgotten, and we never want to be forgotten in any way. For example, the CD that was mentioned earlier—every time the CD is played, who is the referral provider going to think of? Every time the necktie or scarf is straightened in the mirror, who are they going to think of? Every time the plant is watered . . . . Every time the frame is viewed . . . . Every time the hat is worn . . . . You get the point. Assuming that your taste is appropriate, these gifts are both positive and permanent.

Our personal favorite referral gift is a magazine subscription. Each month, magazines arrive on our clients' desks, and they might as well have our picture on the cover. We get *Runner's World* for the runners, *Flying* for the pilots, *American Heritage* for the history buffs, and *The Coconut Telegraph* for the Parrot Heads. We make sure that all gift subscriptions are non-industry related.

A last thought on referral gift giving—most people enjoy being surprised by a gift and, when they are, they usually call to say thank you. When they do call, they often have some other ideas to work on and some additional people to see. And so it goes.

Next, let's cover our final scenario: What do you do when nothing happens—when you are rejected or you do the rejecting?

## When a Sale Doesn't Happen

Sometimes, despite your best effort to help the referral provider qualify the lead, you will be recommended to a misfit account—an account that doesn't meet the criteria established by your client profile.

Perhaps the account is too small; perhaps it is in the wrong industry, or perhaps it is an out-and-out deadbeat account. On other occasions, you will be recommended to an account that you may wish to write; however, it does not wish to be written by you. Perhaps the company is happy with the incumbent; perhaps it is a "lowest bid" buyer, or maybe you just don't get along. Regardless of the reason for the rejection, we have some "bad news" to deliver back to the referral provider.

Earlier in this chapter, we briefly mentioned that we are obligated to follow through on all referral leads, regardless of our desire or ability to actually write the account or develop a relationship with the referral contact. We are bound by our integrity and the strength of our relationship to respect all recommendations and to protect the referral provider's position.

Although this mandate might appear to contradict the precedent that we established in our Channel Marketing and Priority Management chapters, we are investing in the relationship we have with the referrer, which is certainly a high-payoff activity, and the follow-up strategy that we suggest is not terribly involved or time consuming. We need only to close the loop on every referral in a manner that is consistent with our overall value-added service strategy.

For the accounts that you deem inappropriate, send your referral-approach correspondence anyway, and follow up with a phone call. Your discussion with the referral contact should be entirely focused on who the client is and what insurance needs the client has. Once these needs are established, you will be able to determine if they are best served by staying with the current agent and insurance program, or if you should refer them to another agency that could improve their service or program. Whatever the solution is, you maintain the role of insurance advisor, rather than insurance agent. Once you have referred the client to another agency or producer within your network, you have fulfilled your obligation.

In this instance, your follow-up call to the referral provider is very simple:

*"Bob, I spoke with Jack Reynolds over at BigHazard, Inc., and we had a wonderful conversation. What an interesting*

*guy. We reviewed the program that he currently has in place. We agreed that the insurance product was the right one; however, the company needs immediate loss-control help. I gave Jack the names of two loss-control consultants with whom I have worked before and who would be of great value. Jack is going to connect with them and let you or me know what his impressions are. I've already called each of them and briefed them on the company."*

Alternatively, you might say:

*"Bob, I spoke with Jack Reynolds over at BigHazard, Inc., and we had a wonderful conversation. What an interesting guy. Based upon this preliminary review, I told him that I thought he was being under-serviced. I've given him the name of an agent friend of mine who specializes in Bob's industry and can really pull together a great program. I don't have access to the kind of program that Jack will need going forward. Even if the product can't be moved due to the firming market, my colleague will be able to help with proactive risk management and loss control. Jack is going to connect with him and let you or me know what his impressions are. I've already called the agent and briefed him on the company."*

Regardless of the circumstances that you uncover, your opinion and advice is all that is necessary.

Your follow-up conversation regarding an account that you did pursue but didn't get is very similar:

*"Bob, I met with Hilarie Williams over at A1 Riding Stables. We had a great meeting and, in the end, she determined that she is more comfortable staying with her current agent. We did agree to connect from time to time to discuss any new developments, and she indicated that she would enjoy attending our next safety symposium. Thank you so much for the introduction; I absolutely love to meet new people, and I was able to learn quite a lot about her industry. It was definitely time well spent."*

Notice that in all of these conversations, we never let the referral provider feel as if he or she has failed. We must find something good to say about each contact that we make and let the referral provider see how the referral was beneficial for everyone. Finally, please remember to send everybody involved a thank you note, and make sure that your colleagues follow up with every referral that you send their way.

## Summary of the 10-Step Referral-Harvesting Strategy

**Step 1**—Make a list of at least 20 potential referral sources, including:

- Existing Clients;

- COIs;

- Industry Service Providers; and

- Colleagues and Affinity Groups.

**Step 2**—Set a weekly referral-request objective (minimum of one per week).

**Step 3**—Decide when and how to make each referral request—either face to face or over the phone. Never through the mail!

**Step 4**—Prepare a script for your request that:

- Discloses your intention;

- Includes a "relationship reminder;"

- Includes a professional request;

- Includes a qualifying statement;

- Reassures and assists; and

- Includes a professional thank you and a follow-up plan.

**Step 5**—Ask and respond appropriately

- If the answer is "yes," move to Step 6.

- If the answer is "I can't think of anyone," help them think and consider providing a list of desirable prospects.

- If the answer is "I don't give referrals," find out why, accept the reason, and ask for a reference or testimonial.

- If the answer is "I can't recommend you," find out why, and commit to saving the relationship.

**Step 6**—Immediately send a "thank you" letter that includes a description of your continuation plan.

**Step 7**—Send a referral-approach letter to every referral contact, and copy the referral provider.

**Step 8**—Follow up each letter with a phone call to:

- Set an appointment with qualified accounts; and

- Review, advise, and refer unqualified accounts.

**Step 9**—Continue to update the referral provider on the status of each referral, including the "bad news."

**Step 10**—Send, or better still, deliver a personalized thank you gift to referral providers that generate appropriate new business.

Please grant yourself an enormous advantage, and learn to use this referral-harvesting strategy. You cannot be successful or ever realize your true potential unless you have fully developed a system for harvesting and processing referral opportunities.

Any system so dependent on timing requires a tracking system to ensure you don't miss any steps. Otherwise, what has the potential of reinforcing the already favorable impression the referrer has of us can backfire and become a negative. If we promise to send a letter with a cc to the referrer, and we fail to do so on a timely basis, or at all, we leave a bad taste in the referrer's mind. If we commit in our referral-approach letter to contact the prospect within a given time frame but don't, we have undermined all the good things the referrer has said about us. This reflects badly on us and even worse, on the referrer.

If a robust, systematic, referral-harvesting process is a key element of our new business development strategy, we need discipline to keep us on track. We suggest a tracking worksheet like that shown below in Figure 19. The top half of the worksheet records activities related to the referrer, and the bottom half records activities related to the prospects we have been referred to.

Whether you use this worksheet, or one you develop for yourself, use *something*, because, once you start asking for referrals every week, it's easy to miss steps. And then, only bad things can happen.

## Figure 19: Referral-Harvesting Tracking Worksheet

### Referral-Harvesting Prospecting List

| Client Target | Referrer Name | Referrer Phone | Contact Date | Referral (Y/N) | Testimonial (Y/N) | Reference (Y/N) | TY Letter Date Sent | Gift Date Sent | Remarks |
|---|---|---|---|---|---|---|---|---|---|
| | | | | | | | | | |
| | | | | | | | | | |
| | | | | | | | | | |
| | | | | | | | | | |

## Referral Tracking Sheet

| Prospect | Prospect Contact | Prospect Phone | Referred by | Approach Letter | Contact Date | App't Date | Prem/Rev $'s | Commission $'s | Remarks |
|---|---|---|---|---|---|---|---|---|---|
|  |  |  |  |  |  |  |  |  |  |
|  |  |  |  |  |  |  |  |  |  |
|  |  |  |  |  |  |  |  |  |  |
|  |  |  |  |  |  |  |  |  |  |

Because your future depends on it, you cannot afford to be bashful, intimidated, lethargic, or unprofessional about building and working your personalized referral-harvesting system. Such characteristics will only hold you back, so lose them quickly.

Remember that asking for referrals is truly an act of service, not an act of exploitation. You have worked so hard to earn this privilege, but you will continue to work too hard if you do not take the time to harvest such opportunities. Over time, it can and will become your only method for generating new business opportunities, if you follow these guidelines and manage your system deliberately and consistently.

You've come this far—now it is time to assume your rightful and hard-earned position at the top. Your referral-harvesting system will provide you with everything you need to get there and to stay there.

# Chapter Twelve

# Differentiating with Integrity—The Needs Assessment

*"In this life we get only those things for which we hunt, for which we strive, and for which we are willing to sacrifice. It is better to aim for something that you want—even though you miss it—than to get something that you didn't aim to get, and which you don't want! If we look long enough for what we want in life we are almost sure to find it, no matter what that objective may be."*

— George Matthew Adams

The good news is that the business is out there. Every minute of every day, somebody, somewhere, is faced with the grueling decision of how to best insure a company or family possessions. The bad news

> "Your program was the beacon I needed to continue."
>
> *Jason Chevoya*
> *Agent/Producer*

is that many will not be entirely sure of what they are buying, not completely trust who they are buying it from, and sense that "something" is missing from the process. After the transaction, many will be disappointed by reactive and random servicing of their business, feel ignored by the broker, and appropriately question the integrity of the insurance program.

However, there is a strategy that will eliminate these anxieties and negative emotions at the start of the relationship, by providing what's missing. Knowing that traditional insurance selling behaviors often lack the integrity, value, and trust necessary to build client confidence and create durable client relationships, a pre-sale needs assessment helps clients and potential clients to understand that many risks can be positively impacted by improved risk-management and human-resources strategies, and that you are as much about "prevention" as you are about "protection."

Value-added service planning begins by conducting a needs assessment with clients and prospects during the "discovery" phase of the sale. The assumption we are making is that your channel-marketing program has worked. You have attracted a prospect, and you have successfully differentiated yourself from your competitors. You are about to schedule your first visit to the prospective client's office, and it's here that you will begin to demonstrate just how unique you are.

The prospect is bracing himself, nervously expecting an avalanche of product books, carrier contracts, client lists and program announcements. He is expecting that you will request a copy of all current policies, current bid specifications, and five years of loss-runs. He is expecting you to meet with a small executive team, headed by the CFO, to review just enough additional information to allow you to formulate a competitive bid. Finally, he is expecting you to push for a close and to wrap the deal up in as little time as possible.

*You of course, will do nothing of the kind...as your existing clients know only too well.*

Instead, right off the bat, you are going stake out the high ground. How so? By patiently doing the footwork necessary for truly getting to know your prospect, while at the same time allowing the prospect to get to know you. You are courting your prospective client, easing your way into the relationship, rather than trying to sell or bargain your way in.

> *"People who say that life is not worthwhile are really saying that they themselves have no personal goals which are worthwhile."*
>
> —Maxwell Maltz

Enter the needs assessment—a simple and easy-to-execute preliminary step in the sales process that allows you to determine the prospect's corporate culture, composition, and risks. The results of the assessment will allow you to reach beyond the normal process of reviewing existing coverage and rates by obtaining a clear sense of each prospect's operations, convictions, and specific needs. This enlightenment will enable you to specifically tailor programs and strategies designed to proactively protect company assets, prevent injuries, and, ultimately, reduce the cost of insurance. That satisfies the primary interests of the business owner—value and budget.

Of course, not everyone has the same wants and needs. Your needs assessment should be designed and scaled to be user friendly enough for potential clients at all levels in the market, and some form of needs assessment is appropriate for every line of business—including personal lines, BOPs, and small, middle-market companies. Usually, the larger the business, the more exposure to risk, and the more complex the needs assessment becomes.

One company president we know of is an industry leader in the design and use of risk-management/needs-assessment tools. Convinced that his agency could "grow and prosper without additional sales people, that expanded risk-management resources could be the ultimate sales tool that would cement the agent/client relationship," he tracked his agency's performance and compared its results against traditional industry benchmarks. He reported the following:

- Exceptional client acquisition ratios; hit ratios are in excess of 80 percent, compared to the industry average of 30 percent.

- Explosive and efficient growth of new business commissions.

- The agency is perceived to be a trusted colleague, rather than an insurance supermarket. This status occurs as a result of the in-depth analysis of the client's operations, facilities, exposures, and risk-management standards.

- There is no competition from competing agents during the assessment process. The incumbent is typically not a factor.

- The assessment enhances the company's ability to focus on risk-management issues, rather than on insurance products and price.

- A scaled assessment process creates strong, long-term client relationships that evolve from employee, supervisor, and management interviews.

- Insurance companies respect the comprehensive nature of the assessment. It permits them to price a prospect or client more aggressively, expand coverage, and streamline claims and risk-control services as their fixed costs are reduced and underwriting results are enhanced.

- As a percentage, fewer clients will choose to bid out their insurance placements.

- Client satisfaction, as measured by the number of referrals received from clients and COI, is dramatically increased.

- The differentiated, consultative approach is marketable to trade associations and can be tailored to specific industry groups.

- The comprehensive nature of the assessment positions the producer to expand the business relationship into other income-generating areas, including employee benefits, financial services, and personal insurance.

- Client retention rates routinely exceed 90 percent.

## Benefits for Clients:

- The needs assessment provides a tool through which the client can assess the degree to which its risk-management policies, procedures, and controls adequately respond to the firm's exposures and assets at risk.

- Because the assessment is performed away from the insurance "bidding process," the client is fully focused on critical risk-management issues. These include loss-prevention orientation and training, safety committee functions, substance abuse, employment practices, accident investigation, emergency preparedness, and claims management.

- For personal lines, a properly scaled needs assessment permits a review that demonstrates a concern for family members and a sincere interest in "preventing bad things from happening."

- Action plans are developed to address issues arising out of the risk-management assessment process. The plans allow the client to proactively participate in a formal risk-avoidance program.

- Claims frequency and severity are reduced, along with insurance costs. The process gives insurance carriers confidence in reducing premiums, as their underwriting results are improved and fixed costs reduced.

- The information gives the client the ability to negotiate expanded insurance coverage terms and conditions.

- Prospects have the opportunity to observe the professionalism and measure the results of the producer before making decisions about insurance placement.

## Benefits for Carriers:

- Underwriting results are improved, as the needs assessment has identified and addressed critical risk factors.

- Underwriters are comfortable with aggressively, yet responsibly, pricing the risk.

- Fixed/operating costs are significantly reduced in three key areas: underwriting, risk control, and claims.

- Retention of business is increased as interactive, long-term relationships are developed with the client. The client learns to place more emphasis on the carrier's value-added resources and expertise than on the price of the product.

- The assessment pinpoints issues that need attention and provides an action plan for completion.

- The carrier works hand-in-hand with the producer as a member of the client's risk-management team. The carrier has great visibility in the eyes of the client.

- The carrier becomes more comfortable considering broadening coverage and expanding limits if the assessment confirms the client's risk-management practices meet or exceed standards.

> *"Always bear in mind that your own resolution to succeed is more important than any other one thing."*
>
> — Abraham Lincoln

Your needs assessment can and will provide you with similar benefits, as long as you develop it, use it and trust it. Notice that every benefit derived from the assessment enhances one or more of the following objectives:

1) Improved production;

2) Improved account performance and profitability;

3) Improved client retention; and

4) Improved efficiency.

These are good objectives to target, because they are the cornerstones on which your professional success will rest.

## Introducing the Needs Assessment

Generally, you create a needs assessment for qualified clients and prospects. In each case, it is presented as the first and most important step in your insurance-program development process. At the very onset of your discussions, your clients are reminded and your prospects learn that you are interested in custom developing an insurance and risk-management program, and that you are not intending to simply shop and hock an existing policy for a better price.

Based on the time it might take to do a thorough needs assessment and present your findings and recommendations, this strategy also encourages you and the client or prospect to initiate discussions well in advance of the normal harvesting season—allowing you to demonstrate your ability long before your competitors have even considered engaging.

Be prepared. Prior to your arrival, you should brief your client or prospective client on what the objectives of the meeting are. While setting up this appointment, inform them that the appointment will be used to gather some preliminary information that's needed for you to conduct a more thorough analysis of the organization, its culture, its people, and its insurance program. Be matter of fact about it, and make it clear your chief responsibility is to be a good listener. As one exceptional producer puts it, "I'll only be bringing a sharp pencil, a new legal pad, lots of questions, and a clean set of ears." Emphasize that this is not a sales call or a product pitch. At this point, you may describe the process that you are about to walk them through and offer to send along an advanced copy of your outline.

Of course, it will help if you know what the process is and if you have an outline to send, so . . . on to the next step.

### Creating the Needs Assessment:

The needs assessment is nothing more than a series of questions that you and/or other members of your team (if available) will ask about the prospective or existing client that you are interviewing. While the needs assessment process applies to both commercial and personal lines, it is obviously more comprehensive for larger and more complex businesses. For commercial lines, your questions should be designed to provide you with a comprehensive analysis of their corporate philosophy, structure, and exposures. The answers to these questions will allow you to look beyond the issues of policy and rates by gaining a true understanding of their organizational culture and specific needs. Although underwriters favor submissions that include this type of cultural assessment, underwriters do not typically ask them. The questions are intended to provide you with insight that will enable you to specifically tailor programs, services, and strategies designed to protect assets, reduce insurance costs, and bring tangible value to the relationship.

The types of questions and the number of them that you ask depend entirely on you and the nature of the client or prospect you are interviewing. For instance, size does matter—in the insurance business, anyway. As mentioned earlier, larger clients tend to have more complex insurance programs and require a comprehensive assessment to completely identify needs and expectations. Be careful; more is sometimes less, and a few carefully targeted questions may be enough to give you most of what you need to build your plan. You will have ample opportunity to fill in any gaps as your relationship evolves.

Figure 20 indicates some areas to consider investigating when building a needs assessment. The lists of categories are by no means all-inclusive, nor are they all necessary to cover with every assessment. Draw from your own expertise and your own Value-Added Service Menu (see Sample Commercial- and Personal-Lines Menus in Figures 22 and 23), as described and exhibited in our chapter on Value-Added Service Plan, to formulate your questions, and use them as a springboard to educate your prospects and clients, define your involvement, and build the insurance and risk-management program.

## Figure 20: Areas to Consider when Building a Needs Assessment

**Potential Categories for Property and Casualty Needs-Assessment Questions:**

- Relationship with Agent
- Relationship with Carrier
- Buying Practices/Supply Chain
- Knowledge of Existing Program
- Industry and Community Involvement
- Alternative Markets
- Business Practices
- Company Structure
- Cultural Assessment
- The Insurance Marketplace
- Insurance Buying Practices
- Employment Practices
- Claims Management
- Loss-Control Programs
- Orientation and Training
- Environmental Issues
- General-Liability Issues
- Endorsements
- Social-Media Practices
- Business Recovery/Disaster Planning
- Data Storage/Security
- Employee Benefits
- Motor-Vehicle Safety
- Retirement Plans/Fiduciary
- Employee Wellness
- Substance Abuse
- OSHA Compliance
- Policy Review
- Reserve Analysis
- Fleet Safety
- Safety Committee
- Perpetuation Plans
- Expansion/Contraction Plans
- Employee-Development Programs
- Customer Profile
- Service Standards
- Safety-Involvement Programs

## Potential Categories for Personal-Lines, Needs-Assessment Questions:

- Frequency of Agent Contact
- Home Safety Awareness
- Home Protective Devices
- Insurance Buying Practices
- Knowledge of Coverage
- Knowledge of Limits
- Loss-free Discounts
- Computer Coverage
- Credit Scoring
- Home Business
- Watercraft
- Volunteer Work
- Personal Liability Issues
- Payment Plans
- Emergency Planning
- Additions and Alterations
- Wills
- Life Insurance
- Service Expectations
- Environmental Issues
- UM and UIM Coverage
- Rental Property
- Mold
- Earthquake, Flood

- Pets
- Replacement Cost Estimates
- Mortgage Protection
- Retirement Planning
- Greenery Coverage and Debris Removal
- Personal Property Endorsements
- Companion Credits
- Complete Auto Policy Review
- Personal Auto Discounts
- Driver Training Credits
- Seasonal Use Of Vehicles
- Audio and Visual Equipment
- Lease Coverage
- Rental Coverage
- Safe-Driver Programs
- Seminars and Safety Programs
- Vacation Plans/Overseas Travel
- Family Higher Education Plans

## Potential Categories for Employee-Benefits, Needs-Assessment Questions:

- Relationship with Agent
- Relationship with Carrier
- Knowledge of Existing Program
- Industry and Community Involvement
- Business Practices
- Company Structure
- Cultural Assessment
- The Insurance Marketplace
- Insurance Buying Practices
- Employment Practices
- Managed Care Options
- Voluntary Programs
- Flex Spending Accounts
- Dental Plans
- COBRA
- Disability Program
- Employee Advisory Committee

- Section 125 Plans
- Childcare Programs
- Supplemental Plans
- Payroll Deduction
- Vision Plans
- Tuition Reimbursement
- Long-term Care
- Prescription Plans
- Retirement Plans
- Company/Employee Contributions
- Employee Wellness Programs
- Managed Care Options
- Substance Abuse Programs
- Life Insurance Plans
- Bonus/Safety Involvement Programs
- Employee Compensation
- Claims Management

Keep in mind that traditional underwriting questions are focused on coverages. You are not asking coverage questions here. The answers to your needs-assessment questions will provide the information needed to create a customized, value-added service plan, which:

1) Establishes tangible performance benchmarks for you and your prospects and clients;

2) Proactively schedules and defines your service activities;

3) Differentiates you from your competitors;

4) Enlightens the carrier with regard to your prospects' and clients' culture, and improves their marketability;

5) Gives the prospect a demonstration of your expertise, integrity, and ability to proactively build a partnership;

6) Reduces the frequency and severity of claims; and

7) Saves lives, prevents injury and illness, and helps avoid financial hardship for your clients and prospects.

To develop your own needs assessments for personal-lines, benefits, life, surety, small commercial, middle-market, and large commercial accounts, build an inventory of questions for each pertinent category identified in Figure 20, using the value-added services shown in Figures 22 and 23 in our chapter on the Value-Added Service Plan to "prime the pump." Then select the appropriate number of questions to include from each category. Please remember that these are only sample topics and questions. Make your list of questions as extensive or as abbreviated as you deem necessary, and add or delete categories as needed. Scale is very important. For a routine personal-lines account, you may have less than 10 questions, while a large commercial account could have 50 or more. If you are uncomfortable about a specific topic or a series of questions, bring along an expert. Many carriers will be more than happy to send a representative, and some will let you borrow a loss-control specialist for your appointment.

## Conducting the Needs Assessment

As mentioned previously, the larger and more complex the prospect or client, the larger and more complex the needs assessment, and the more time it will take to complete it. Be thorough, and take your time to get current programs and future needs right. Interview employees at varying levels within the organization, so that you gather a healthy sampling of perspectives and experiences. You may wish to sit in on a safety-committee meeting or to visit each location in a multi-site organization. Working with a pre-selected carrier, study prospect/client nuances, and conduct a comprehensive loss-control analysis. You will certainly want to educate throughout the process by explaining various coverage options and the pros and cons of each, updating them on the insurance industry and marketplace, introducing risk-management and loss-control suggestions, and so on. Upon completion of the needs assessment, you will want to summarize and present your findings (good and bad) and provide an itemized list of suggested corrections and enhancements to their current insurance and risk-management program. Your ability to customize your prospects'/clients' programs will increase the more thorough and formal you are with your assessment, and the deeper you drill down into the organization.

Time is the issue—the time it takes to do this right and to do this well. This is time that is not available during the normal harvesting season (90 days or less before expiration). Sure, you can try to rush through it and pull something together in time to obtain a quote, but the value of the process will get lost in the shuffle; the information that you gather will be cursory; the prospect will probably find you more annoying than helpful, and you will not differentiate yourself as a value-added provider because you will have had no time to demonstrate your capability. It will look like what it is—a selling tactic. That's the last thing you want.

Instead, do it right. This assessment is best done mid term or earlier, when the prospect is not trying to balance competing producer inquiries while worrying about an impending expiration date. Present it for what it is—an in-depth, cost-free analysis of their entire insurance program, complete with expert ideas and unbiased suggestions. The prospect should quickly grasp the significance of what is being offered, see the value in participating, and willingly engage in the process long before he or she normally starts thinking about the renewal. When this happens, you're in. Better yet, you're in for the right reasons. When it doesn't happen, you are competing against traditional insurance buying practices, and it may take a year or more to fully evolve the buyer. If you feel that the prospect is worthy, it is worth the wait.

A word on smaller prospects and clients: Admittedly, these clients and prospects, whether commercial or personal lines, do not necessitate an extensive assessment and therefore will not require a great deal of time to implement the survey strategy and summarize the results. Timing, then, is much more discretionary; however, the process remains the same. Ask questions that will help identify valued services, and then include these services in your proposal. Remember, this is your best chance to differentiate yourself from peddlers looking for clients and prospects that are yours for the asking.

Once you decide to move ahead with the needs assessment, follow these implementation steps:

## Step 1—Assessment Orientation:

Rather than rush right into the assessment questions (which can feel like a bright-light interrogation to the recipient), it is advisable to conduct a preliminary meeting with the decision maker(s) and key staff members so that you may define the objectives of the investigation and describe what and who will be involved in the process. Large, comprehensive assessments may involve a number of interviews and visits by an assessment team and therefore require an established timeline and a disciplined approach. Use an action plan to map out the roles and the goals of each participant in the process to help ensure proper coordination. Sharing this information with the team helps to avoid uncomfortable moments during the process.

What if you don't have a team? Great question—not everyone has those kinds of resources. Carriers that see the value in partnering with you will commit the time to help you. This, of course, requires you to pre-select a carrier; however, the benefits of doing so out-weigh the risks of choosing an unsupportive carrier.

Good underwriters will help you to a degree; great underwriters will support you however they can, and, as described in our chapter on Carrier Connection, a true partnering underwriter will prioritize your submission, defend a referral when needed, and round out your relationship with the prospective client. It's all good, and everybody wins.

## Step 2—Implementing the Needs Assessment:

Larger prospects and clients require a carefully coordinated implementation plan that usually involves a series of meetings and a number of people on both ends, while smaller property, casualty, and personal-lines accounts can be assessed without a lot of formality. Still, you should conduct the assessment as a separate and distinct step in the development of a customized insurance and risk-management program.

Rather than lumping it in with all of the other activities associated with quoting (current policy review, loss review, etc.), it is highly recommended that you conduct the assessment during a separate meeting, and that you make it the only agenda item for that meeting. This helps to ensure that prospects and clients take the assessment seriously and give it the weight that it deserves. Additionally, this is the point in the sales process that you gain a distinct advantage over competing agents, so you should highlight it and not camouflage it with other routine account development activities.

To be effective, you will need the full attention and cooperation of those participating in the assessment. It is best to conduct it in a relaxed environment, where you can protect participants from ringing phones, text alerts, to-do lists, knocks on the doors, and other interruptions. If available, a conference room seems to work best. If a "neutral" space is not available, consider going to breakfast or lunch, or meeting in your office. Since most of the information that you need is in prospects' or clients' heads, there is no need for them to lug a briefcase full of policies, files and documentation. This is a paperless visit; you will review all of the above at a later date.

Clients and prospects experiencing this process for the first time may feel they're entering uncharted territories here. Being unfamiliar with this level of diligence, it is quite natural for any participant in the assessment to be a little defensive and guarded. Ease them into the process by reviewing your objective and the intent of the assessment—you are there to help, not to pass judgment.

The assessment is a tool that helps you design an insurance and risk-management program based on the needs of your clients and prospects. You are not interrogating, you are learning. Remind the prospect that your objective is only to provide enough information to make an educated decision about their program. It is not to sell a cookie-cutter policy. Essentially, what you're doing is talking about their business. Who has ever met an entrepreneur or business owner who doesn't like talking about his or her business?

To further ease any anxieties, bring a standard "Confidentiality" agreement with you, and sign it for them. Much of the information that you are asking for might be "sensitive," and it is critically important that they feel you can be trusted. As the relationship blossoms, they will of course come to trust and respect your integrity. However, at this stage in the relationship, it is best to provide a hedge against any doubt. Besides, it's an effective way to convey that you have the business owner's best interests at heart.

## Summarizing the Needs-Assessment Findings:

Upon completion of the assessment, it's show time. Call together all members of the assessment team, along with the decision makers for the prospective company (or family). At this meeting, you will present your findings in the following:

1) An overview of the assessment process—who met with whom, when and where;

2) A copy of the assessment tool or questionnaire;

3) A summary of what you discovered—what they were doing well; where you feel they have some good things in place but could be improved, and where there is an opportunity to bring something new, different, and/or especially meaningful to the table;

4) Itemized recommendations and adjustments to their current insurance and risk-management program, along with your reasons for making the recommendations (these include coverage and carrier recommendations);

5) Recommended program objectives for the next policy year and beyond; and

6) Finally, and perhaps most importantly, your schedule of actions, activities, and events that will support the accomplishment of the objectives. ***This becomes your Value-Added Service Plan***.

## Preparing to Build the Value-Added Service Plan:

Why do most client-service programs fail? As noted before, it's because they don't effectively define and measure up to clients' service expectations. Most often, this results from never asking and/or assuming client expectations. Big mistake. The message the client absorbs is that we are arrogant. "Imagine," the client thinks, dark clouds forming in his mind, "This clown thinks that he is going to represent me, but he doesn't even know me."

Fortunately, the needs assessment allows us to create a much different impression. We diplomatically uncover erroneous reserves, loss-control issues, and gaps in coverage without coming off as pushy or critical. The needs assessment allows us to experience and define the culture of the organization and its people. It establishes very specific product and program benchmarks. It educates us, and, most importantly, it helps us to articulate and validate the client's service and support expectations. Knowing these in advance, rather than discovering them following a service disappointment, enables us to build a plan of action that proactively fulfills and, in most cases, exceeds them.

Let's assume that you have completed a needs assessment on "Company 1" In addition to product, price, carrier and coverage recommendations, your assessment uncovered the following:

- There is no standing safety committee.

- Back strain "lifting" injuries account for an unusually high percentage of claims.

- Driver-safety training is sporadic and not conducted by the incumbent carrier.

- The incumbent agent only visits the home office and only does so at time of renewal.

- Internal customer-service representatives who have never visited the client handle account administration.

- There is no posted procedure for emergency medical care.

- There are no formal security programs for visitors.

- Many claims are stale dated and appear over reserved.

- There has been no formal training in the following:

  1) Slip, trip, and fall;

  2) Sexual-harassment prevention;

  3) Diversity;

  4) Crisis management;

5) Bloodborne pathogens;

6) Claims management/reporting;

7) Proper social media behavior; and

8) Disabilty/Return-to-work management.

## Sample Recommendations:

Based on the above findings, you would make the following recommendations within these Priority and Impact rating categories[2]:

## Priority Rating—High

### Impact Rating-High

1) Establish a formal, employee-led, safety committee that meets once per month. This will dramatically improve the organization's "safety consciousness."

2) Create a safety participation program to improve the workplace safety culture, and establish formalized risk-management training programs and initiatives. Monitor and analyze trends, workplace injuries, and incident-reporting standards.

3) Conduct documented, quarterly risk-management and loss-control training for all employees. Invite appropriate managers to all agency-sponsored training events. Design customized program templates for implementation and documentation of all workplace safety initiatives.

4) Conduct regularly scheduled reserve analysis with claims adjusters for all reserved claims and adjust as needed.

---

2 "Priority" and "Impact" ratings are assigned based on the significance of the finding and the potential effect that the corrective action will have on the cost of insurance incurred by the client. A typical list of recommendations for a client of this size would usually be more extensive and include lesser priorities as well. Also, where possible, the recommendation description would be followed by a statement describing the benefit of the recommendation.

5) Provide a template for effective human-resources practices dealing with preventing sexual harassment, hiring/firing, disability management/return to work, and social media. Coach existing staff on how to customize the template to their environment

## Priority Rating—High

### Impact Rating-Significant

1) Establish safe lifting standards. Train and reinforce safe lifting techniques and mandate use of loading docks for all deliveries. Consider replacing manual off-loading system with a mechanical "roller" system or other lifting aid. Deploy loss-control engineers to design and monitor a comprehensive program.

## Priority Rating—High

### Impact Rating-Moderate

1) Conduct driver-safety classes for all drivers twice a year, and invite managers to attend an incident investigation webinar or seminar at the end of the year. Equip all vehicles with incident reporting kits, including disposable cameras, reporting guidelines, etc.

2) Schedule quarterly reviews to monitor and assist with the implementation of loss-control initiatives, review claims, and conduct site visits. Coordinate these sessions with the service team and loss control. Attend a minimum of two safety-committee meetings annually.

3) Establish, post, and train standardized emergency medical-care procedures.

4) Develop a standard approach for recording and monitoring all visitors to each location. Create visitor parking areas, sign in/out logs, identification badges, reception area, hardhats, etc.

Now it's time to begin sowing the seeds of all your hard work. Having thoroughly reviewed and presented your findings and recommendations to the client or prospect, including everything that the team found to be positive and adequate, you now steer the discussion away from the current program by outlining your vision of the possible future program. At this point, the client or prospect is convinced that you know the organization and its people better than any producer who has ever come before you. He or she is impressed by your thoroughness and honored by the time and attention that you have invested in the company. You are clearly different and believably better. Clients and prospects have first-hand experience with your professionalism, integrity, and value. They are probably ready to turn over a broker of record (BOR) or agent of record (AOR) based on the work that you have already done. Wonderful! And it's about to get even better.

# Chapter Thirteen

# The Value-Added Service Plan –
# Bringing it all Together

*"To give real service you must add something which cannot be bought or measured with money, and that is sincerity and integrity."*

—Douglas N. Adams

There's no shortage of companies that have earned household names based on their ability to provide service and value to their customers. Consider Federal Express, the parcel delivery giant that was founded on the premise it

> "[This] is an ongoing process that improves the way we do business."
>
> *Robert M. Dietzel*
> *Managing Partner*

would "absolutely, positively" get your package to its destination by 10 a.m. the next morning. That service model made history—and billions for the company.

Then there's Ford Motor Co., the firm that founded the customer-service model back when the term rarely passed the lips of captains of industry—if they knew it at all. Not Henry Ford. Here's what he had to say about the value of service: "The trouble with a great number of us in the business world is that we are thinking hardest of all about the dollar we want to make. Now that is the wrong idea from the start." The person with "this idea of service in business is the biggest guarantee of success."

Of course, titans like Ford "walked the talk." They made service and value a high priority and prospered. That's one reason why the greatest compliment you can receive from your clients is that you "walk the talk." This means you aren't coming to the table empty-handed—that you have demonstrated a unique level of personalized service they value and appreciate. It also means that you have reached beyond the normal boundaries of a client/provider relationship to form a personal bond that is mutually productive and equally beneficial.

It is amazing how little effort is needed to create and manage these high-level, service-focused relationships. If you knew how easy it is, you would kick yourself for waiting this long to make the break from the traditional service philosophy. Of course, it's not that you're complacent; most feel a sincere obligation to take care of their clients and to meet their expectations. But service (particularly personalized and proactive service) is always a struggle when you're immersed in a jumble of shifting priorities, crises, and needs.

As soon as you shift to the sales, service, marketing, and priority-management systems that are the cornerstones of this book, however, you will become more consistent, efficient, productive, and available. You will learn to use the same activities to attract and develop a client as you do to service a client. This is because you will integrate your service activities and value-added service plans with your sales and marketing plans to create one seamless, proactive, client-management strategy.

> *"One way to keep momentum going is to have constantly greater goals."*
>
> — Michael Korda

For example: If you're hosting a client roundtable or a workshop, you will invite prospective clients as well as existing clients. You will send your electronic newsletter to both groups, and you will regularly give advice and assistance to those who need it and will use it—regardless of whether you close any business. Inevitably, you will attract clients who are comfortable with your methodology and recognize its value. You will retain them as clients because you will consistently deliver the value that attracted them in the first place. It is a superbly efficient and incredibly effective way to do business.

The right clients will appreciate early demonstrations of value, integrity, and trust, followed by a comprehensive plan to deliver even more. What they don't want is a bid, a pitch, or a phone number. Over time, you will come to understand why the value-added approach is so powerful compared to the "pitch and pray" system. Let's examine why our system, and the value-added service plan that results works so well.

## The Psychology of Service

What's more appealing, price or value? In other words, when you buy something, what do you consider most important, the price that you pay or the value that you receive from the product? How much weight do you give to the reputation and credibility of the seller? (Consider the rankings of online sellers: The higher the seller rating, the more confidence one has when making a purchase.) Do you evaluate competing products and services on cost alone, or is quality a determining factor as well? What about the social implications of your selection—will you compare your purchase to what other people have bought, and is the status of your selection a priority to you?

The answers depend on what you are buying. In most cases, the size of the purchase and the complexity of the product or service determine the degree of consideration given to these and other "look and feel" conditions. Smaller, "simple" sales, such as pencils, speaker wire, fast food, cab rides, and chewing gum, tend more toward the commodity, price-driven factors, because the decisions are low risk, and the differences among competing products are reasonably obscure. Look and feel characteristics do exist; however, they are not given much weight.

On the flip side, larger, complex sales, such as cars, computers, insurance, homes, vacations, weddings, and college educations, are nearly always determined by look and feel attributes first, price second.

Marketing, advertising, and public relations firms have been aware of consumers' buying patterns since cavemen first grunted "how much?" to the traveling sharp stick salesman. It's no secret that product branding and corporate identity are the most vital components of any strategic marketing program—including yours.

To gain traction in any market that is already occupied, providers of products and services must differentiate their offerings based upon look and feel factors and create an exclusive "space," or niche, for their offering. That is how they attract and retain a client base—by creating brand loyalty.

When a company fails to differentiate its brand with look and feel, it is almost always slapped with a "copycat" label and forced into the "low-cost provider" space in the market, where price, not perception of value, motivates the buyer. Unable to recognize any significant difference between products, these buyers focus only on price and tend to float from one provider to another in search of financial value. As a market segment, these consumers tend to view products and services as commodities to be bid and bargained for. They are fickle, volatile, transient, and disloyal. As a client base, such consumers are a disaster.

That's why nearly every section of this book hammers home the point that this is not a good space to be in if you are a provider of insurance programs. Still, we worry. There are enough of your comrades trapped in conventional insurance agencies to fill a dozen football stadiums. There's also an abundance of companies that still depend upon price rather than value to attract and retain their clients. As Mr. T said, "I pity the fools." Because the market continues to shift, as it always will, insurance buying practices shift dramatically in favor of proactive, value-driven, risk-management-rich insurance programs.

Insurance buyers will soon realize that the most effective method for controlling premium levels is to proactively address and reduce the frequency and severity of claims. Thus, the end game is clear. Those of you who are willing and able to participate and manage these preventive programs and specialty services will attract and retain clients. Those who can't won't. Fools indeed.

Although there will always be a justifiable, price-driven, "insurance is a commodity" buying attitude in some markets, this space is not large enough to accommodate all of the players who are looking to exploit it.

> *"The only true measure of success is the ratio between what we might have done and what we might have been on the one hand, and the thing we have made and the thing we have made of ourselves on the other."*
>
> — H.G. Wells

Okay, you might be wondering what any of this has to do with service. Remember the "special sauce" that made the "Big Mac" a best seller? Our model has one, too. Its special sauce is the infusion of principled, proactive, year-long service strategies into each element of the program. These collective service strategies define your "value proposition."

Our objective all along has been to help you establish and consistently maintain a unique and highly personalized value proposition in your selected market. Your value proposition creates your space and allows you to effectively differentiate. Your sales, marketing, and referral-harvesting plans are all designed to attract qualified clients to your value proposition. Your value-added service plan will be crafted to retain them.

## What is Value-Added Service?

Simply stated, providing value-added service means making a sincere, consistent, and proactive commitment to understand your clients' needs and to meet them as they change. Think about the term "value-added." It tells customers they can expect the rock-solid basics—good products and services, fair prices, and good customer service—but that's not all it's telling them. Value-added service also means adding additional ingredients to that special sauce we were talking about. It means telling clients you'll do what it takes to keep them happy—that you'll go out of your way to add extra services and attention to the relationship. It tells them that you are serious about keeping the rapport growing and mutually beneficial. That's where integrity comes in.

---

### Value-Added Service is Not

- Good administration
- Reactive responses to requests
- Routine claims advocacy
- Focusing primarily on price
- Answering the phone
- Trying to be all things to all clients

---

To be sincere, your motive must be to build a relationship based upon mutual trust and integrity—a relationship that is not contingent on any particular sales event, now or ever. In a value-added sales environment, relationships occur when individuals and organizations form a cohesive bond and agree to work together toward a common objective.

## Value-Added Service Is

**Initiatives that:**

○ Serve our primary purpose

○ Have a measurable impact

○ Build a sense of value, integrity, and trust

○ Anticipate and answer clients'/prospects' needs and expectations

Though products, services, money, and information are exchanged, the exchange is a result of and not a cause for the relationship, or the objective. The healthier the relationship, the more these exchanges take place, and vice versa. If you have followed the steps in this program to this point, then you have already created your value-added sales, service, and channel-marketing system.

Think of your business as a pyramid. With your sales and channel-marketing plan serving as the foundation, use the same blueprint to build your value-added service plans. In fact, the proactive service activities that appear on your channel-marketing plan are the same activities used to build your value-added service plans.

Essentially, your sales plan is also your service plan. Your activity is fully integrated, consistent, and productive. You remain uniformly visible and viable, both before and after every transaction that takes place during the client/prospect relationship.

No doubt by now you've noticed that value-added service is much more comprehensive than simply taking care of a client claim or question, chasing a certificate, or checking in at time of renewal. These activities and others like them are considered normal administrative servicing practices—the "basics," or routine things that must be done to keep the policy in place.

Don't misunderstand us, good administration is critically important, and you won't get anywhere without it. However, good administration is only doing what you should do and what the client anticipates will be done. Some would say it's simply the "price of admission."

When contrasted against a fully integrated, value-added service strategy, we quickly see the difference between reacting to an administrative responsibility and proactively satisfying client needs.

Figure 21 compares the characteristics and perceptions of a traditional sales and service model with our value-added approach:

## Figure 21: Traditional Versus Value-Added Sales Approach

| Initial Client Contact | | |
|---|---|---|
| | *Traditional Approach* | *Value-Added Approach* |
| **Motive** | ✘ *to make a sale* | ✔ **to build a relationship** |
| **Focus** | ✘ *on the product and the price* | ✔ **on the client and the client's need** |
| **Behavior** | ✘ *high pressure* | ✔ **conversational** |
| | ✘ *rushed/frenzied* | ✔ **patient** |
| | ✘ *opinionated* | ✔ **consultative** |
| | ✘ *overbearing* | ✔ **listens, questions** |
| | ✘ *attempts to close* | ✔ **agreements reached** |
| **Post-Sale Activity** | | |
| **Service Behaviors** | ✘ *Reactive — issues are responded to as they develop, no news from clients is considered good news.* | ✔ **Proactive — client interactions continue. Needs are constantly assessed, anticipated, solicited and creatively satisfied.** |
| **Producer Focus** | ✘ *The relationship is dormant; producer contact is limited to renewal activity, special requests, or problems.* | ✔ **The relationship blossoms; contact is frequent. Client communication and consultation continue.** |
| **Producer Behavior** | ✘ *Other sales activity significantly limits producers' available time. They become elusive and pass off most service requests. New business is generated the old fashioned way.* | ✔ **Producers are accessible and highly visible. They continue to service the relationship and utilize existing clients to attract new business opportunities.** |
| | ✘ *A client's value is determined by the level of premium paid and by what they can do for the producer in the short-term.* | ✔ **Clients are catered to and invested in. Relationships are established with the intention of creating a long-term partnership.** |

| Results | | |
|---|---|---|
| **Client Perceptions** | ✗ *Buyer remorse is high. Clients feel cajoled and doubt the decision to enter the relationship.* | ✔ **As the relationship grows, client loyalty deepens. The decision to enter into the partnership is trusted.** |
| | ✗ *There is no perception of value. The decision to buy was based on price. The decision to renew will also be based on price.* | ✔ **Value far beyond the original need for coverage is clearly apparent and trusted, regardless of price.** |
| | ✗ *Clients feel abandoned, ignored, patronized, and sold to.* | ✔ **Clients feel spoiled, cared about, listened to, and informed.** |
| | ✗ *Producers are associated with invoices, claims and additional expenses.* | ✔ **Clients view the producer as an informed and interested business partner and consultant.** |
| | ✗ *There are few, if any, opportunities or attempts made to cross sell, harvest referrals, or differentiate on anything other than price.* | ✔ **Exchanges continue to occur as client needs evolve. Referral business is a normal outgrowth of the relationship.** |
| | ✗ *Accounts are highly susceptible to internal and external competition. Retention is average, bids are common, and renewal times are stressful.* | ✔ **Retention is extremely high. Value, not price is the buying motive. Competitors are rarely received, bids are infrequent, and expiration dates are just another day.** |

It should be obvious by now that an agency that decides to use a value-added approach will have a much easier time building and maintaining mutually beneficial relationships with clients and prospects. Clearly, one should seek to emulate a value-added approach as soon as he or she leaps out of bed in the morning. Unfortunately, common sense is not always common practice.

Though recognition of the benefits associated with providing value-added service is generally acknowledged, consistent practice of these principles remains rare due to an industry addiction for instant commission dollars on any investment of time and attention. Building value-added relationships takes longer, and the payoff isn't a near-term one; it's a long-term one. However, when the payoff does materialize, it is usually here to stay.

As tempting as it may be, you can't leap back and forth between the two philosophies, painstakingly attending to an abundance of shifting priorities while attempting to identify true opportunities. The predictable result is a haphazard, reactionary approach to service that quells the disturbances but camouflages the truly rewarding opportunities. Before long, you lose focus and lapse back into old, failed habits.

We know that won't work. And we're not casting aspersions here, either. Many organizations, sales individuals, as well as sales and service teams, earnestly attempt to differentiate through service, and almost all are truly concerned about the welfare of clientele. This is not a case of "good versus evil." Most are unsuccessful in their efforts, because their approach to service replicates their selling habits—load up with clients, build a cookie-cutter, one-size-fits-all service program, and deal with the problems as they develop. While the intentions may be honorable, they're not very workable. Certainly, they're not proactive.

Organizations that are successful use a different strategy, one that's based on relationship building. First, they recognize that people, not product and price, are the most important variables in any sales or service model. Consequently, they make it a priority to identify with these people and understand their likes, dislikes, culture, habits, and expectations. When it comes to providing service, experience has taught them that different people have different expectations regarding their relationship with the insurance industry. Successful organizations recognize that the difference between ordinary service and extraordinary service is simply a matter of clarifying each client's expectations at the beginning of the relationship and proactively integrating them into the development of their insurance programs. The client, not the service department, establishes the service standards, best practices, and performance benchmarks.

Second, successful service providers realize that client expectations are fluid and dynamic, changing as the relationship matures. As a result, they need to be consistently redefined and discussed. Organizations that thrive take nothing for granted, routinely verifying their service assumptions, rather than presuming that in the absence of a crisis or an obvious conflict, all is well. Doing their homework and studying their clients' peccadilloes and preferences, they don't confuse "quiet clients" with satisfied clients. Instead, they regularly investigate what is working, what isn't, and what can be done better. They start proactive, and they stay proactive.

Finally, healthy and successful organizations acknowledge imperfection. Nobody can do it all, and nobody can do it perfectly, right? So they accept the reality of their own limitations, and they establish these service parameters early in the relationship with the client. Having identified the client's expectations, smart sales and service people honestly and diplomatically outline their own capabilities and expectations. That alleviates surprises and takes the unknown out of the equation early in the relationship, minimizing the potential that either party will be disappointed in the future.

Okay, time out for a disclaimer. A magic pill doesn't exist. There is no ironclad service plan that successfully anticipates every service issue. Nor can such a plan be created. Let's face it, ours is not a perfect world, nor will people or circumstances ever be entirely predictable. Even with the best planning, things can and will go wrong. Unforeseen service gaps will occur; problems will arise, and crises will happen—in spite of your proactive service posture.

Unfair as it may seem, this is a part of doing business, and it is a part of life. So, as you develop your value-added service plan, be realistic with your expectations about what the plan will and will not do. Your plan *will*:

- Enable you to integrate your proactive sales and marketing plans with an equally proactive, custom-developed, needs-based, value-added service strategy.

- Be your blueprint for scheduling consistent value delivery to your key clients over time, ensuring that you are visible and viable.

- Make it possible for you to establish well-defined, client-service expectations and manage them as they change.

- Provide your clients with an unprecedented level of insurance program management and support focused on protection (insurance) and prevention (risk management).

Your value-added service plan *will not*:

- Be that "magic bullet." Certificates will still get lost, and some claims will be denied or delayed. Clients will still miss payments, and carriers will miss deadlines. You will still not be able to control the uncontrollable and predict every contingency. However, you will be able to better influence those around you to become more responsive and work more proactively. Things will never be perfect, but they will be consistently better.

- Meet every client expectation. Despite your efficiency and effectiveness, you will never be able to be all things to everybody—nor should you desire to be. You will always have limitations on your available time and resources. Limitations, however, do not have to lead to client disappointments if they are communicated up front.

- Remain etched in stone. Circumstances change for you and for the client on a regular basis— your value-added service plan will undergo regular revisions.

- Be appropriate for every client. The activities and client-support strategies included in your plan are time consuming and require careful coordination. They cannot be effectively or efficiently applied to a large group of small clients who have little appreciation for the extra steps you will take and probably have little use for the added value that you will bring to the relationship.

These plans are meant for mid-size, larger, complex, long-term clients. They are not meant for low premium, price-focused, fickle clients. That's not to say the value-added services for smaller, commercial-, and personal-lines clients should be ignored. On the contrary, it's just that services might be different, more rationed, and administratively less involved (newsletter, six-month "check up," clipping file, e-mail, etc.)

Your value-added service plan will create a uniquely personalized foundation for mutually beneficial exchanges of value, integrity, and trust with those clients who are worthy of your time and attention. It will not prevent or predict human error or systems malfunctions, nor will it convert low-end clients into favorable ones. But it will give you an advantage over the rest of the field. When things do go wrong, practitioners of a value-added service philosophy—those who have created a more sophisticated level of client interaction and empathy, are able to easily insulate the client relationship from the service glitch. They enjoy higher levels of client loyalty and lots of "wiggle-room" within the relationship, because they have consistently demonstrated their commitment to their clients. They are forgiven for the small slips, because they take care of the big stuff.

## A Final Plug for Consistency

Like channel marketing, providing value-added service requires consistency, patience, determination, and an honest desire to help. Because we have removed the sales event as the demilitarized zone between what is selling behavior and what is service behavior, the activities and tactics that we use to attract new clients and develop a relationship with them are the very same ones that we will do to provide value-added service and continue to develop the relationship. On both sides of the initial transaction, our motive is the same, and the desired result is identical—to provide our clients with consistent and proactive demonstrations of value, integrity, and trust. The activities that we engage in to support this common objective should also be similar.

Can the system or plan serve a dual purpose? Absolutely. By design, the target channel-marketing plan that you have created should also be equally effective as a value-added service plan. In fact, that is exactly what happens. Not only is the message and activity consistent from the first introduction to the last referral, you also save countless hours and huge redundancies by eliminating the need to manage separate sales and service functions.

## When to Start

The value-added service plan is essentially your client-management strategy for your key clients. Every qualified client receives a customized plan that is constructed to proactively fulfill each expectation that was identified during your needs assessment. Therefore, you design and present your plan to the client before any transaction takes place and usually before the client has selected you as a BOR. Remember that you are selling *you* and your ability to bring value, integrity, and trust to their insurance program—they need to see evidence of your ability prior to buying.

The evidence is your value-added service plan. Your customized, proactive, client-management plan is designed specifically to reduce the frequency and severity of claims, prevent accidents and injuries, and reduce the cost of insurance over time—the right way. For commercial clients, your plan will, in most cases, improve morale, reduce employee turnover, improve quality and service, and create new efficiencies that will travel directly to the organization's bottom line.

These "softer" benefits result from taking a harder look at how and why they do what they do in the way that they do it. They adopt a "critical eye" approach that breeds new ideas and creates new solutions to existing problems. It's empowering, dynamic, and extremely effective. For personal-lines clients, your plan will anticipate and deal with risks that are often overlooked, provide a comforting "someone cares about me and my family" feeling, and remind clients throughout the year that you are there, thinking about and working for them.

We know that the best way to manage claims is to prevent them from ever happening. Our value-added service plan is used to schedule the action items we intend to deploy on a monthly basis to proactively manage the insurance program while continuing to build and maintain the client relationship. Here is how to create one:

**Start** by making a list of all activities that could be incorporated into a commercial-lines account. It should reflect services that your carrier partner, your agency, and even you personally will bring to the table. Clearly, the more you specialize, the more you have to offer. Think of it as your value-added service "menu," as shown in Figure 22. Some commercial-account examples include:

## Figure 22: Sample Value-Added Service, Commercial-Lines Menu

| | |
|---|---|
| 1) Establish a safety committee that meets monthly. | 6) Conduct quarterly employee training. |
| 2) Establish and implement safe lifting standards. | 7) Design customized work-place safety initiatives. |
| 3) Conduct twice-annual driver-safety classes. | 8) Establish emergency medical procedure. |
| 4) Conduct quarterly account reviews with team. | 9) Create standards for improving security and monitoring visitors. |
| 5) Attend safety-committee meetings. | 10) Conduct scheduled reserve analysis with claims adjusters. |

**Next**, add to the list any agency-wide initiatives that could be planned and would be appropriate for this class of prospect or client. These might include:

| | |
|---|---|
| 11) Semi-annual risk-management workshops<br><br>12) Quarterly client roundtables<br><br>13) Monthly electronic client newsletter | 14) Annual client picnic<br><br>15) Semi-annual needs-assessment updates<br><br>16) Monthly progress reports |

**Finally**, add any additional services that could be specific to some clients or prospects or conducted on an as-needed basis and that do not need to be scheduled on your calendar but could be considered high-payoff activities. These might include:

| | |
|---|---|
| 17) Work with carrier and client to create needed risk-management program templates.<br><br>18) Conduct specialized training for new safety committee. | 19) Establish workplace safety participation program.<br><br>20) Create and supply incident-reporting kits for vehicles. |
| 21) Send weekly "check-in" e-mails to the safety program coordinators.<br><br>22) Post claims hot-line number in all departments.<br><br>23) Attend industry manufacturers' annual convention. | 24) Maintain clipping file and forward as appropriate.<br><br>25) Request referrals.<br><br>26) Update and rehearse crisis-management plan. |

The same approach applies to creating a Value-Added Service, Personal-Lines Menu. A sample of such a menu is shown in Figure 23.

## Figure 23: Sample Value-Added Service, Personal-Lines Menu

| | |
|---|---|
| 1) Personal-lines monthly e-newsletter | 21) Work with carriers and clients to create needed risk-management program templates. |
| 2) Identity-theft tool kit | |
| 3) Conduct driver-safety classes | 22) Provide discount or free coupon for smoke detectors/ carbon monoxide detectors. |
| 4) Conduct mid-term account review. | |
| 5) Fire-safety home checklist | 23) Create and supply accident-reporting kits for vehicles. |
| 6) Update unsafe travel destinations list. | 24) Send monthly "check-in" e-mails to all life clients. |
| 7) Home risk-management inspection | 25) Post claims hot-line number in all client homes. |
| 8) Establish emergency medical procedure. | 26) Attend client and community gatherings. |
| 9) Home security inspection | 27) Maintain clipping file and forward as appropriate. |
| 10) Cross-referral program | |
| 11) Semi-annual risk-management workshops | 28) Request referrals. |
| | 29) Update and rehearse crisis-management plans. |
| 12) Quarterly client roundtables | 30) Send birthday cards and holiday cards to all clients. |
| 13) Long-term care workshop | |
| 14) Annual client picnic | 31) Conduct a detailed client survey once annually with all clients. |
| 15) Needs-assessment updates | |
| 16) Claims reviews | 32) Send service correspondence; make service call, or send greeting card for non-contact months. |
| 17) Participate in client charity drive. | |
| 18) Coverage-gap analysis | |
| 19) Monthly calendar of events | 33) Send pre-approach and other correspondence. |
| 20) Neighborhood crime-watch programs | |

And so on. Your numbered list of value-added services should be as comprehensive as possible, without being overwhelming. These services and the schedule to deliver them are of little use to anybody if they cannot be effectively and efficiently facilitated. Nor should they be "fluffy." Your inherent value is your ability to manage a plan of activities that ultimately has a measurable, positive, bottom-line impact. Your visits have purpose and add value; they are not the drop-in-bring-donuts-to-say-I-was-there type of visit. Yes, we need to be visible; however, it is equally necessary to remain viable.

To test the integrity of any particular event or activity, ask yourself: "What purpose does it serve, and what effect will it have?" If the purpose is definitive and the results are tangible and measurable, you have a winner. For instance, conducting bi-annual needs assessment updates will enable you to identify new exposures and expectations, make the necessary changes to your current plan, further enhance the organization's ability to proactively manage the risk and insurance program, and help to eliminate the potential for service problems. It will also give you a chance to evaluate the client's perception of the service that you are providing and make any adjustments. "Is what we are doing worth the time that we are spending?" is a question that can be asked and answered. The quarterly account reviews will allow everybody to take a "step back" and evaluate progress against the program benchmarks. "Are we getting the results that we expected?" Should we do more or less? Is there anything that needs to be done differently? The answers to these questions will provide you with the information that you need to allocate and reallocate your most valuable asset—your time.

Remember, this listing of value-added services is *your* list of possible value-added services. It is not to be distributed to prospects or clients. The services don't all apply and would be overwhelming at best and impossible to deliver at worst. Once your "menu" is complete and you have used it to develop your needs-assessment questions and client's/prospect's needs, you are in a position to identify the appropriate value-added services—specific to each client and prospect. Translating your Value-Added Service Menu to a customer-specific Value-Added Service Plan or Schedule is when the "special sauce" is applied.

As you prepare to present your plan, ideally in the form of a schedule of events planned for the following year, take steps to emphasize the big picture. Make sure that they see your vision. When presenting this customized, assessment-based list of initiatives, connect each one to an impact statement to ensure that they fully comprehend the value that you are providing. You, or a representative from your team, are not attending safety-committee meetings just to be nice; you are doing so in order to train them and guide them to become a self-managed, proactive, viable, and efficient risk-management team. Ultimately, they will prevent people from being injured, reduce claims, and shrink the cost of their risk-management and insurance program. And so it should be for each activity.

Having itemized the services and correlated each with a tangible result, the next step is to create an implementation schedule that you will present. Remember, client and prospect service schedules represent many of the same services. This is nothing more than pre-scheduling each client or prospect activity into a monthly calendar, as shown in Figures 24 and 25:

## Figure 24: Value-Added Service Schedule for Commercial Client

| January | February | March |
|---|---|---|
| Establish Safety Committee.<br><br>Training—Slip Trip and Fall<br><br>Client Roundtable<br><br>Newsletter<br><br>Progress Report<br><br>Emergency Medical Plan Introduction | Establish Safety Committee.<br><br>Safe Lifting Program<br><br>Agency Workshop<br><br>Newsletter<br><br>Progress Report<br><br>Visitor Security Introduction | Establish Safety Committee.<br><br>Driver-Safety Program<br><br>Account Review<br><br>Newsletter<br><br>Progress Report<br><br>Loss-Control Visit |
| **April** | **May** | **June** |
| Safe Lifting Program<br><br>Client Roundtable<br><br>Newsletter<br><br>Progress Report<br><br>Reserve Analysis | Attend Safety Committee<br><br>Training—Sex Harassment<br><br>Newsletter<br><br>Progress Report<br><br>Loss-Control Visit | Account Review<br><br>Newsletter<br><br>Client Picnic<br><br>Assessment Update<br><br>Progress Report |
| **July** | **August** | **September** |
| Attend Safety Committee.<br><br>Safe Lifting Program<br><br>Client Roundtable<br><br>Newsletter<br><br>Progress Report | Driver-Safety Program<br><br>Training—Diversity<br><br>Agency Workshop<br><br>Newsletter<br><br>Progress Report | Attend Safety Committee.<br><br>Account Review<br><br>Newsletter<br><br>Progress Report<br><br>Loss-Control Visit |
| **October** | **November** | **December** |
| Safe Lifting Program<br><br>Client Roundtable<br><br>Newsletter<br><br>Progress Report<br><br>Reserve Analysis | Attend Safety Committee.<br><br>Training—Claims Reporting<br><br>Newsletter<br><br>Progress Report<br><br>Loss-Control Visit | Account Review<br><br>Newsletter<br><br>Assessment Update<br><br>Progress Report |

**Figure 25: Value-Added Service Schedule for Commercial Prospect**

| January | February | March |
|---|---|---|
| Newsletter | Newsletter | Newsletter<br>Pre-approach Correspondence |
| **April** | **May** | **June** |
| Client Roundtable<br>Newsletter | Safe Lifting Program<br>Newsletter | Birthday Card<br>Newsletter |
| **July** | **August** | **September** |
| Holiday Card<br>Newsletter | Training—Diversity<br>Agency Workshop<br>Newsletter | Newsletter |
| **October** | **November** | **December** |
| Newsletter | Newsletter<br>Loss Control Visit | Newsletter |
| **Other Initiatives:**<br>Attend annual convention<br>Maintain clipping file and forward as appropriate<br>Association leadership activities<br>Publish insurance column | | |

Now you have your plan—all scheduled and ready to deliver. Let's take a moment to acknowledge that these plans are very involved and busy—intended only for a client or prospect who is worthy of the time and attention, understands and appreciates the value that you will provide, and represents enough of a commission on the account to make it all worthwhile. Smaller, less complex clients and personal lines require a much more efficient, less intensive plan. The plan for a personal-lines client may only involve monthly e-mails (done in a group for all clients), twice annual visits, a newsletter, quarterly phone-account reviews, two client workshops, and a birthday card.

We recommend that you regularly evaluate the appropriate level of service for each account to ensure that you are being compensated for your time. In short, there must be a "quid-pro-quo" established for every service plan. This does not mean that you charge fees. It does mean that you provide strategic levels of service only to those who are worthy of your time and attention—those who recognize your value and offer enough income to support the plan.

---

### Author Snapshot: Steve Thompson

"Each client has individual needs that vary from time to time. For example, having a mix of 10 large and 30 or so mid-sized clients will require higher levels of service for certain clients in some years than others. Rather than solely allocating services based on specific clients' revenue, calculate total revenue received from all clients, including all of their business lines (personal lines, benefits, etc.), then allocate a percentage of that to providing value-added services. This enables "touching" all clients, and also spending time where specific needs are developing."

---

Also, be flexible. Consider the initial plan to be only a draft and, as you present it to the client, let it be known that you would like them to adjust it as they see fit. Is it too much? Too little? Rather than guess, ask. The client may also want to add ideas that, upon delivery, will further enhance the perception of value.

Now, back to you.

How do you manage all of this activity efficiently and still sell? Let's start the discussion by remembering what you are selling—you are selling this plan and your commitment to it. The insurance product is important, but it is only a piece of this much larger picture.

As an example, for new business development, let's assume that you have done the market research necessary to identify some key prospects for the coming year. You are also actively working your referral-harvesting program. Through blending the two strategies, you have developed a list of 25 key prospects that you intend to approach. Following the recommended steps outlined in the channel-marketing and referral-harvesting chapters, you send out an invitation to an agency event already scheduled for clients and invite your prospects. Using this one strategy—you eventually gain an audience, administer the needs assessment, and create the prospect's value-added service plan. Regardless of the expiration date of the existing policy, the plan starts, and you provide the services outlined. This may mean that a significant amount of time elapses before you actually take over the account at expiration date, or you could get a BOR letter on day one. The delay is actually preferable, because it leaves time to demonstrate the effectiveness of the plan, build the value, and truly differentiate. If we have done our homework on the prospect and we trust that they fit our profile, then it is usually safe to invest our time and attention prior to getting paid. Most often, after seeing you in action, the prospect comes to you on a BOR letter long before the harvesting season arrives.

## Managing Value-Added Service Plans

Okay, you have created plans for your key clients (we suggest starting with 15) and prospects (15). You are faced with the daunting task of proactively managing 30 distinct plans and all that they contain. It feels overwhelming and, suddenly, you are dispirited. This is understandable, but don't despair. We are about to let you in on the final tool of this book—the one that we have been building to all along. It will allow you to incorporate everything that we have reviewed into a concise, coherent, consistent, and manageable format. To visualize this, we have provided a simple calendar of events for commercial clients and prospects, mapped out for the year, broken down into months for easy integration into your weekly calendar and Ta-Da list in our chapter on Priority Management. In fact, the entire master, value-added service plan for all 30 accounts (15 commercial clients and 15 commercial prospects), and more if needed, can be contained on two pages. Figure 26 provides an example; then we'll walk through how to build one for you.

## Figure 26: Combined Client and Prospect Value-Added Service Management Plan

| Client Name | JAN | FEB | MAR | APR | MAY | JUN | JUL | AUG | SEP | OCT | NOV | DEC |
|---|---|---|---|---|---|---|---|---|---|---|---|---|
| Client 1 | 1,6,8,9 | 1,2,9,7 | 1,3,4,20 | 2,10,23 | 5,6,20,30 | 4,15,22,23 | 2,5,25,26 | 3,6,21,28 | 5,4,20 | 2,10,29 | 5,6,20 | 4,15,31 |
| Client 2 | 5,6,16 | 15,18,21 | 4,10,20 | 5,16 | 6,18,28 | 4,17,20,32 | 5,16 | 15,18,21 | 4,6,26 | 5,16,29 | 10,18,20 | 4,6,31 |
| Client 3 | 4,7,10 | 5,18,20 | 16,17,22 | 4,25,29 | 3,5,7,15 | 10,16,28 | 4,18,21 | 7,26 | 5,16 | 4,21,15 | 3,18,31 | 5,16,20 |
| Client 4 | 6,18,28 | 4,16,23 | 5,10,25 | 3,7,21 | 4,6,16 | 18,25,30 | 5,10,21 | 4,6,7,15 | 3,16 | 18,32 | 4,6,31 | 7,22,15 |
| Client 5 | 4,20,30 | 5,6,21 | 7,16,28 | 4,15 | 5,10 | 6,18 | 4,16 | 5,6,31 | 7,15 | 4,18 | 6,21 | 5,10,16 |
| Client 6 | 5,7 | 4,10 | 6,15 | 5,20 | 4,7,30 | 6,28,31 | 5,10 | 4,8 | 6 | 5,15 | 4 | 21,30 |
| Client 7 | 6,15 | 7,8,18 | 4,16 | 5,29 | 6,20 | 4,10,31 | 7,15 | 5,16 | 4,18 | 6,28 | 21,30 | 4 |
| Client 8 | 4,6 | 5,15 | 7,20 | 4,10,18 | 5,16 | 7,28 | 4,6,31 | 15,29 | 5,30 | 4,10,18 | 7,16 | 5,21 |
| Client 9 | 5,10 | 4,6 | 7,15 | 5,16,30 | 4,18 | 6,17 | 5,21 | 4,31 | 15,16 | 6,28 | 4,18 | 20 |
| Client 10 | 7,28 | 8,18 | 4,5 | 6,31 | 9,15 | 4 | 7,20 | 5,21 | 4,18 | 6,30 | 15 | 4 |
| Client 11 | 4 | 7,16 | 6,10 | 4,18 | 5,20 | 6,30 | 4,16 | 10,28 | 5,21 | 4,31 | 6 | 18 |
| Client 12 | 6 | 4,28 | 5,17,30 | 10,29 | 4,18 | 5,20 | 6,31 | 4 | 15 | 5,21 | 4 | 16 |
| Client 13 | 9,18 | 10,30 | 4 | 5,15 | 6,31 | 4,28 | 7,30 | 16 | 4,18 | 6,20 | 15 | 4 |
| Client 14 | 16 | 5,21 | 6 | 4 | 7,30 | 10 | 4,17 | 5,31 | 20 | 4,18 | 28 | 15 |
| Client 15 | 4 | 20 | 18 | 6 | 4 | 16 | 5,21 | 6,30 | 4,31 | 28 | 7 | 10,15 |

**Figure 26: Combined Client and Prospect Value-Added Service Management Plan (Part 2)**

| Prospect Name | JAN | FEB | MAR | APR | MAY | JUN | JUL | AUG | SEP | OCT | NOV | DEC |
|---|---|---|---|---|---|---|---|---|---|---|---|---|
| Prospect 1 | 7 | 7 | 7, 35 | 7, 37 | 7, 38 | 7, 32 | 7 | 7, 39 | 7 | 7 | 7, 20 | 7 |
| Prospect 2 | 33 | 33 | 33 | 33 | 15,10,18 | 7 | 17 | | | 15 | | |
| Prospect 3 | 33,26 | 33 | 15,10,18 | 4,7,20 | | | | | | | | |
| Prospect 4 | 33 | 33 | 33 | 17 | 33 | 33 | 15,10 | 1,7 | 1 | | | |
| Prospect 5 | 33 | 15,10,18 | 4,7,20 | | | 26 | | | | | | |
| Prospect 6 | 33 | 33 | 33 | 33 | 15,10,18 | 4,7,20 | | | 15 | | | |
| Prospect 7 | 15,10,18 | 4,7,20 | | | | | | | | | | |
| Prospect 8 | 33 | 33 | 33 | 15,10,18 | 4,7,20 | | | 15 | | | | |
| Prospect 9 | 33 | 33 | 33 | 33 | 33 | 33,17 | 33 | 15,10,18 | 7 | | | |
| Prospect 10 | 33 | 15,10,18 | 4,7,20 | 33 | 26 | | | | | | 15 | |
| Prospect 11 | 33 | 33 | 33 | 33 | 33 | 33,26 | 33 | 33 | 15,10,18 | 4,7,20 | | |
| Prospect 12 | 33 | 33 | 33 | 33 | 33 | 33 | 33 | 33 | 33 | 15,10 | 4,7,20 | |
| Prospect 13 | 15,10,18 | 4,7,20 | | | | | 15 | | | | | |
| Prospect 14 | 33 | 33 | 33 | 15,10,18 | 4,7,20 | | 4,7,20 | | | | 15 | |
| Prospect 15 | 33 | 33 | 33 | 33 | 33 | 15,10,18 | 4,7,20 | | | | | 15 |

Your Combined Client and Prospect Value-Added Service Management Plan is a comprehensive account of every individual, value-added service schedule that was custom developed for each client and prospect. The monthly activity numbers shown are directly related to the numbers originally posted on your Sample Value-Added Service Commercial-Lines Menu (Figure 22). It is a snapshot of all scheduled activities for the year, and, used effectively, it is the coup de grace of differentiation. The plan enables you to see at a glance what you need to do each week, month, quarter, and what you need to do semi annually and annually. It is perfectly suited to serve as an input to your weekly priority-management process (Ta-Da list and Calendar).

While especially helpful for planning commercial client and prospect activity, you can use the same approach for personal lines, albeit containing less planned activities. When properly integrated into your weekly calendar planning process, this tool will allow you to proactively coordinate all activities with all service providers and carriers, track performance against established benchmarks, and correlate your activity to a bottom-line impact for clients and prospects.

The combined plan shown in Figure 26 is an elaborate one that is loaded with activities that involve interaction with the client or prospect. While your master plan may not be as involved, the impact and the client's/prospect's perception of value will be similar when their specific plan is presented. This positive effect specifically results from the proactive, well-planned, customized approach that you are taking. Notice that none of the activities is "spectacular" or especially unique—many can be considered normal account-management events that you have seen before and may currently practice. In and of themselves, they do not effectively differentiate you from other service-focused producers. Instead, it is the strategically laid-out plan, the proactive and predictable approach that ties it all together and, most importantly, differentiates you from the peddlers calling on your customers and prospects.

Take care not to over-allocate your resources. Time, your most limited resource, must be carefully preserved and only invested in activities with clients who are worthy of the attention. You cannot be everything to everybody, nor should you try to be. This level of service is not appropriate for clients who don't value it (regardless of the size of the account).

Be very, very careful to adequately segment your book of business and plan accordingly. The opportunity cost associated with not doing so is horrific. If you are investing time in over-servicing, you are taking time away from another client where your impact and value could be much greater. So pick your spots, and pick them carefully.

Notice that on the sample plan, the clients and prospects are "ranked," 1-15. Note that the level of contact and service is most intense and complex at the beginning of the plan and becomes less involved as you work the plan down to number 15. This is not accidental—it is strategic. Generally, the larger, or more complex, the greater the impact, and the more time and attention that is warranted.

## Constructing Your Plan

Now that you've seen the plan and what it can do, let's begin at the beginning to construct your own plan. Constructing your plan starts with an unbiased segmentation of your existing book of business and your list of prospects. We suggest you rank each account based upon two criteria:

1)  Size and complexity, an potential for opportunity; and

2)  Perception of value for services and cultural compatibility.

## Size of Account and Potential for Opportunity

Ralph Waldo Emerson once said, "Every act rewards itself." What he meant was that we get paid for what we are worth—once we prove our worth. Our plan recognizes this and understands that nobody works this hard for free, so you must be compensated for your time. Obviously, commissions are higher for larger clients (or a group of combined clients), and therefore should merit a higher ranking—providing that they meet the cultural compatibility requirement and appreciate the value that you are bringing to the table. Opportunity, however, comes in many guises. For instance, suppose that you have approached a sizable client and they, being impressed by your message, have given you a piece of the overall account—perhaps just one line of business. They might be testing you; they might have scattered expiration dates for different lines, or maybe they have to "ease" their way out of an existing relationship with an incumbent broker or carrier. On paper, they aren't too impressive; however, the potential to round out the account as the relationship progresses could be magnificent and, therefore, would merit a higher degree of time and attention than might otherwise have been allocated.

Some suggest that you could and should charge fees beyond the commission for these value-driven, account-management activities. Some discount the commission at time of sale and charge a "pay-as-you-go" account-management fee. The fact that this is a common technique indicates that there are circumstances where it can be applied successfully. However, we believe that this practice greatly diminishes the perception of value that is the foundation of your message, and it too often focuses the client on payment amount, rather than what you are doing. It's your call.

Centers of Influence should also experience your premier service plan, for it is they who will endorse you, encourage you, educate you, and lead you to your cornerstone accounts. They need to know how good you are, and you need to show them how good you can be.

## Perception of Value for Services and Cultural Compatibility

Sometimes, large clients don't translate into large commissions. Likewise, a large prospect or client does not automatically qualify. "Good" prospects or clients are those that are able to rise above the narrow confines of the common "insurance is about price and product" perspective and view the entire insurance program—both its prevention and protection elements. They will comprehend the inherent value of your plan and its positive implications for the organization. At some level, such clients view you as a "partner" rather than a policy pusher, and they will actively participate in the development and implementation of the insurance program. Price will matter, but it will be considered as a part of the overall landscape rather than a world unto itself—one of many factors that will enter into the buying decision, rather than the single greatest one. Good clients want you to actively and consistently participate in their program; others would prefer to be left alone unless something breaks.

Agreement to and participation in the needs assessment provides you with a clear indication as to which side of the line they are likely to fall, but it is no guarantee. Most people and companies are somewhere in between the extremes of what constitutes "good" and "bad," and most can be moved up the scale and get better over time—providing that they are willing and able.

With these two qualifiers in mind, segment your book of business, and rank your clients. Use a simple system to grade each client, as follows:

Great Opportunity, Culturally Compatible

Good Opportunity, Culturally Compatible

Great Opportunity,
Culturally Questionable

Small Opportunity,
Culturally Compatible

Good Opportunity,
Culturally
Questionable

Your ranking system is customizable and completely up to you. The objective is to scale your book of business so that you can efficiently allocate your resources. If you are concerned that you have not completed a needs assessment and cannot make a fair or convincing assessment of potential or compatibility, now is a good time to set the appointment and get the process going. Even if you have a good feel for your clients and how to rank them, conduct the needs assessment on those who have not had it as a first step to introducing your account-management strategy. You'll be shocked to discover how many once-dormant clients suddenly spring to life around your program.

Having segmented your clients, it is time to take a hard look at those on the low tiers. We have previously acknowledged that we cannot be all things to all people, that investing our time and attention with those clients who are most worthy necessarily means less or no time spent with those that are not. Now we are looking at the lowest tier of our segmentation plan, made up of our worst performing and least compatible accounts, and it's not a pretty sight, especially as some of these accounts are also our "noisiest." Administratively unorganized and risk-management inept, their service "program" has historically been limited to responding to the crisis of the moment, in the moment. These are the clients that put the "fun" in dysfunction—always needy, always late, always reactive, always calling, sometimes rude, perpetually non-renewed, rarely loyal, and never learning. In short, they're the clients you're better off without. The revenue or money that we make hardly covers the cost of the time that they take.

What to do, what to do . . .

End it. Retaining these clients is asking for trouble in any market where profitability means leverage and favorable treatment with every carrier. Move them to a service center or third-party administrator; suggest another broker; give them to a new producer to cut their teeth on, or provide them with administrative services only and cut off (or severely limit) any access to your time. At this end, you simply cannot afford to give too much and have your best clients suffer as a result.

Building a book of business should not mean building an ever-expanding client list—keeping all that you have and constantly pushing to add more. This common business practice is what causes most of the traditional service problems. Rather than focusing on the number of clients, your strategy demands that we continue to focus on quality and the right size of clients. Keeping the number of clients consistent by replacing poor performers or those that are poorly qualified with better ones will help you steadily grow your business without cheating anybody, including yourself.

Practicing this strategy might someday make today's middle-of-the-pack client your worst performer. That's fine. In fact, what does that tell you about the quality and the performance of the clients that you have built on top of this one? It should tell you that you have done a masterful job of focusing on the right relationships while building new ones. Manage yourself and your business accordingly.

Once you have decided which of your key clients and prospects are going to receive your value-added program, list them in ranked order on your Combined Client and Prospect Value-Added Service-Management Plan, as shown in Figure 26.

## Planning the Service Activity

At this point, you have a number of activities created from nearly every chapter in the book, and possibly you will have some client-specific activities from conducting needs assessments. Collectively, it's a lot of stuff—stuff that needs to be organized efficiently.

For clients, start by making a list of all of the activities that you have created, similar to those shown in Figure 22. Some of these activities will be applied universally across the client list. Others have limited or specialized application, resulting from a specific need that arose from an assessment. Some can be generalized, rather than appearing specifically as described in the client's individual plan. For example, in Figure 26, Client 1 has two specific training topics listed on the individual plan (Value-Added Service Schedule for Commercial Client); however, the activity shows up as "Conduct Quarterly Employee Training" (Item 6) on the Sample Value-Added Service, Commercial-Lines Menu (Figure 22). However you design your Value-Added Service Menu, make it functional, and keep it to one page if possible.

You now know what you are going to do, and you have identified to whom you are going to do it. Let's determine when you will do it by scheduling the activities and events on your calendar. Here are the steps:

1) **Identify the scheduled activities that are unilateral and consistent.** The activities that apply to everyone at consistent intervals throughout the year (in Figure 23, Sample Value-Added Service, Personal-Lines Menu, these are activity numbers **11, 12, 13, 14, 19, 24, 32**, which respectively include: semi-annual risk-management workshops; quarterly client roundtables; long-term care workshop; annual client picnic; monthly calendar of events; monthly "check-in" e-mails to all life clients; service letter/call/greeting card for non-contact months). Although these activities definitely appear on the individual client plans, we are creating a footnote on the master plan to avoid unnecessary clutter on the matrix.

2) **Identify unscheduled activities that will be deployed on an as-needed or random basis** (in Figure 26, Combined Client and Prospect Value-Added Service Management Plan, such as activity **32**, sending service correspondence, service call, greeting card). Once again, to avoid unnecessary clutter, we have elected to create a footnote for activities on the master plan.

3) **Use the individual, value-added service schedules that you created for each , and place the activity codes in the appropriate month of delivery for each existing client.** Again, notice in our example in Figure 26 that the higher-ranking clients receive more face time and more services than others do. As you work your way down the list, the activity becomes less frequent and less complex.

4) **After ranking your prospects using the same criteria used when evaluating existing clients, plot out their contact schedule and marketing touches, which lead up to an estimated time for their initial needs assessment.** Assuming you have created a Value-Added Service Schedule for prospects, as in Figure 25, post these activities to your Combined Plan. Note that after conducting the needs assessment, you will be in a position that is sufficiently informed to build the remainder of their plan (as shown with "Prospect 1") on

our Combined Client and Prospect Value-Added Services Management Plan in Figure 26. We can also safely predict the activity for any new account in the first few months following the needs assessment, and these events are also shown; however, that is all we can safely anticipate at this point. Keep in mind that the "blank" months are not truly empty—you will continue to provide all of the footnoted activity each month, as appropriate.

When allocating your time and attention and determining the level of services that are appropriate for each client, be conservative. Though the needs assessment may have uncovered a long list of issues in need of attention and some significant holes in the current program, you cannot fix it all at once. Pace yourself and your client; prioritize the objectives, and stretch out the initiatives to ensure that you can manage the program consistently and effectively. Some objectives will have to wait, and they may have to wait until years two, three, and four of the program. It is better to start slow and build than to over commit and become frustrated at best and disillusioned at worst. If necessary, start with five clients and five prospects, and build from there.

This is not to suggest that we abandon the lower-ranking clients or those that do not make the Combined Client and Prospect Value-Added Service Management Plan. The weekly, monthly, quarterly, semi-annual, and annual activities are intended for every client and meet our objective for consistent client contact over time. Additionally, these unilateral activities add a significant level of value on their own and are the core activities for prospects contained in our channel-marketing plan. If these baseline activities successfully attracted clients, they will also retain them. Let's be clear on this, no client is getting cheated. All are getting the level of service that is appropriate for their circumstances.

You now have your plan, and you are equipped with the tools that you will need to execute it consistently. Similar to your weekly plans that you created in our chapter on Priority Management, your master plan and the individual client and prospect plans are going to remain fluid rather than fixed. Your plans are based only on what is known to be true for today and on what can reasonably be expected to occur in the future. We are never exact with our forecast, nor should we be too confident in our assumptions and expectations. You will change; clients will change, and underwriters will change—as will the market itself. Everything will adjust, and you will need to make adjustments. Not all of your highest-ranking clients will respond as expected; consequently, they will need to move down in ranking. Conversely, some clients that currently rank lower will embrace, respond to, and perform for you. These you will move higher.

You won't be successful with every prospect, and your pool of prospects will change as time rolls on. New ideas will creep into your plan, new value-drivers that will develop from your experience and from that of your clients. Some established activities will fade due to ineffectiveness and/or inefficiency. In short, you'll grow, and your clients will grow. Their needs will change, and your plan will change to accommodate. It is how it should be.

Not shown in our plan are the inevitable ad hoc meetings that you will have to have with clients, underwriters, prospects, and colleagues. Not shown in our plan are the day-to-day administrative tasks that are inevitable. Not shown in our plan are the crises, the phone calls, and other interruptions that require you to drop what you are doing and spring into action. Not shown is a perfect plan.

What is shown is a client- and prospect-management process that, though flexible, will keep you focused on doing the right things, in the right way, for the right reasons, at the right time, with the right people—in short, fulfilling your primary purpose, day in and day out. What is shown is a way out of the traditional sales and service model that defeats too many and benefits too few. What is shown is a proven formula for achieving a level of success beyond your wildest dreams—in any market. What is shown, in combination with all that we have delivered to you throughout this book, is the best possible advice you will ever receive—and, quite possibly, the most rewarding.

# Chapter Fourteen

# Final Thoughts

*"My thought has always been completion. Maybe you have to rebound better, shoot better, hit free throws, handle the ball, defend better. You have to do all those things in the course of a game."*

—Isaiah Thomas

It's time to congratulate yourself. You have established your objectives and created a priority-management system that will direct your personal and professional activities toward their achievement. You have researched and analyzed the marketplace and designed a service-driven, channel-marketing system that will attract and embrace the clients that are worthy of your time and attention. You have created a comprehensive needs assessment for these clients that enables you to reach far beyond issues of policy and

> "[W]hen you actually practice what they preach, IT WORKS!... our results in a very difficult market have been astronomical—more than that our customer satisfaction is off the charts and retention is close to 100%. We believe in [this] philosophy and will continue to use it as we grow."
>
> *Paul Michaels*
> *Industry Expert*

price to custom develop a proactive, tangible, risk-management and service program for each of them. Using this information, you have produced a value-added service plan that establishes performance benchmarks, specifically defines activities and schedules contacts, and correctly manages insurance-program cost by proactively managing the frequency and severity of claims.

You have done it all and done it well. Your client and carrier relationships have evolved to become partnerships, and you are now in a position to reap the rewards of doing the right thing, in the right way, for the right reasons, with the right people.

With years of experience instructing and coaching this process, we are elated to make it available to you. Although nothing that you have designed could be categorized as "radical," much of what you will be doing certainly flies in the face of conventional wisdom and legacy behavior. Indeed, chances are good that you will upset the organizational apple cart. Though most eventually do come around and see the merits of your approach, it doesn't happen overnight, which can be a bit discouraging. The following section will help you understand what is happening and offer you some tips to get through it.

## Terrorized by Change— The Dilemma of Internal Innovation

The greatest single deterrent to organizational growth is the refusal of an organization's members to accept the change that facilitates growth. We speak endlessly of new plateaus, new horizons, new business, and a new breed. Yet most prefer to follow the familiar routine. We build magnificent plans, copy models, develop logos, create teams, conduct countless meetings, ... and never move forward. We shake things up, only to watch in frustration as those around us settle back in. Sometimes the mere suggestion of a simple adjustment in strategy is enough to make you wish you hadn't. Is it all worth it?

The answer is: absolutely. In a market characterized by chaos and searching to find itself, improved efficiency and effective differentiation are prerequisites to survival. Is there anything you can do to resolve the conflict between internal innovation and pre-conditioned responses to change? Not likely. Human nature prefers an established comfort zone and a predictable world. You can, however, lighten your load a bit by understanding the resistance, while you continue to hold your position. Listed below are the three greatest challenges those who dare to be different face, along with some ideas on how to manage the negativity.

Remember, stick to your guns, trust your instincts, and no . . . nothing is easy.

> *"It generally happens that assurance keeps an even pace with ability."*
>
> — Samuel Johnson

## Challenge # 1—Everyone's a Critic:

Defending status quo by attacking the unfamiliar is the world's oldest *pre*occupation. Change shatters the illusion of control, safety, predictability, and wisdom found in all comfort zones. Although we no longer execute our pioneers, people still line up to terminate a new idea. Be leery of the "it-will-never-work," Eeyore-worshiping, rain-on-any-parade, Chicken Little-like crowd, and hang with the believers. For those who understand what you're doing and support you in that effort, no explanation or justification is necessary. For those who don't and won't understand, no explanation is possible.

## Challenge # 2—The Illusion of Perfection:

Do it right the first time and every time, right? Not. Especially not when you are creating, researching and developing. Trial and Error are our greatest teachers, and they demand flexibility, perspective, patience, and tolerance from their students. Perfection is a state of mind. You cannot and will not design and implement a new strategy that answers every contingency and fulfills every expectation. Your innovation will develop over time, not over-night. You are initiating and managing a process of change—an evolution, not an event. You must manage your expectations accordingly. Things in life rarely follow your plan exactly, and people never do. Expect perfection, and you'll always be disappointed. Loosen up; life is far too short to sweat every moment.

## Challenge # 3—Measuring Success:

Defining success as anything other than a tangible goal achieved or a positive result attained might seem absurd to the casual observer; however, traditional measurements of day-to-day success are not appropriate for innovative works in progress. Our greatest achievements, discoveries, and adaptations usually result from things gone slightly awry, rather than according to plan. Our success is our participation in the process, and our greatest measurement of that success is how well we participate.

## Traits of Successful Sales and Service People

Though each person we have coached has been unique with respect to their backgrounds and their tenure in the industry, we have been able to identify some common traits exhibited by our most successful sales and service people. These traits mirror those that we have identified in the many hundreds of other participants who graduate from our programs conducted around the country each year. You might be surprised by the fact that these behaviors are not complex, mechanical or process/gimmick-driven strategies. Instead, they are elementary habits that work well without regard to product, price, market conditions, education, style, finesse, hype, or height. You should also know that although no single sales/service person displays all of these traits all of the time, we can say that they do have an uncanny ability to develop and consistently apply most of them over time.

## How Successful Sales and Service People View their Goals

Success in life, both professionally and personally, is determined by our ability to establish crystallized objectives, develop a plan to achieve those objectives, and discipline ourselves to execute the plan. All too often, life's preoccupations and distractions derail our plans with an earsplitting crash, and we fall victim to the noise. Others' priorities overwhelm our own; a need for instant gratification erodes the promise of patience and cumulative results; urgency and emergency replace systematic assessment and provocative thought. As we work our way through the wreckage, it is easy to settle into believing that it was never meant to be. Great sales and service people, however, view their goals differently in at least 10 ways:

1) They are on a mission. They decide what they can have, believe that they should have it, and then go and get it. No excuses.

2) They have goals that far exceed others' often understated expectations.

3) They are never content or comfortable with today's progress.

4) They review their goals and measure their progress daily.

5) They visualize achieving their goals and are guided toward them by an internal compass.

6) They evaluate their performance and the quality of their activity regularly.

7) They celebrate victories.

8) They are disciplined daily—even on Friday afternoon.

9) They run marathons, not sprints.

10) They are emotionally attached to their objectives. They may give in, but they never give up.

## How Successful Sales and Service People Work

Time is our most valuable possession. It is the measure of our existence on the face of this earth, and the decisions that we make about how to allocate our time ultimately determine the quality and usefulness of our stay. Given that we begin each day with the same 24 hours and that it elapses at exactly the same rate for all of us, what we do with each moment is the single greatest and most controllable variable in our formula for success. Great sales and service people worship their time and protect it well. They establish priorities based upon how well the task or project will move them toward accomplishing their objectives—rather than upon ease, expediency, preference, or pleasure. Great sales and service people see the light... usually the first light:

1) They start early every day—7 a.m. or earlier.

2) They "sell" during selling hours. Housekeeping hours are before 8 a.m. and after 5 p.m.

3) They are "selling" at least 70% of the time.

4) They remember to have fun, and they plan for it.

5) They return their calls quickly—not every call, but every high-payoff call, usually from a cell phone.

6) They look for efficiencies. They are consumed with finding a better way, not an easier way.

7) They are always learning, and they learn by doing.

8) They are stable and consistent.

9) They do their homework... at home.

10) Sales people spend a minimum of 50 percent of their time outside of the office.

## What Successful Sales and Service People Work On

In the beginning, there was the cold call. It was intrusive, inefficient, and discomfiting for peddler and prospect alike. Most have justifiably abandoned this legacy prospecting tool in favor of a more palatable one. That said, we continue to find that a "cold-call mentality" still dominates in a majority of alternative marketing and prospecting systems. The basic premise is that selling is a numbers game. Cast a wide net (through mass mailing, advertising, volume quoting, and extensive bidding), reel it in, sort it out, and work frantically to find a keeper. Although this method generates an impressive amount of work, it does so by exacting a huge opportunity cost on efficiency and client quality while creating a culture of urgency and desperation. This game of numbers simply does not and will not provide enough quality return for the time and attention invested.

Great sales and service people are consistently more selective—maintaining what Stephen Covey refers to as "an abundance mentality." They understand that opportunity is limitless and timeless. After all, everybody needs what we have to offer, and they all have to buy it every year! They identify their niche markets, learn and stay educated about the unique needs of their markets, and become specialists in serving those markets. Great sales and service people work with a scalpel, not a machete:

1) They know their product, their competition, and their market, inside and out.

2) They selectively quote. They analyze and pick every shot.

3) They are calculated and figure angles. They find and work from positions of strength.

4) They look to be unique and search for unique opportunities.

5) They show up when everyone else has given up.

6) They speak of a selling process, rather than transactional selling events.

7) They thrive on new activity, not old.

8) They enjoy the challenge of complexity, flourish on creativity, and are bored by normalcy.

9) They know what others don't, or they will take the time to find out.

10) They quickly move away from lost causes and focus on developing opportunity.

## Who Successful Sales and Service People Work With

The most dynamic, unpredictable, and fascinating components of any sales process are the relationships—relationships between people who sell things for a living and people who buy from them. Ordinary people, perhaps, at first glance. But if you dig below the surface a bit you'll find an extraordinary glossary of experiences, motives, values, behaviors, habits, beliefs, ambitions, fears, emotions, expectations, likes, and dislikes that combine to form the core of their existence and define who they really are. It is at this level that decisions are evaluated and made, and, though this may appear obvious, it is also the "human element" most ignored by those of us whose livelihood depends on our ability to influence the decision-making process.

Great sales and service people seem to do a better job than most at attracting, creating, and maintaining long-term client, industry, organizational and personal relationships. While many focus on product, policy, price and transactions, great sales and service people focus their attention on the people and their needs and expectations. Further, great sales and service people demand the same from those who work with them and for them. As a result, they tend to work with fewer, more carefully selected clients. Great sales and service people build networks with like-minded professionals and usually attract new clients through referrals and reputation:

1) They don't discover clients; they create them.

2) They fish in stocked ponds, not open oceans.

3) They work exclusively with clients who will work with them.

4) They know that some relationships come and go. They focus on the comers.

5) They conduct a formal client needs assessment prior to making product recommendations.

6) They educate rather than "sell"—providing their clients with enough information to make informed decisions.

7) They view each relationship uniquely.

8) They are heavily networked within the industry and their community.

9) They go beyond product to provide their clients with value, integrity, and trust.

10) They are magnets for new and creative opportunities.

## How Successful Sales and Service People Think

Some of the most positive, well-balanced people we have ever had the opportunity to meet are at the top of their game. Knowing that they didn't start there, we asked them how they, above most others, overcame the challenges, frustrations, turmoil, and anxiety inherent in building a career and a stable book of business. The answer to this question is always the same—they simply never believed they couldn't. The power of positive thinking and its associated benefits are well documented and affect everything that we do. Great sales and service people are very positive people:

1) They never believe they "can't" or they "won't," so they don't... fail.

2) They aren't consumed by what's on their desk; they are consumed by what isn't.

3) They are competitive, internally and externally.

4) They have a decent boldness; they often say "no," but rarely hear it.

5) They view their profession as challenging, but not difficult.

6) When others would take the day off, they charge ahead.

7) They are proud, determined, and appropriately entitled.

8) They depend on faith and work, not luck and circumstance.

9) They find success; they do not wait for it to find them.

10) They have bad moments, not bad days.

Great sales and service people have methods that are simple, the ideas logical, and the potential for personal and professional growth phenomenal. In our years of coaching, supporting, and training, we have had the wonderful experience of watching good sales and service people become great sales and service people, the luxury of watching the impossible become probable, the theoretical become practical, and the gap between performance and potential become forever bridged with countless participants.

Simply doing the best that you can do with what you have, moment to moment, day to day, and week to week, until it is time to do something else, is a fabulous achievement.

> *"No man, for any considerable period, can wear one face to himself, and another to the multitude, without finally getting bewildered as to which may be true."*
>
> —Nathaniel Hawthorne

## Staying on Course

Staying on course is perhaps the most challenging aspect of change. When the initial thrill of learning new tools and practices gives way to the daily routine, complacency sometimes creeps in on us, and we slide back toward what is most familiar and least challenging.

As we work our way through the debris of such shortcomings, it's easy to settle into a belief that the new path we are trying to follow was never meant to be. But the good news is this: Once you begin to practice these behaviors, they take on a life of their own.

Providing service with integrity instead of selling product, and striving to maintain quality relationships with your clients have an exponential effect: a momentum that requires minimal maintenance. The beauty of this approach is that if you "fall off the horse," you can get right back on using what you've learned about goal setting, scheduling strategic, high-payoff activities, and practicing priority management.

The idea is that, once you've created a thorough foundation, *it* will support *you*, offering newfound freedom. You won't be chasing after business or clients, so you'll have less stress, and you'll be able to focus more on *purpose*—saving lives, preventing injuries and illnesses, and protecting clients from financial hardship. And, let's not forget that you'll have more time and resources to enjoy all those personal priority activities you calendared at the beginning of this process.

While these outcomes alone will motivate you to stay on track, equally inspiring will be the dignity you cultivate as a result of having defined and developed your own worth. Now that you know exactly what you have to offer and to whom, fear will be replaced by faith that even if your enthusiasm occasionally wanes (as it will inevitably do), and even if you are temporarily blindsided by exigencies, your efforts won't be derailed. Remember, this is a process—a way of life, not a program. It doesn't require perfection, only progress—and the more you rely on it, the more you will come to trust it to keep you on course.

Oh, this can be so much fun, or it can be miserable; the choice is yours. Choose fun!

# Epilogue

More than a decade has passed since our initial printing of *Hard Market Selling: Thriving in the New Insurance Era*. Yet, it feels like yesterday that we ripped open the boxes of books from our publisher and leafed through the newly minted pages. Little did we know then that we would require three additional reprints, and the book would actually become popular enough to stand the test of time. After all, it's a book about insurance stuff.

Still, too much has changed in our industry, our world, and our lives to present the old model as a truly comprehensive one. We've experienced devastating natural disasters around the globe, along with 13 named hurricanes and countless tornadoes, blizzards, droughts, and floods in the U.S. While these events literally and figuratively changed the landscape, a near total economic collapse proved humbling to even the mightiest and forced us all to think more deeply and reorder our priorities.

As an industry, we've responded well. We've cycled through an extended soft market, introduced new products and services, and emerged stronger than ever before. Technological advances have made communication more efficient and effective; new websites and cloud computing have helped us to become much more interactive, and a wide array of social media platforms allow us to transmit messages to large audiences at the speed of light. These new tools have leveled the playing field a bit—small brokers can appear larger than they are and cover more ground than ever before; large brokers can personalize their approach and customize services like never before.

So, while the times have gotten tougher, our industry, our capability, our service levels, and our commitment have grown stronger. This didn't happen accidentally. It happened because our belief in our primary purpose—to save lives, prevent injuries and illnesses, and to help our clients avoid financial hardship—never wavered. The industry is strong because you are resilient and unwavering in your determination to take care of your clients. Through thick and thin, good days, bad days, and going half-mad days, you have served and served well. I am proud of you and honored to have shared the industry with you for as long as I have.

Now, it is time to up our game. The co-authors of this book have taken the best of what made us great and combined it with new insights, strategies, and concepts to help us become even better. Richard Coskren, Bob Teschke, and Steve Thompson are dear friends and colleagues whom I've had the privilege of working with for most of this past decade. I have been blessed by their companionship, kept fresh by their creativity and energy, and stayed strong with their gentle guidance and leadership. My hope is that their words will prove equally meaningful for you and help you to become the spark that ignites a passion for improvement at your desk, in your agency, and in our industry.

Be well, feel the love, and keep the faith.
Scott Primiano

# Index

# O

# P

# R